Smart
Business
Solutions

Financial Management

RIVKA TADJER

PUBLISHED BY
Microsoft Press
A Division of Microsoft Corporation
One Microsoft Way
Redmond, Washington 98052-6399

Library of Congress Cataloging-in-Publication Data
Tadjer, Rivka.
    Smart Business Solutions for Financial Management : how to harness
  the power of technology to put your small business in the black /
  Rivka Tadjer.
        p. cm.
    Includes index.
    ISBN 0-7356-0682-X
    1. Small business--Finance.   I. Title.
  HG4027.7.T33   1999
  658.15'92--dc21   99-22894
                                                                       CIP

Printed and bound in the United States of America.

1 2 3 4 5 6 7 8 9   MLML   4 3 2 1 0 9

Distributed in Canada by Penguin Books Canada Limited.

A CIP catalogue record for this book is available from the British Library.

Microsoft Press books are available through booksellers and distributors worldwide. For further information about international editions, contact your local Microsoft Corporation office or contact Microsoft Press International directly at fax (425) 936-7329. Visit our Web site at mspress.microsoft.com.

Acquisitions Editor: Christey Bahn
Project Editor: Kim Fryer

This book is dedicated to the memory of my father, Dick Tadjer. He was the consummate entrepreneur who taught me that two essential things are borne from independence: freedom and original thought. I have come to believe that these two elements are not only the key to my own happiness, but that they must both exist and be nurtured in any culture in order to create an evolved, enlightened society.

Contents at a Glance

Contents

Contents

Part 5

Tricks for Today, Plans for Tomorrow

Acknowledgments

I want to offer not just thanks, but credit, to Amy Oringel, for being my research assistant on this project. There's no way this book would have gotten done without her.

I'd also like to offer thanks to Bill Hancock, who has taught me everything I know about how security is breached and privacy is invaded in electronic commerce.

Introduction

So, you've cashed out. It's a big step, saying "Check, please!" and joining the 8 million or so Americans who have forsaken the safety of a corporate conglomerate job in order to forge ahead independently, taking the risk of an entrepreneurial life. Maybe you're working in your home and doing whatever it is you do for a smattering of clients instead of for one boss. Or perhaps you've had the business idea of a lifetime and have rented some office space to start a whole new venture. Maybe you've invented something or are pursuing creative interests. Or perhaps you've been in your own business for a while. One thing is clear: You are not a foot soldier for someone else's agenda. You are your own boss, and the moment this became true was one of your life's great moments.

And like all of life's great moments, the day you declared your independence was filled with unadulterated insecurity and the deep-rooted fear that quitting your nice, safe job may actually have marked your worst act of insanity yet.

Well, if it's any consolation, someone once said that there is a fine line between insanity and genius. Some of you entrepreneurs who have traveled further along the independent-lifestyle path realize that maybe there is no difference at all—and that you like it that way. Odd as it may sound to new entrepreneurs, it is downright inspiring to have time for your thoughts, time for true abstract thinking. Yes, it is scary to be on your own, but the ideas that come to you living this way are unmatched.

If you haven't already, you'll wake up one morning and know independence is the best path. I promise. Three years into my independent life, I can no longer even imagine working for a large organization, where I have little stake in its growth, little say in its direction.

If this description sounds familiar, then indeed you qualify as a small business entrepreneur. Whether you own an architectural firm, a law firm, an accounting business, an insurance business, a retail store, or a consultancy, you are a small business. Whether you are a writer, graphic artist, actor, or hotel or inn owner, you are a small business. Whether you work one day a week or all seven days to earn your living, however you define that living, you are a small business.

A small business, according to The Wharton School of Business at the University of Pennsylvania, is defined as a business with 100 or fewer employees and $15 million or less in annual revenues. This is a good workable definition, but it doesn't quite capture the true characteristics of many small businesses, which are often one-person entities, clad in bathrobes and slippers, working in what used to be the spare bedroom or dining room or whatever area in the house the entrepreneur has appropriated to earn a living.

Perhaps most important, the Internal Revenue Service has many definitions for small businesses (which we'll get to in Chapter 5). In essence, though, if you are working independently to earn a living—if you are self-employed in any way—you are legally a small business of some kind.

The types of self-employed people who will find this book useful run the gamut. I think of a small business as anyone selling goods or services, with employees or without them. I consider partially self-employed people (who are making money on the side while they hold down corporate jobs) also part of this group.

Why will small business owners and self-employed people find this book useful? Because gaining control over your financial matters is the key to running a well-oiled machine of a business, no matter how big or small that business is. This book shows, in a step-by-step manner, how to create financial management strategies and then employ the right tools to execute those strategies. The concepts are flexible—they can be scaled up or down to meet the needs of individual self-employed people or small businesses with 100 employees. Not only are the strategies flexible, but the management and tracking tools are, too. The only hard-and-fast rules that will be widely different for, say, a home office dweller and a 100-employee business owner are those that the IRS imposes. Those differences are addressed in this book as well.

Remember that businesses with the proper financial management infrastructure know where they stand and can build on that infrastructure. Control of finances is also the key to freedom—freedom to spend your time the way you want. It is very important for self-employed people—including owners of businesses with 100 employees—to think of their businesses in terms of their independent lifestyles. The business should feed your lifestyle, not overwhelm it.

Control Money to Live within Your Means

The truth is, there has never been a better time to become—or remain—independent. The economy is strong, and efficient telecommunications methods mean that you can stay in touch with clients easily, no matter where you choose to live and work. Telecommunications methods also mean that the scope of your clientele is no longer limited to close physical proximity. The advances of the Internet and electronic communication in general have made local physical boundaries and limited resources—two traditional obstacles for small businesses—less problematic. The playing field for conducting business is leveled. You can reach people you couldn't have reached five years ago, and you can build your brand name (yes, even single entities need a marketing strategy today) to compete with much larger companies.

Anyone, for instance, can design and manage a Web storefront that looks of the same caliber as a much larger company's Web store and earns the same revenue (see Part 4). Location is not an issue on the Web, and neither is visibility. Any consumer can go to a search Web site such as Yahoo! (*www.yahoo.com*), type in "books," and get a list of Web bookstores. Yes, Barnes & Noble will appear as an option, but so will any mom-and-pop bookstore that registers its Web site address (also called a universal resource locator, or URL) with Yahoo! Since Internet shoppers aren't getting in their cars and driving to a store to shop, Barnes & Noble on the Web has no inherent advantage over the mom-and-pop Web shop. Jeff Bezos, the thirtysomething founder of Amazon.com, proved that concept by starting his own Web bookstore a few years ago. Today, Barnes & Noble must face the fact that Bezos' Web-only bookstore may be its most ferocious competitor. The Internet, in short, provides any entrepreneur access to a universe of potential clients and customers.

But before we get ahead of ourselves and start building on the revenue side of your business, we have to step back and start at the beginning, which is getting systems in place to properly manage the finances of your business. Maintaining an independent lifestyle, no matter how good the surrounding economic conditions, starts with money management. If you don't properly manage $100,000 in annual revenues, which specifically means living within your means, you won't be able to manage $1 million in annual revenues, either. It is a big mistake to think that more money will solve any problem.

Control over any finances you have, whether great or small, builds good habits, and good financial habits must be in place for your company to remain in the black. There's no getting around it.

Now, I'm not discounting the importance of earning money. Independence and freedom to pursue your own interests cost money, for sure. But earning money is still just the beginning. If you've taken off on your own, you've thought the earning part through: Either you've figured out a way to make money running your own business, or you have made the decision to make do with less in order to go after a dream.

Next on the list after earning money is managing it. The key to managing money is gaining control over it. The key to control is knowledge— knowledge of how much you have at every turn, how it is being spent, and whether or not there are better ways to spend or retain it. As an independent with limited resources, your mantra, when it comes to finances, must be "Maximum profit, minimal expense."

This is a tough order to fill. Even a single person's finances can become unruly very quickly. I use every trick in the book, and I'll be honest: My desk is stuffed with paper. Okay, not just my desk. My *life* is stuffed with paper. No matter how many systems I use, there are always surprises—a bill that got lost in the mail; a tax I didn't think about; a computer that crashed, forcing me to buy another one at a time when I didn't count on spending the money.

Money is a slippery thing, and life's inherent chaos makes it more so. If you have a business with employees, these surprises expand exponentially, and control can seem more elusive every day.

But if you want to be successful, you cannot become daunted and give in. You must set out to seek maximum control so that monetary surprises decrease over time and have less impact when they hit.

Consistency Is Key to Successful Strategies and Systems

In order to gain control, you need consistency. For everything you can predict, there should be a standardized system in place to deal with it. This is how major corporations manage money in order to be profitable, and there is no reason for you to handle financial situations any differently. A scaled-down version of how corporate conglomerates run is exactly what every entrepreneur needs to put into place. The "system for everything you can predict" is the absolute key to gaining and maintaining control over your finances, especially for the liability side of your life and business. Remember the phrase "a system for everything you can predict."

Systems start with an idea—a strategy—of how you want a particular business function handled. That part is up to you. Then tools come into play to execute the strategy, thereby setting the system in place. Then that system, if it was devised properly, should run itself, with minimal manual maintenance.

Here's a classic example: Your monthly bills are absolutely predictable. The amounts may not be, but the fact that they'll arrive like clockwork and need to be paid is predictable. So, you need a system for paying your bills, and when it comes to systems, you want the most efficient ones possible, because you don't want to spend your whole life dealing with your finances. What would be the point of an independent lifestyle if you spent your newfound freedom handling finances? For bill paying, the strategy is to automate the process so that checks are cut and sent without human intervention. The tool for executing this automated system is Microsoft's Money software program. You set up all the accounts once, and then bill paying is automated.

Some business functions will require a much more extensive strategy than simply loading a software program and learning how to use it (which this book explains for every software program mentioned). But the process is the same. You start with the problematic business function, devise a strategy, and then execute a system efficiently using technology.

Remember that if you set up a system and it ends up being more of a burden than the disorganized way you handled the business function before, then the system has failed. In this case, the whole thing must be rethought from square one—the strategy phase. The biggest mistake people make is to cling to a failing system and try to make the technology stretch and bend to fix all the problems. Technology doesn't do that. Technology is not an inventor; it is an executor.

Microsoft Office 2000 and Other Technology Tools

Talking about technology as the executor, not inventor, raises the central issue about technology that I believe is critical for people to remember. *Efficient*, in our electronic age, means employing technology. It means using software tools and using the Internet. It also means using electronic payment systems, such as credit and debit cards, or direct deposit for employees. But technology never works alone. Throwing technology at a problem is useless unless the business strategy is in place first. Technology can actually harm productivity unless it is employed correctly. Your business sense drives your business; technology makes the ride smoother and easier.

This book will show you how to use technology to solve your current financial management problems and create new revenue streams. However, the answers will never start with the technology, because the biggest myth of our technological age is that technology in and of itself is a cure-all. The last thing you want to do is spend more money on technology that won't help—or worse, that will create systems you and your employees will do anything to circumvent. One of the most common problems with technological solutions is that the business strategy wasn't thought out before the technology was deployed. Companies that make this mistake—from small businesses up to Fortune 1000 corporations—pay dearly for it. They end up spending a lot of money for a system that doesn't work in their business processes. Remember our mantra: "Maximum profit, minimum expense." Expense here also refers to employee productivity.

This book starts with the business strategy, then brings the right technological tools to bear on the situation. For small business financial management, there are two cornerstone technologies: Microsoft's new Office 2000 suite of business programs and the Internet.

Both of these technologies are perfect for any small business. Although the Internet doesn't seem like a technology brought to bear on a particular business function, it is. For managing investments (covered in Chapter 9) to tracking revenue from a Web storefront (Chapter 15), the Internet is front-and-center technology.

How You Can Save Money Using This Book

One of the advantages of financial management technology systems is that they can save you money. If you can't really afford an accountant on staff or a monthly bookkeeper, Office 2000's Financial Manager applications, used with Money, can enable you to keep accurate books. By the time you get to that once-a-year need for an accountant for tax preparation, your finances will be in such top order that the accountant's job will take far less time, and therefore cost you less. You can even automate your quarterly estimated tax payments by filing them electronically with the IRS (see Chapter 6).

Every system and step-by-step technique you need to be a do-it-yourself bookkeeper is covered in this book. However, the cost savings go way beyond that. A key component to managing your investments, for instance, is using online discount brokerages to buy stocks. You can keep track of your portfolios, transfer funds electronically, and much more. This book will show you how.

And forget just saving money. This book can help you increase revenues by showing you how to set up a Web storefront so you can conduct electronic commerce. By selling your goods or services over the Internet, you will create a new distribution channel for your business—and then you can track those revenues in Office 2000.

The point is, the strategies you learn in this book all work together, with the technology as the linchpin. You will create one system for all your financial management needs, with mini-systems to handle each component. All those mini-systems work together under one umbrella. You will not create a single balance sheet or budget that can't be transferred from one software program to another. For instance, when you track your expenses in one program, that "expense" file can simply be brought into your tax preparation program, intact.

I promise that if you follow the guidelines set out in this book, you will become organized and efficient with your finances.

How This Book Is Organized

This book is divided into five parts:

Part 1: The Lay of the Land: What You Need to Survive (Chapters 1 and 2) discusses what small businesses are up against, with particular attention to what the IRS wants from your life, as well as what new business challenges the twenty-first century will force you to face.

Part 2: Accounting for Small Businesses (Chapters 3 through 8) includes step-by-step instructions on how to use Microsoft Money and Microsoft Office 2000, set up automated bill paying, establish an electronic bookkeeping system, and prepare and file taxes electronically.

Part 3: Investing (Chapters 9 through 11) covers managing personal and business investments, buying stocks over the Internet, and tracking all your investments electronically.

Part 4: Web Storefronts (Chapters 12 through 17) discusses when you need a Web storefront and how to set up its electronic commerce component so you can accept credit-card transactions over the Internet and track revenue in Office 2000. It also helps you decide whether to manage your Web store in-house or hire an Internet service provider (ISP) to run the show. This part also teaches you all you need to know about the proper security systems you'll need for your Web store, including strategies and tips gathered directly from FBI Web security experts. At the end of this section is an electronic commerce resource list, including helpful ISPs, useful electronic commerce Web sites, and examples of successful Web storefronts.

Part 5: Tricks for Today, Plans for Tomorrow (Chapters 15 through 21) looks ahead to give you an idea of what's coming next in financial management.

In each part, you will learn proven strategies and systems for each business function mentioned. Because I believe that simplest is best when it comes to financial management, these systems are the simplest ways to get each of the jobs done, using the technology that is the linchpin of every strategy (software, online services such as tax-filing, ISP services, Microsoft commerce servers, and so on). Any of these strategies can be customized to meet unusual needs your business may have. The point is that they are fundamental strategies, designed to be flexible.

You will also see real business case studies that illustrate how small businesses have handled each task, as well as tips from what those businesses learned.

Why These Five Parts Are Included

When I was asked to write this book, I was asked to come up with a comprehensive look at what small businesses need to know about managing finances. *Comprehensive* is a frightening word for any writer, and my M.O. is to try to keep things simple. As a journalist who covers the trials and tribulations of small businesses trying to make their way in a ferociously competitive world of marketing and big brand names, I took a studied look at the 200 or so small businesses I am in touch with—businesses and entrepreneurs I talk to consistently in order to keep up with their challenges and how they're dealing with them.

What I realized was that the concepts that make up the five parts of this book are those that concern businesses when it comes to finances. Is the book comprehensive? Well, I'm sure that any small business owner who reads this book could come up with many additional questions for me, but this book will help businesses get their essential financial management systems up and running. How, in particular, those systems must evolve to meet changing needs is another issue.

The systems outlined here are designed to be flexible and simple for exactly that reason: to allow for inevitable changes that are still unknown. But for now, let's take the task at hand, which is to set up your systems to make sure that you can put, and keep, your business in the black.

Part 1

The Lay of
the Land:
What You Need
to Survive

Chapter 1

What Small Businesses Are Up Against Today

Small businesses and home office dwellers have more to contend with than ever before when it comes to handling finances. Keeping the books and managing investments are just the beginning. The technological age has introduced many new variables: online bill paying, online tax filing, and remote employees and subcontractors to track; Web storefronts to manage; and cash-alternative payment methods (for the payments small businesses accept) to handle. All these new variables, of course, offer enormous benefits, but that doesn't detract from the challenge they pose to entrepreneurs who are already juggling far too much and wearing many hats each day. Still, do keep in mind that although the learning curve for managing finances can be steep, the result is efficiency, which eventually means you get to devote less time to thinking about it—a boon in and of itself.

The learning curve for any or all of these new financial factors tends to go something like this: It starts by sounding overwhelming and expensive, so you put it off. Then, with a little bit of knowledge and insight into the benefits of facing your financial demands, it starts to sound appealing, though daunting. Then you start the process, and it seems like it's all possible. Then you get into the thick of learning how to use software and setting up systems, and it sounds daunting and unattainable again. Then the first month goes by when you don't have to sit down and write a bunch of checks—your automated bill-paying system kicks in—and you're motivated again. Then you see the light at the end of the tunnel—that each system will take patience to set up, but it will be well worth it. Next, the brass ring: You see how methodical the whole process is, and you dig in. Finally, you have an efficient system for each and every financial function in your business.

So, how do we get you from daunted to efficient?

Since it tends to hold true that context sheds light, and having light shed on a subject in turn helps you think clearly, let's start by talking about these New-Age challenges that will affect the way you think about the strategies and systems you want in place. The crux of giving context to financial management in this chapter is really to help you think about what is viable in terms of your budget and your human resources, taking all your factors into consideration before deciding what systems you want to start setting in place. It may well be that you need to start slowly, applying only a few systems detailed in this book and saving others—such as Web storefronts and credit-card acceptance—for later in the year or next year, when your budget allows.

The point is to get everything, including a realistic look at what everything will cost you, out in the open. As you may remember from the Introduction, a crucial factor in financial management is to minimize the kinds of financial surprises that leave you short on cash, or worse, in debt.

So let's demystify the key issues before we get to the nitty-gritty of setting up systems.

Cut to the Chase: What Uncle Sam Wants From You

The first step in understanding the challenges to your finances today is to understand what the IRS thinks about you. The IRS is all about definitions (which we get very specific about in Chapter 5).

The main thing you need to know now is that IRS officials, namely tax auditors, are skeptical when looking at small business and individual returns that include home office deductions and other entrepreneurial expenses. In short, a small business tax return raises red flags at the IRS. The reason is that apparently there is a great deal of fraud, especially by people who claim to work at home and deduct everything they do in life, including vacations and other non-deductibles, in the name of business expenses. (Note: If you own your own home, you may not necessarily want to take the home office deduction every year, because of the tax implications should you sell your home.) Furthermore, taxpayers—both the home office dwellers and small businesses with leased commercial space and employees—overestimate deductions. Even though some of these mistakes are made honestly, they encourage scrutiny from the IRS.

Toeing the Line

Say you live in a city in a small apartment that doubles as your home office. It is very likely that a large portion of your apartment is truly devoted to office space. Yet, if the IRS sees that you're trying to deduct a high percentage of square footage as a home office, they may flag your return for scrutiny or trigger an audit. One year, I tried to get 80 percent of my apartment as a home office deduction past my accountant. My former apartment in New York was small, and 80 percent was an honest, if not conservative, estimate of how much of the space I used for a home office. (We're talking about pretty much every room except my bedroom, bathroom, and kitchen!) Yet my accountant shook his head and asked me to lower that estimation.

At first I was angry, to be honest. I believe very strongly that our society should encourage small business owners and entrepreneurs of any kind. I was being totally truthful about my deduction and struggling to make my entrepreneurial life work while saving money by not renting a separate office, effectively forcing me to live amid a sea of computers and papers in my apartment.

After all, if it weren't for entrepreneurs, the nature of capitalism and competition in this country would change drastically—perhaps even making corporate oligopolies the norm, with very little room for true competition, which, in turn, would result in fewer choices for consumers and less creativity and invention in our society overall. If you look at the technology industry alone, you see how much invention comes from small businesses.

Anyway, my accountant nodded his head in sympathy at my philosophical diatribe about the importance of entrepreneurs in a free-market society, then told me once again to change the percentage on my return. Well, I didn't, but I understood that I was taking a chance. The reason I took the chance—aside from strong conviction—is that my apartment space fit the IRS requirements to the letter.

The point of this anecdote about home office deductions is that there are a million details involved in dealing with the IRS as an entrepreneur. The more careful and detailed you are, the better off you will be. Keep this in mind when you decide what kinds of ledgers you want to set up and what line items you will track.

Pay Taxes Online If You Want the IRS to Love You

The other way of avoiding intense IRS scrutiny is to make sure your tax returns are error-free. Many audits start because an auditor finds an honest mistake. Once the auditor is focused on your return, the IRS might go through it with a fine-toothed comb.

The good news is that the likelihood of an audit is actually less if you file your taxes electronically (which you will learn how to do in Chapter 6). According to H&R Block, which is responsible for handling more than 50 percent of all electronic returns filed with the IRS, the error rate on electronic returns is less than 1 percent, but it is 22 percent on print returns. The reason the error rate is lower for electronic filers is simple: If your return is in electronic form, it means you've keyed all numbers into an electronic form, then let the computer program do the calculations automatically. Checking and double checking are built into the process. Plus, if you've put a deduction in the wrong schedule, the computer program alerts you.

No great cost is associated with either electronic bookkeeping or electronic tax filing, so at the very least—if you do nothing else this book suggests—make these two projects your top priorities for financial management.

One other piece of information to bear in mind if you're starting to worry about scrutiny of your tax returns: You do not have to feel guilty or second-guess yourself if you are audited. As long as you have receipts proving your expenses and have taken legitimate deductions, you'll be fine. What an audit does mean is a headache—and that brings us back to our point about keeping fastidious books electronically and filing electronically to avoid errors.

New-Age Employees and Other Disasters

After getting your mind around the basics of electronic bookkeeping and tax filing, start thinking about some of the other issues small businesses face today. At the top of this list are employees who want lots of freedom (just as you do) and the new people the age of technology will inevitably force you to hire (even if you're a home office dweller).

These two factors are exactly what they sound like: cost centers. So, as you get a feel for the realities of these factors, keep your budget in mind. Some of these cost center items may have to wait.

Give Your People Freedom—Or Lose Them

Let's start with employees who want more freedom. As an entrepreneur, you have a good sense of how the American workforce is changing. More and more, people want to work from their homes, whether they own their own businesses or work for corporations as telecommuters.

Some analysts predict that in the next 10 years, close to 40 percent of the service industry workforce will telecommute. For small business owners with employees, this means you will need to accommodate changing lifestyle needs in order to acquire and maintain good talent. For small businesses in particular, no asset is more valuable than intellectual property—the people.

What are these changing lifestyle needs? Telecommuting is a big one. You can count on the fact that your employees will want to work at least part of the week at home. Whether the reason for wanting to work at home is as simple as easing a long commute or as complicated as having to juggle child care obligations, the result is the same. You will need to provide means for your employees to work at home.

One of the consequences of our telecommunications age is that the workforce at large has "seen the light"; everyone understands very clearly that standards of living can be raised with the aid of technology. The means you will need to provide could include new laptop computers or telecommunications access to your databases so that your employees can get at the reports and other documents that "live" in your office computers. They'll need e-mail and maybe a second phone line for faxing or Internet access. These needs add up to capital expenditures—which you'll need to budget for and then track.

The Right Person Might Not Be in the Right Place

This concept of employee telecommuting goes a step further. Say you need to hire someone with particular skills—maybe a salesperson with a lot of experience in your industry. Say the person you really want isn't local and isn't willing to move, but he or she would be extremely valuable to your business. You could end up with a remote employee, one whose relationship to you is primarily conducted via telecommunications methods, namely e-mail and phone. In this

7

scenario, there could be even greater benefits to you than simply having the right person doing the job. From a financial perspective, you might be able to cut a deal with this potential hire to work as a subcontractor, which of course means you don't need to pay benefits. If you and the subcontractor work out such an agreement, you'll need a system to track subcontractors separately from your regular employees.

When it comes to telecommuting employees, remote employees, or the employees who work at your office every day, even more issues arise: You'll need to pay these folks, and most of them will want direct deposit of their paychecks to their bank accounts. This means setting up accounts in Office 2000's Financial Manager.

You'll start to see that the linchpin of all the financial systems you'll invent for yourself—including the one we'll discuss next, the Web storefront—is Office 2000.

The Web Storefront: Albatross or Money Machine? It's Up to You

Another cost center to plan for is your Web storefront. A Web storefront is a Web site for your business that allows people to buy goods and services from you directly over the Internet. Like any good Web site, your Web storefront is a brochure for your business as well. What distinguishes a Web site that's simply a brochure from a Web storefront is the capability to buy products or services.

Selling goods and services through your Web storefront usually means setting up a credit-card transaction-processing system on your Web site. Say you're a small retailer that sells crafts. Potential craft buyers can surf to your Web site, look at pictures and descriptions of the items you sell, choose the ones they want to buy by "clicking" on them, and then key in credit-card or debit-card numbers (totally securely, of course), which are sent to you over the Iternet with the orders. You fulfill the orders and probably send the customers back e-mail receipts.

You can have a Web storefront of sorts without accepting credit cards. Instead, you can simply take orders for goods over the Internet, then send the goods C.O.D. or have a salesperson call the customer to get the credit-card information. Although you can argue that this is indeed a Web store, it isn't really conducting electronic commerce. It actually makes the whole traditional phone-ordering or fax-ordering concept more complicated by adding another step. You might find this concept worthwhile nonetheless, because a Web site itself is a terrific marketing tool; it gives your business worldwide exposure to people you may never otherwise be able to reach.

However, taking the whole order, from start to finish, over the Internet is often the best way to go. It requires much less in terms of human resources, for instance. One of the greatest assets of Internet sales for small businesses is that they require you to have fewer people manning the phones for orders. Web storefronts also provide new revenue streams. (We go into detail about Web storefronts and how to set them up in Chapters 12 through 17.)

What Will It Cost?

The thing you need to remember about Web storefronts is that they cost money and require effort to set up and run. The good news is that over time, they've gotten much cheaper to implement. Here's the bottom line: You can get a Web storefront up and running for about $300 per month. A Web-hosting company (which may or may not be an Internet service provider) will host the whole thing for you, plus provide the Internet access you'll need. That access rate will need to be faster than simply dialing in on a regular phone line. You will need a digital line of some kind, as explained in the Web storefront part of this book. A Web-hosting company will also arrange for your back-end accounting system, which routes the credit-card purchases directly from your Web storefront to the banking system. These same Web-hosting companies often provide reporting as part of the service. This means the host will send you statements of all sales made to integrate into Financial Manager. The reports also tell you valuable marketing information, such as what items are selling best and who's buying what.

The total monthly cost for a Web store varies according to your Internet access speed. Just keep in mind that you'll be spending $300 per month (including your Internet access), at least, when all is said and done.

Will It Pay Off?

How to gauge whether this expenditure will pay off for your business is the key issue for Web storefronts. Knowing the estimated return on your investment will play a part in how you negotiate with Web-hosting services. For example, most Web-hosting services will offer you a better deal per month if you sign on for a full year. However, it may be smarter for you to pay a slightly higher per-month fee in order to test the waters for three months or so to see if you sell anything at all.

Getting a headache yet from all this new information? Don't fret, and don't try to assimilate all these bits of information in your head right now. All the factors related to Web storefronts will be made clear and given to you in bite-sized, easily digestible morsels in the Web storefront section of this book. By the time you're done reading that material, you'll have a step-by-step guide of what to do and when to do it for maximum profit and minimal expense to your business.

The only thing you should make a mental note of right now is that $300 monthly cost. It's a realistic cost. Toss out the lowball figures, such as less than $100 per month, that you've heard at cocktail parties. That kind of unrealistic price leaves some vital component out of the equation, such as Internet access costs or the price you pay as a merchant that accepts credit cards over the Internet. Any credit-card payments you accept cost you. The catch with Web storefronts is that the fee the credit-card companies charge for Internet sales is higher than the fee they charge in the physical world. So, say Visa charges 1.5 percent per sale for items consumers buy in a physical-world retail store. The percentage may be 2.5 percent for similar items sold via the Internet.

Visa, MasterCard, and American Express officials attempt to explain this discrepancy by saying that their risks are different on the Internet because it is a less proven, and therefore higher-risk, sales vehicle. This reasoning is what I affectionately refer to as "banking industry logic"—a breed of reasoning formed by what I believe are extraterrestrial beings who have somehow earned MBAs. Like it or not, though, it is a fact of life. These same credit-card companies offer "reassurance" by claiming that as the Internet proves itself as a marketplace and they gather more data showing payment patterns on which they can base predictions (as they do in traditional retail sales), they might lower that percentage to be on par with physical-world sales.

Why credit-card companies can't use the predictions they make about over-the-phone credit-card sales and apply them to the Internet is beyond me. Essentially, the Internet is a phone network, with Web sites as text-based (instead of voice-based) message systems. Your computer is the phone. This analogy makes sense to the telecommunications industry, but alas, bankers are a different breed.

My point is that there are costs people leave out when they give you too-good-to-be-true estimates for Web storefront costs. You may want to kill the messenger—which would be me—for giving you less optimistic news about per-month fees, but at least you won't have nasty surprises later. My estimates will be your actual costs; I won't leave anything out, so you won't experience sticker shock once your Web-hosting company sends you the real, live bill.

If it ends up costing you a little less than my prediction, well, that's the kind of financial surprise that tends to sit well.

While we're on the subject of monthly costs for new things, let's go to the last cost center: new employees you're going to have to hire.

Technology Means You Need to Hire People, Like It or Not

No matter how much of an electronic do-it-yourselfer you become after reading this book, I cannot save you from one inevitable cost center: technical support staff. One truism about technology is that things inevitably go wrong. Another truism is that small businesses can't do everything themselves—we just got through talking about hiring a Web-hosting company, for instance.

The Catch-22 is that even if you arranged to implement a Web storefront in-house, you'd absolutely, positively—no question about it!—need an in-house technical person on staff to make sure it runs correctly. Don't listen when vendors tell you their systems are so easy to use that you won't need a technical support person. They're wrong.

And that's the point here: These technological benefits mean you will need to hire support staff to handle technical tasks—whether it's contracting a Web-hosting company, hiring a part-timer for tech support, or simply paying extra (up to $1,000 per year at the low end) for access to emergency on-site computer repair services.

Technical support staff doesn't become a need solely if you have a Web storefront (though that makes support staff particularly imperative). The minute you rely on computer systems to run your business—even if it's just loading Office 2000 on your system and keeping your books on it—you need to be able to keep that system up and running all the time, because if your computer network goes down, so does your business. Home office dwellers with one or two computers, a printer, and Internet access are no exceptions.

Thinking about computer tech support as something on which you'll spend $1,000 per year is a wise way to plan ahead. You can buy contracts for such support from the people you buy computer systems from. This kind of arrangement is usually called a *maintenance contract*. If you think computer maintenance is not something worth budgeting for, you should consider the possibility (or the likelihood!) of some kind of computer disaster that will grind your business to a halt—a hard drive crash, a software program on which you store everything you need and which suddenly won't open up—at which time you will be flipping through the Yellow Pages, desperately trying to find anyone who can fix your problem. Such a crisis management service, if you find one, will cost you about $95 per hour, plus a fee just for someone to show up at your door.

You will pay less if you think ahead. Maybe it will cost you $1,000 per year, or $2,000, or for some home offices, $500 or so. The price will vary according to the complexity of your computer network setup. But whatever you pay planning ahead will be less than you would pay dealing with computer repair people once you ran into an emergency.

Bottom line: The day you start running your business electronically is the day you add a technical maintenance line item to your budget. Part of this maintenance budget might go for backup systems—Zip drives, for instance. Once you have a technical support person advising you, you'll know what you need for your situation.

The benefits to these expenditures are many. Perhaps you will even be able to upgrade less often because your systems will be better maintained. Simply cleaning a computer system properly can prevent problems such as hard drive crashes.

So, add $500 to $1,000 per year to your budget for computer maintenance. Later chapters go into detail about how to find these mysterious technical support people. You'll have a resource list at your fingertips by the time you're done reading this book.

With This Context in Mind, Time to Move On

Now, without further delay, let's get to the systems and how they work. Let me quickly outline what you'll be looking at in the next few chapters.

The next chapter, Chapter 2, is devoted to telling you about the features of Office 2000 and the Microsoft Money program. The chapter starts with a detailed description of these two programs because they are the linchpins of setting up your bookkeeping system. Once you understand what these programs offer, it will become clear how each financial management function is tracked as you read the various sections of this book. You'll have context needed to understand what you're reading, and you'll know the capabilities of the software.

Chapter 3 takes you step by step through the process of installing the Money software and setting up your accounts. Chapters 3 and 4 discuss issues you'll want to consider when you set up your books. So let's get started.

Chapter 2

What's New in Money and Office 2000 for Small Business Owners

Y ou should keep two essential ideas in mind when it comes to using any software program: First, it's just software, and no matter how unlikely it seems at the start, you *can* learn how to use it—master it, even. One of the biggest problems people have with any software program is that they don't understand the range of what it can do, so it often seems that the software isn't doing what it's supposed to do. Knowing what a program is capable of doing is critical to using it efficiently and effectively, even if the process of acquiring that knowledge is a little tedious. Until you fully understand the software's functionality, you can't take advantage of everything it can do.

The second thing to keep in mind is that it won't help to remain in denial about needing to understand your software's capabilities—I, for one, often complain about the difficulty of using software. However, the reality is that software is getting easier to use all the time, but it's still not a matter of simply launching the program and learning by osmosis. You must study what the software does and look at the whole program or, in the case of Office 2000, the suite of programs, in order to get the most from any software package.

If You Understand It, It's Your New Best Friend

I have to admit I am one of the worst at practicing what I preach when it comes to installing software. Typically, I get a new program, and without even opening the manual, I install it, find the one or two key elements I need, and never figure out what else it can do. Then, invariably, some friend of mine with the same program will call me. (I am lucky to have technical friends with endless patience for fiddling with software.) The friend will ask if I like a certain really cool aspect of the software. My response is often, "What? It does *what*? I didn't know that. I can't believe I went out and bought a different program to do that!"

Then, of course, I blame the friend for not telling me about the software's functionality before I went out and bought an additional program. Better to blame others than myself, I always say.

For a supposed technical expert, I spend a lot of time looking like a moron. My little secret is that I'm lazy, which is why I bought the software in the first place—to take over tasks I'm too lazy to do myself.

So, over time, after suffering endless embarrassment in front of colleagues who are much more thorough than I am, I've learned the hard way that truly studying what the software can do before starting to use it makes a big difference in terms of what you get out of it. That's why this chapter reviews the features and functions of the suite of programs that make up Microsoft Office 2000 and Microsoft Money 99, without going into the step-by-step set-up process. Keep this information in the back of your mind for now; don't let it overwhelm you, and don't worry about the details of how to actually use the software. Keeping an open, uncluttered mind regarding the software now will help you make decisions about the systems you need to set up later, once you understand how you can put Office 2000 and Money to work for you.

Your life is supposed to get easier once you use a software program. A software program that takes over functions of your life—in the case of Money, financial management—should impose a sense of organization on the way you think, and it should do so comprehensively. With a software package, the function should become mostly automated, predictable, and reliable. If your life doesn't get easier—and I mean after you really understand how to use the software thoroughly—the program is no good.

One of the shortcomings of many software programs is that they do some of what you want and need, but not all. Or they're too stiff—you can't customize them for the inevitable idiosyncrasies of the way you like to organize things. With one disclaimer in mind—which is that no software to date has succeeded in catering to the whims of your mind, because software simply isn't that advanced yet—let's take a look at Office 2000 and its essential companion program, Money 99. It is arguable that with this suite of software programs, you will come the closest you can to having a truly comprehensive financial management package.

Bear in mind that I call Money the essential companion because you really can't run your business on Office 2000 alone. Money is the indispensable bookkeeping component of the equation. Many people may choose to start with Money and then buy Office 2000 later or not at all, depending on their needs.

With that in mind, let's look at the features of Money. Particularly for home office workers, Money may well be the only software program a small business person needs in order to get a handle on finances.

Money, That's What You Want

Figure 2.1 is a "screen shot"—literally, a snapshot of what your computer screen looks like with a particular software program loaded. In this case, it's what the screen looks like right after you start Money 99. The beauty of Money is that it's organized like a Web site, with the features labeled so that you can simultaneously see everything the software can do. And as you do when you visit a Web site, all you have to do to use Money is point your cursor and click a button or a link to move to another part of the software.

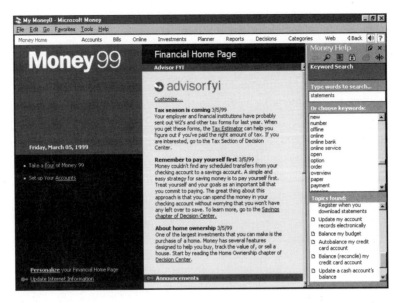

Figure 2.1

The screen you see when you start Money 99.

In fact, Money is more like a Web site than you may realize. For instance, when you click Bills on the navigation bar, you will go to the Bills & Deposits area of Money. Once you're there, you can click another link that will log you into the Internet (assuming you have an Internet account and you have set up the correct information in Windows to access it). Then Money will open your electronic account in the financial institution you use so that you can pay bills while you're in Money. So, when you access the Bills feature of Money, it's as though you are on a Money Web site, paying bills through your financial institution without ever leaving the program.

But I'm getting ahead of myself. Let's go through what Money can do, feature by feature. If you already have Money installed, you can see that the navigation bar tells you everything the program can do, in shorthand. If you don't have the program yet, you'll want to get it once you read through this chapter. Chapter 4 will help you install the Money software on your computer.

Money Home

Starting from the left on the navigation bar, Money Home represents your Financial Home Page. This page is what you'll see when you start the program, after you've set it up. Money Home gives you a starting point for all the features Money puts at your fingertips.

Accounts

The Accounts feature is next on the navigation bar. The Accounts place is where you manage all your accounts—up to 15 different types. When you click Accounts, the Account Manager page opens; here you create new accounts or delete accounts you no longer need. For each account you set up, Money creates a file. You simply open each account and add monthly items, calculate your registers, and keep an ongoing register for each of your creditors.

The 15 account types Money can track are:

- **Assets,** or the things you own, such as cars, computer equipment, or your home. This information comes in handy if you ever need to make an insurance claim or calculate your net worth.

- **Bank,** which tracks accounts you may have with banks other than the usual checking, savings, or line-of-credit accounts. An example is a CD account, which you may cross-reference with Money's Investment account.

- **Cash,** which includes day-to-day cash expenditures (such as ATM withdrawals)and an investment account's associated cash account, which is considered the amount of cash you have on hand, totally liquid (in other words, money not tied up in stocks or mutual funds).

- **Checking,** which tracks your checking account transactions, including day-to-day spending and bill paying.

- **Credit Card,** which includes a separate account for each credit card you have.

- **Employee Stock Option,** which tracks stock shares with a vesting schedule that you've received from a company. This feature is useful for home office dwellers who are still tied to another company.

- **House,** which keeps tabs on house expenses, home office expenses, and lines of credit taken against the home. House is linked to Money's Mortgage Account.

- **Investment,** which includes stocks, bonds, mutual funds, CDs, money market funds, and so on.

- **Liability,** which tracks money you owe but on which you don't pay interest, such as short-term loans from friends or family.

- **Line of Credit,** which includes your line of credit from a bank.

- **Loan**, which includes any loan you have that you are repaying on a regular schedule with interest, such as car or student loans.

- **Mortgage**, which covers amortized real estate loans and is linked to a corresponding House account.

- **Retirement**, which tracks tax-deferred savings, such as 401K, 403b, IRA, SEP, Keogh, or RRSP accounts. Retirement can be cross-referenced with Investment accounts for a full view of your investments in one window. However, the Retirement category exists separately because retirement accounts have different tax implications—namely, none!—when you file returns with the IRS.

- **Savings**, which include interest-earning savings kept in a bank.

- **Other Accounts**, which is a category designed for flexibility, so you can track accounts particular to you that are not included among the other options listed.

Bills

We've already touched briefly on the Bills & Deposits feature, which you can use to pay bills and transfer money (from, say, a checking account to a savings account) online. The four essential functions of this feature are Direct Statements, Web Statements, Direct Bill Payment, and Web Bill Payment. The first two deal with making bank deposits and transferring funds from one account to another; the second two deal with paying your bills:

- **Direct Statements.** This feature lets you find an account's current balance and get information on cleared transactions. For instance, if a creditor says you never paid a bill, but you did send the check, you can see whether or not the check cleared your bank. You can also transfer funds from one account to another and e-mail messages to your financial institutions. Think of Direct Statements as a full-service capability, not just a function in a software program. Essentially, the Direct Statements service allows you to send the bank information you've already entered in Money.

- **Web Statements.** This feature allows you to link directly to your financial institution over the Internet while you remain in the Money program. So, even though using Web Statements is like visiting your financial institution's Web site, all you see is the same familiar Money program screen, rather than unfamiliar and different screens for every institution with which you do business. Think of it this way: Your financial institution is set up to communicate with the Money program, so you never have to exit the program to deal with your bank. Depending on the services your bank offers, you can use this feature to check balances, get information on cleared transactions, transfer funds, and send e-mail messages to your bank.

- **Direct Bill Payment.** This feature lets you pay all your bills while you sit at your computer. Requiring no postage stamps or paper checks, you simply sit down and fill out little electronic forms that look like checks, and then press a Send button, which zips your "checks" off to whichever creditors you've set up accounts for. The check's amount is deleted from whatever account from which you wrote the check, and the cleared transaction appears when you download your bank statements (which you do via either the Direct Statements or Web Statements features).

  The Direct Bill Payment feature also lets you schedule automatic payments to be made to any or all creditors for up to a year. For each creditor, you set up an account and log it in your Account Register, which is located in the Accounts section, and then you enter the amount to be automatically paid each month. Automated payment is a good feature to use if you have monthly bills that are always the same, such as a car loan, a home mortgage, or a computer equipment lease. But don't worry if your checking account balance is too unpredictable to make automated payments. (Most of us know the feeling of having to wait a week before mailing out a bill!) You don't have to schedule automated bill payments, and you can start an automated bill-payment schedule and cancel it later. Or you can just sit at your computer each month and pay your bills online, creating records in your accounts as you do it.

- **Web Bill Payment.** Like the Web Statements feature, Web Bill Payment links you to your bank's Web site but lets you work in the Money program while you pay your bills and schedule your advance payments.

You need to remember the difference between the Direct Statements feature and the Web Statements feature, as well as the difference between Direct Bill Payment and Web Bill Payment. For the direct functions, you are simply dialing directly, via modem, to your bank or other financial institution to perform transactions; for the Web functions, you are linking to an institution's Web site and conducting the transaction directly on that site. The cool thing about Money is that to do the Web transactions, you never have to leave the Money program or interface.

One other note: If you've used Quicken, another popular accounting and bookkeeping program, you can easily transfer those files—both the bill-paying files and the account registers themselves—into Money. Remember, though, that in order to use Money's funds transfer and bill-payment features, you will have to set them up in advance with your bank. We'll get to that topic in more detail in Chapter 4.

Online

Consider Money's Online feature your "communications central." When you click Online, you open the Online Financial Services Manager place, which enables you to set up online transactions with financial institutions. This is the feature you use to set up direct dial-in connections as well as Web site connections for each financial institution with which you deal. Each time you want to add a bank to your arsenal of online resources, you go to the Online place.

Investments

The Investments feature exemplifies just how much Money resembles a Web site. When you click Investments, the Portfolio place opens. You can choose from among several categories that give you information and news on investment-related topics, including Subscription Services, Stock Research, Investment Finder, Market Update, Investment Insight, and Online Trading. If you have an Internet account, when you click one of these categories, you link to that Microsoft Investor Web site. There you can research investments and even buy and sell stocks live online, and then go back to Accounts in Money to track the transactions in your Investment accounts.

It's a wonder people ever leave their houses anymore, isn't it!

Planner

Planner may take some getting use to, but once you are accustomed to it, you'll find it a very valuable feature. When you click Planner, the Financial Planner place opens. It has three options: Lifetime Planner, Debt Reduction Planner, and Budget Planner.

The Lifetime Planner is for planning your retirement, college expenses, or other long-range goals. The Debt Reduction Planner is a budgeter of sorts that allows you to schedule debt-reducing payments to creditors so that those payments work within your budget. The Budget Planner helps you budget everything from housing expenses to groceries.

The beauty of these planners is their built-in calculators, which automate the process of assessing budget options. My recommendation is to start with the basic Budget Planner, and then use the Debt Reduction and Lifetime Planners after you've gotten your basic monthly costs in order.

Reports, Decisions, and Categories

The Reports, Decisions, and Categories functions of Money are what I call the "keep you honest" features. Reports will show you your spending habits and where your money is going . By creating tallies of what you're spending and who is getting all your money (as depressing as some of these reports may be), you can tell whether or not you are living within your means, which is truly the crux of money management. With the Reports feature, there is no fudging: The cold, hard numbers sit in front of you, and you are presented with a bird's-eye view of where you're spending too much or too little (too little may mean that you're not paying off debts fast enough to live up to your budget goals).

The Decisions option shows another bird's-eye view—a comprehensive look at various categories of financial management you should be taking into consideration. It's a good way to check yourself and make sure you've covered all your bases.

Finally, the Categories feature shows you all the categories you've set up for budgeting, bill paying, investing, and accounting. If, for some reason, the way you've organized your financial management system isn't working, you may want to go into Categories and see if you find intuitive the way you've divvied the components of your financial plan. For instance, let's say you've created different tracking categories for capital expenditures (such as new computer equipment) and major debts. You may want major debts to be the primary category and the capital expenditures to be a subcategory under it if, for example, you are paying off computer equipment in scheduled payments.

Another—and perhaps the most important—way Categories comes in handy is to set up all categories to match the way the IRS will look at your expenses and revenue. If your categories match the IRS's, taking the next step and transferring the information to your tax returns becomes a no-brainer. It's a good idea to learn what categories the IRS wants to see and set those up first. If you have categories left over that don't seem to fit in any of the IRS requirements, create your own categories. However, you will probably find that the IRS categories are sufficient, at least as primary categories, and the leftovers will become subcategories.

Becoming the Best Bookkeeper Your Accountant Has Ever Seen

It is important to think of all your financial management in terms of what the IRS wants from you. Not only will that make your life easier during tax season, but it will get you used to thinking about which expenses are advantageous to you in terms of deductions and which aren't.

I know it starts to sound like all financial management practices are focused on the IRS, and frankly, they are—especially when you're planning budgets and creating expense-tracking systems. If you can get a grip on what the IRS wants and needs in the early stages of setting up your systems, it will teach you to think and act differently and more advantageously. You may start to save receipts every time you park your car or take a taxi, or you might lease computer equipment instead of buying it because it's a better tax write-off. As a person flying solo in the business world, you want and need those sound habits in order to stay solvent and then thrive.

Office 2000: The Mother of All Financial Managers

Office 2000 has been evolving into the premier suite of office productivity applications for some time. When you load Office 2000 onto your computer, you have pretty much everything you need to run your business, from Microsoft Word to Microsoft Excel to far more elaborate customer management and direct-marketing programs.

For the purposes of financial management, though, we'll focus only on Small Business Financial Manager, which is a set of features designed specifically for small business owners' money management needs in the latest version of Office 2000. Financial Manager requires that you use Microsoft Money, because Financial Manager springboards from Money's accounting, bookkeeping, and bill-paying features to add very sophisticated functions that small businesses—mainly those with employees—need.

The "What-If?" Factor

Financial Manager works with Excel in order to make better use of your accounting data. Financial Manager is capable of bringing spreadsheets to life, making them dynamic. You can create customizable financial reports and charts by asking Excel one question: What if?

Think of your accounting spreadsheets—which you take directly from Account Manager in Money—as a vast database that you need to mine. Then imagine that you can ask that database business questions in the form of "what-if?" scenarios, in order to find out what will happen if you adjust some of the numbers to meet a specific goal.

For example, say you're looking at a spreadsheet that lists your employees' salaries. You know you need to hire a few more people, but you can't decide whether you can afford two or three. Or perhaps you are trying to decide whether to hire one upper-level management person or two lower-level administrative types. You can key in average salaries for each category and ask the spreadsheet "What if?" for as many combinations of new employees as you can think of. Excel can calculate what any combination of new employees will cost you, how those salaries will change the average salary in your office, or any other financial questions you may have about how employee salaries will affect your business.

When strategizing for your business growth, for anything from new employees to making sales projections, this "what-if?" scenario function is critical because at the core of any new business decision is the question of whether it's affordable. The five types of "what-if?" analyses that can be performed are profitability, accounts receivable/payable and inventory, financial, expenses, and buy vs. lease. The features in Financial Manager that help you with the "what-if?" scenarios, from creating them to executing them, include:

- **What-If Analysis Wizard,** which is the feature that lets you test decisions before making them.

- **Report Wizard,** which creates customizable financial reports, such as income statements and balance sheets. Using a built-in sales analysis reporting tool, Report Wizard also lets you see where sales are coming from.

- **Business Comparisons,** which let you compare your business against industry averages by using a common-sized income statement, balance sheet, and four key ratios: Current, Debt to Equity, Sales to Total Assets, and Percentage of Profit Before Taxes to Equity.

- **Financial Projection**, which projects and forecasts future results based on historical accounting data, combined with any growth rates you key in (a critical part of a "what-if?" scenario). You can do projections for periods of up to five years and then see them in report form.

- **Preset Graphical Charts**, which include Revenue Expense Trend, Cash Flow Trend, Sales Composition, and Balance Sheet Composition pie charts.

Poof! Transform Yourself into a Financial Strategist

With Money and Office 2000's Financial Manager, you will transform yourself into a financial strategist. This software combination frees you to think out loud while the software automatically performs the calculations your ideas require.

Once you have these programs set up properly, all of these reporting functions will become habitual. For now, though, as we move onto the nitty-gritty details of what the IRS wants and how to set up accounts in Money, keep Financial Manager's data-mining capability in the back of your mind. It will free you to be as imaginative and elaborate as you want with the systems you set up.

Part 2

Accounting for Small Businesses

Chapter 3

Step-by-Step Guide to Using Money for Account Bookkeeping

By the time you have completed this chapter, you will have installed Microsoft Money and set up all the accounts you need. You will know how Money works and will actually look forward to using it—it will have that novelty of a new toy that you have mastered and want to play with.

Working with the Software

I know this sounds like a cheap pep talk, but, hey, pep talks can be helpful. The bottom line here is that it's just software; it can't do you any harm. I admit that's not *entirely* true. Computers often seem like a vast wasteland—you put your precious data inside them and then they crash, or software programs self-destruct and your data can become corrupted or seemingly irretrievable. But those are the exception, not the rule.

It's Just Software—But Do Back It Up

Before we start using Money, you need to back up all the software you put on your computer. Unfortunately, this is a lesson I recently learned the hard way. I got lazy about backing up data as I started writing this book. After three weeks of research—catching up with the IRS to make sure I was on top of all the new laws that apply to small businesses and writing it all down on my trusty desktop PC—my hard drive crashed. I woke up one morning and tried to turn on my computer. Nothing. No screen, just a horrible, strained whirring noise coming from my hard drive. I stared out the window, unable to even contemplate what might have just happened. I tried to think. When was the last time I backed up everything on my other computer? The reality hit: It had been weeks ago. After taking my computer to the recovery experts, I phoned them for the prognosis. The friendly, soft voice on the phone described my hard drive as having "severe damage." Words like "crunched" and "gouged" were used. I felt like I was sitting in a hospital waiting room while a family member was in critical surgery. The worst part: About 30 percent of my data was gone forever. Of the salvageable data, the recovery experts weren't sure what shape it would be in.

A whopping $2,300 and a week and a half later, I was sitting at my computer, putting in the CD that said "good recovered data" on it (the other two said "bad recovered data," and I couldn't face those). Imagine if every paper and folder in your office were thrown up into the air and landed on the floor in one huge pile. Then picture that every heading on every piece of paper said "filoool.chk" instead of informative things, such as "Q1 report." Then imagine yourself trying to find your critical documents in that pile. Suffice it to say, I'm *still* looking for some of my files.

Have I scared you enough yet? I hope so, because once you put all your financial information into a software program, you never want to be in a position where that data has vanished into the ether. I can assure you that my terribly kind editor at Microsoft Press was far more understanding than IRS auditors will be if you tell them that all the numbers on which you were based your tax return got "lost" and they'll have to wait until you make up new ones.

Your New Backup Routine

My quick recommendations for backing up data: If you're on a network, back up everything to a server, every day. For extra protection, get a Zip drive. Hook it up to the PC that you use for Money and Microsoft Office 2000, and back up all the data. There's also a very cool Web site service called @BackUp (*www.atbackup.com*). For a fee, you can back up critical data to that Web site. Essentially, @BackUp gives you a membership that allots you a "briefcase" of space on its site. You send data to this site via e-mail, and you can update the data whenever you want. The beauty of this backup option is that it's off site. If there's a fire in your office or home, there's no risk that you'll lose your mission-critical electronic documents, because you'll have backups stored at @BackUp. I recommend using this service in addition to backing up to a server or Zip drive. Call me paranoid, but I'm planning on never again losing the data on which my livelihood depends.

Okay, lecture over. Let's put in that Money CD and get started.

It's Easy to Install

Put in the Money CD in your computer's CD-ROM drive and follow the instructions that appear on your screen. Note that I am using Microsoft Money 99, so if you're using an older version of the software, some things may be different.

Once the CD is in the drive, Money will ask you a few questions:

1. Where should it install the program? (You want to install it in your Program Files folder on your hard disk, which is usually the C drive.)

2. What is your CD key? (The key is printed on a sticker on the back of the CD's plastic case. Just type the key into the box that appears on screen.)

3. Shall it continue to load the program? (Click Yes.)

All the questions Money asks during the installation process are this simple. It takes only a couple of minutes to install the program.

Tip

If for some reason the setup does not begin automatically when you insert the CD, go to the lower-left corner of your desktop screen and click the Start button. Then click Run on the Start menu. The Run dialog box appears. In the Open box, type the drive letter for your CD-ROM drive, followed by a colon (:), a backslash (\), and the word "setup." For example, if your CD-ROM drive is drive letter D, type the following into the Open box:

D:\setup.

Then click OK. Money should start the installation process.

Put It on Your Desktop

After you've installed Money, a process that takes only a few moments, you can create an icon for it on your desktop so you can start the program easily by just clicking the icon. This process is called creating a shortcut. It's easy. Just follow these steps:

1. Right-click the My Computer icon on your desktop.

2. Click Explore on the drop-down menu. This opens Windows Explorer.

3. If you've installed Money on your C drive, open the C drive by double-clicking its icon. Otherwise, double-click the icon for the drive on which you installed Money.

4. Open the Program Files folder. You should see the Microsoft Money folder listed. If you don't, you've installed Money to another folder.

5. Select the Microsoft Money folder. The files in the Microsoft Money folder will appear in the right pane of Windows Explorer.

6. Left click the Msmoney file and drag it onto the desktop. Windows will create a shortcut for Money on your desktop. From then on, when you want to launch the Money program, you simply click the Money icon on the desktop.

Setting Up Your Books Using Account Manager

Open the Money program. Go directly into the Accounts section by clicking Accounts on the navigation bar near the top of your screen.

The Account Manager place will appear. See Figure 3-1. Click the New Account button at the bottom of the page. Have your bank account statements ready, because you're about to create an account in Money.

Figure 3-1
Account Manager helps you track all of your financial accounts.

Create the Account

Once you click the New Account button, a wizard will take you through the process of setting up an account, step by step. The first thing you will do is enter the name of your financial institution. If you don't know whether your bank or other financial institution (depending on what kind of account you're setting up) participates in online services, click the Financial Institutions button. It will give you a list of banks and other financial institutions that participate in online banking services. If your bank is not on this list, you will not be able to get statements via the Internet or do online bill paying with Money. Without these services, Money is only partially useful. It is worth opening at least your primary checking account—the account from which you pay bills—at one of the listed banks. There is bound to be one located near you.

Let the Wizard Do It

After you've entered the name of your financial institution, just follow the wizard. It will give you options regarding the kind of account you can set up (detailed in Chapter 2). You'll need to enter your checking account number and current balance. Then you'll have an option to connect to the online services of your bank via the Internet. Click on that option (you'll need to have an Internet account and your modem connection set up to do this). Money will automatically locate your bank's Web site and connect you (as long as it's one of the financial institutions that support Money).

After you've set up the first account, click the New Account button in Account Manager to create another account. When you're done setting up all your accounts, you can view your full list of accounts in Account Manager. Click View, and then click All Accounts. To open up any particular account, just click its icon. A register will open, and you can enter items in it. Just remember to save the file after each change you make. Money will calculate your new balance after each debit or deposit you enter in the account.

Congratulations. You have now taken the first step to better bookkeeping. Your first electronic system is officially in place. Each month, you can download statements from your bank and save them in the account folder you've set up. In the next chapter, we'll see how to set up online bill paying, the second must-have system. But before we do that, one quick word on security and training.

Other People Who Have Access to Your Books

You definitely don't want to be the only person in your office who knows how to keep your company's books—unless it's a home office and you don't want anyone else to be involved with your finances. In a small business, you may want an administrative assistant to handle the monthly maintenance of keeping your accounts straight or have a bookkeeper come in once a month. If you decide to give others access to your books, sit down and walk them through the process of working with Money. You don't want them making notes or keeping ledgers anywhere else but in Money; otherwise, it defeats the purpose of setting up the system.

In addition, talk to the other bookkeepers about being sure to back up their work using whatever back-up scheme you've decided on. You should also talk to them about security. You can password-protect your Money documents, just as with most other Windows-compatible documents. If you do so, make sure the people you trust with this password don't share it with anyone else. I know this sounds slightly paranoid, but it's not. Your bookkeeper could unwittingly give the password to someone with an unsavory agenda, so better that your bookkeepers not share the information with anyone.

One of the reasons small business computers are at greater risk of being accessed by the wrong person is the familial culture in which small business owners work. As the FBI is quick to point out, more than 80 percent of all break-ins are inside jobs. When it comes to small businesses, the culprit is usually a friend of an employee, who, say, comes in the office for lunch and swipes a password printed on a note left out on a table. (Chapter 16 goes into great detail about what the FBI says to do to protect your business from hackers and other thieves.)

Don't ever underestimate how vulnerable electronic documents are to tampering and theft. Be careful whom you trust with access to your Money accounts; this is your *money* we're talking about. Make sure a loud-and-clear company policy about snooping in those files is in place. It might sound silly to have official company policies in businesses that may have just two or three employees, but to the contrary, such policies help everyone develop security-conscious habits that will protect them as well as the business.

Okay, now on to bill paying.

Chapter 4

Setting Up Electronic Bill Paying in Money

I hate paying bills. In fact, I hate every aspect of it—setting aside a perfectly good morning at the beginning of the month, pulling the stack of bills from their cubbyhole in my desk, writing the checks, addressing the envelopes, and searching for the book of stamps of which I never have enough for the number of payments I need to send. Most of all, I hate how depressing it is to watch the balance in my checking account dwindle away with each check I write.

You'll Never Want to Write Another Check Again

So, it is without exaggeration that I say that aside from the wheel, the telephone, air travel, and good coffee, online bill paying is the best invention of civilization to date.

Think about it: You sit at your computer, you fill out a couple of electronic forms, hit Send, and it's over. No opening envelopes, no writing checks, no licking envelopes to seal them, no searching for stamps, no need to remember to go to the mailbox.

Personally, I like bill paying to be fully automated—any payments that are the same amount each month are automatically deducted from my checking account and sent on their way without my intervention. I set up automatic payments for a year at a time, but that isn't necessary. If your checking account balance is not very consistent, you can sit down at the computer every month, on whatever day works for you, and pay your bills.

Your Bills Will Never Be Late Again

If you use electronic bill paying, you should also get overdraft protection on your checking accounts. If you can get overdraft protection, I recommend setting up automated payments for certain bills a year in advance. It is truly liberating to never think about certain bills again. Because you don't rely on yourself to remember to pay them, they will never be late. You can travel and have your bills paid without worrying. It's like that old TV commercial for self-cleaning ovens, where the woman is out shopping and she says, smiling, "You know what I'm doing? I'm cleaning my oven!"

Now, bear in mind that the year-in-advance method is useful only for bills that are the same amount each month, such as a mortgage, car payment, insurance payment, or cable TV bill. You can set up automated payments for bills that have a fluctuating monthly balance, but you will have to guess the amount to be automatically deducted from your account each month, because that amount will vary.

Tracking Is Automatic

There's more good news. Bill payment tracking is automatic in Money. When you fill out an electronic check in the Bills & Deposits place, Money asks you if you want to record that amount in Account Manager. When you click Yes, Money automatically deducts the amount from the account you're using and then it calculates your new account balance.

First Get the Terminology and Choices Straight

Before using Money to pay your bills, you need to understand your choices regarding electronic payments. You can make electronic payments directly from Money or you can go to your financial institution's Web site and pay your bills.

With the first option, you work in Money using electronic checks. You can choose between two methods of payment: Epay (electronic payment) or Apay (automatic payment). When you choose Epay, your bank will make an electronic payment to your creditor (assuming the creditor is in the United States). If the creditor does not accept electronic transfers, your bank will send a check instead. When you choose Apay, your bank will follow an automated payment schedule that you set up (you can cancel this schedule at any time).

With the Apay option, you pay your bills on your financial institution's Web site, using the electronic forms that are there. If you choose this option, you will need to reenter all your bills in your Money Account Register. So why, you ask, would anyone bother to pay bills on a Web site? Essentially, this option exists for people who aren't using a program such as Money. If, for some reason, you opt for the Web site payment method, it's a good idea to keep track of the electronic checks you write. Otherwise, the only records you'll have are the statements you get from your financial institution.

Step by Step, Let's Pay Your Bills in Money

To get started, start Money and click Bills on the navigation bar. This opens the Bills & Deposits place. If it's not already selected, click Pay Bills, which is on the left side of the screen. This opens the Upcoming Bills & Deposits option. Once you've entered the recurring dates a bill is due, Money will remind you each month to pay that bill by the due date.

To enter a bill, click New at the bottom of the screen. The Create New Scheduled Transaction wizard will appear, as shown in Figure 4-1. Just follow its instructions. Remember to have your account number and all your creditors' account numbers handy. Also remember to choose either Epay or Apay in the number field on the electronic check.

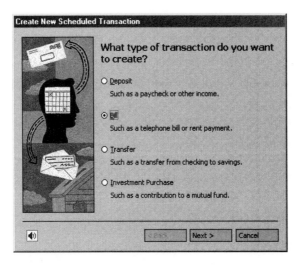

Figure 4-1

The Create New Scheduled Transaction wizard will help you enter your bills.

In a few steps, the wizard will ask you what type of payment you would like your financial institution to make to the creditor. The choices will be Write Check or Direct Debit. If you're not sure whether a certain creditor will accept a direct debit (an electronic transfer from your account to your creditor's account), choose Write Check.

Tip

You may want to ask your financial institution whether charges are involved before choosing an electronic payment method. Some institutions charge for cutting a check but don't charge for an electronic transfer. Others charge for both.

When you're done with each bill, click the Record Payment button at the bottom of the screen. This is what tells the program to record your electronic check in your Account Register.

Setting Up the Online Connection in Money

To actually send your bills, click Online on the navigation bar. Double-click the name of your financial institution. Then choose Investigate Offerings and connect to your financial institution via the Internet to see what instructions it gives.

Tip

Remember to open your Internet connection before you click Investigate Offerings. Otherwise, a box will pop up telling you Money cannot locate the financial institution. Any time you get this warning, check your Internet connection to verify that it's active.

If you've chosen to pay some bills automatically each month, you will need to go through this process only once for those bills. Otherwise, each month when you pay bills through Money, you must remember to actually send them by clicking the Online button. I've made this rookie mistake before: I recorded my payments, saw them nice and neat in the Account Register, and forgot to send them!

The beauty of this system is that once you send the bills, that's it. The payments are recorded in Money's Account Register automatically. You'll also see the transactions in your monthly statement, which you can download on the Web site of your financial institution.

Caution

Be sure not to trust electronic payments altogether. Carefully compare your monthly statements to your Account Register in Money to ensure that the payments have been made.

Online Deposits and Money Transfers

In the Bills & Deposits place, you can make deposits and transfer funds online or simply record deposits you will make in person at your financial institution. For instance, I don't get direct deposit for the money I earn from my freelance contracts—I get checks. I enter them in Money's Bills & Deposits place by using the Create New Scheduled Transaction wizard. When I click the Record Deposit button at the end of the wizard, the deposit is added to my checking Account Register.

You can transfer funds between cooperating financial institutions online for any number of purposes, including transferring money from your checking account to a savings or investment account. Or you can win your employees' hearts by giving them direct deposit for their paychecks.

Win Your Employees Over by Setting Up Direct Deposit

Technically, there isn't much difference between online deposits and money transfers. If the whole process is electronic—and you're not just recording a deposit you made—they are all transfers of funds. So, giving your employees direct deposit can be as simple as setting up recurring payments from your checking account to their checking accounts, which is precisely the same process as setting up bill payment. The only difference is that when you open the Create New Scheduled Transaction wizard, you choose Deposit rather than Bill as the type of transaction you want to create. Then you go through much the same process as you do to pay a recurring bill: You tell the wizard that the deposit is a recurring payment, and you enter each employee's checking account number, financial institution, and amount of the deposit.

There is, of course, a catch: You have to make sure that your financial institution deals with each of your employees' financial institutions. Often this information can be found on the Web site of your financial institution. If all your employees have accounts with the financial institution you use, the process is much simpler. There's less chance of error, and your financial institution is less likely to charge for the service.

Caution

If you talk to a teller or other representative at your financial institution about depositing your employees' paychecks, make sure that you are clear that you want to arrange an electronic transfer. Every business has its jargon, and you don't want the person you speak with thinking you plan to come in person and deposit money for your employees every week or month.

Get in the Habit of Checking Your Statements

When you set up new, complicated electronic transactions—bill payments, transfers, and the like—you should get in the habit of visiting the Web site of your financial institution once a week to make sure that your statements accurately reflect all this electronic activity. Remember, it's not "reality" until it appears on your statement. Earlier, I promised that this electronic money-management system would mean you spend less time, not more, checking your finances, but a quick look at statements online is a good idea when you set up new recurring payments. After a few months, you can cut back on how often you check. But do check at least once a month at the outset.

Every time you make a non-recurring online payment or transfer, check a few days afterward to ensure the payment was made. It's a good idea to see that the transfer went through before the bill becomes late and causes you problems. Hey, I've had bills I sent out that got lost in the mail. Creditors call and ask where the check is, and I've had to mail another check on more than one occasion. This is much the same situation. Think of checking your online statement as getting a receipt for your transaction.

Getting a bookkeeper is sounding better all the time, isn't it?

Chapter 5

The Entrepreneur's Ultimate Challenge: The IRS

There's no getting around it. This chapter, which will tell you everything you need to know to deal with the IRS and track it like an Uber-accountant, is long and detailed because the IRS operates on a foundation of minutiae, and if I were to skip details I would be doing you a disservice.

I have tried to break the information in this chapter into chunks, which you can skim now and come back to later and use as worksheets of sorts. It's important to read the chapter through once, though, because it will plant concepts in your head—important concepts that will help you remember the implications of your spending habits on your small business.

Put it this way: Every time I get out of a cab—I live in Manhattan, so I get out of cabs often—I think of the IRS, even if it's for only a split second, and I ask for a receipt. As an entrepreneur, my business-related transportation is deductible.

As a small business owner, you need to have the items and paperwork the IRS demands from you so ingrained in your thinking that you automatically do the "right thing" to get the maximum financial benefit. If you're worried that you'll turn into a miserly, obsessed person who thinks about little else but receipts and deductions, don't. It is actually far easier to think of your taxes whenever you spend money as a small business owner than it is to sit down at tax time and wonder why you have no deductions. The latter attitude creates much more angst, I assure you.

This chapter will help you manage your finances better and make your life as a small business operator profitable.

How the IRS Defines a Small Business

The IRS is all about definitions. Every cent you have, every cent you earn, and every cent you spend is analyzed and categorized and scrutinized by the IRS. This is a dangerous institutional disposition for entrepreneurs, because we, as a group, often intertwine our personal and professional finances. Every tax return from a small businessperson raises an eyebrow at the IRS because of this truism. The IRS tends to assume that you as a small business owner will take too many liberties, so they are watchful. Never forget that.

On the other hand, you don't have to be too defensive. Just because IRS personnel carefully scrutinize your return doesn't mean that you haven't been honest in your claims. What you need to be is *clear;* you need to give the IRS folks the information they want in the language they use and in the categorical method they understand.

My father, a successful entrepreneur himself who represented the third generation of Tadjers to become entrepreneurs, once told me: Never do business with others until you speak their language.

I think it's some of the best advice I've ever received. He meant it somewhat literally; he spoke five languages because he did business in other countries and never wanted to be at a disadvantage. You have no convincing power and no possibility of bonding, he told me, until you speak the language of your target business partners and customers and you understand exactly where they're coming from and what they want.

Bonding with the IRS may sound like a horrific proposition, but it makes sense. If you understand the way IRS personnel think and how they communicate among themselves, you can interact with them more effectively. The IRS is essentially a business partner you didn't choose but with which you're stuck.

So, let's start with how the IRS defines small businesses. As you may have already guessed, the IRS doesn't have a simple, five-word definition for what it considers a small business. Instead, the IRS borrowed its definition from the Small Business Administration (SBA). The bad news is that the SBA is not much less convoluted than the IRS.

Here's the delineation: Small businesses are typically defined according to the number of employees or the amount of revenue they generate. A quick-and-dirty definition for a small business is one with fewer than 500 employees. But there's a more scientific way of looking at it.

The Small Business Act, which created the SBA in order to aid, counsel, assist, and protect the interests of small business concerns, also defines a small business as "one that is independently owned and operated and which is not dominant in its field of operation."

The Act also accounts for the differences between industries in determining what is a small business. A small farm, for instance, will earn far less revenue than a small bank. For each industry, a small business is defined numerically by either the designated number of employees or the amount of annual revenue. This definition is called a *size standard.* Companies that meet the definition of the size standard are able to receive SBA and/or federal support designated for small businesses. Size standards are categorized by industry division and are indicated with a four-digit code. Industries that don't fit into any of the given divisions are given the code 9999 and set at the standard size of $5 million in annual receipts.

The Office of Size Standards follows three publications to determine what businesses can in fact be called small: the *Table of Small Business Size Standards*, the *Guide to SBA Definitions of Small Business,* and *Small Business Size Standards and Regulations.*

What all of this means is that if your business doesn't command a lion's share of any given market segment and you have fewer than 500 employees, you can qualify as a small business, according to the IRS.

Forms You Need to Fill Out

You need to have three basic categories of forms for the IRS if you operate a small business:

- **Income forms.** This includes Form W-2 (Wage and Tax Statement) and Forms 1098 (Mortgage Interest Statement) and 1099 (includes Miscellaneous Income and Dividends and Distributions).

- **Employment taxes.** You need Forms 940 (Employer's Quarterly Tax Return) and 941 (Employer's Record of Federal Tax Liability) for employment taxes. If you are a home office dweller, you don't necessarily need these forms.

- **The basic tax return itself.** This is Form 1040 (U.S. Individual Tax Return), with Schedules C (Profit or Loss from Business [Sole Proprietorship]), CE-Z (Net Profit from Business [Sole Proprietorship]), and SE (Self Employment Tax).

Defining Home Offices

Time for a distinction between the general small business and the home office, which is a subset of a small business. This is important because it has everything to do with whether the IRS will let you count your operation as a small business. Furthermore, home offices are entitled to certain deductions that other small businesses are not, and vice versa. Home office dwellers may have to fill out different forms, perhaps fewer forms, than general small businesses (for instance, a home office dweller may not have to fill out the employment tax form). Home offices are the most difficult businesses to define because these are the people whose personal and professional finances are the most intertwined.

The crux of the deduction issue is whether you can deduct a portion of your home as a business expense or not. You need to know if you fit this profile before you go any further. Figuring out whether you qualify is complicated. First, you must fit a general profile. Then you must define yourself as one of two categories under that general profile.

General Profile Requirements

Not every person who flicks the on switch to his or her personal computer every third day is considered a home office worker by the IRS. You've got to prove you do more than check your voicemail before eating dinner. To claim business use of part of your home, you have to meet a variety of requirements.

Your use of the business part of your home must be exclusive, regular, and for your trade or business (outside of a few exceptions). It also must be your principal place of business, a place where you handle patients, clients, or customers in the normal course of your trade or business, or a separate structure you use in connection with your trade or business.

If you are an employee of another person's company but use a part of your home for business, you may be able to add it to your deductions. However, the rules for this group are tough. You have to meet each of the above criteria, and your business use must be for the convenience of your employer—not *your* convenience, which is a galling part of the law. You also cannot rent all or part of your home to your employer and use the rented portion to perform services as an employee.

Two Different Breeds of Home Office Worker

If you meet these criteria, you just opened up a whole array of new tax deduction opportunities. However, a variety of situations within these specifications define different types of home office worker; each type has different obligations to the IRS as well as being entitled to different deductions.

If you use a specific area of your house solely for your business, you can deduct certain expenses on Form 1040. But wait, it's self-evaluation time again. Are you self-employed or an employee? Different tax rules apply to these two groups, so make sure you follow the section that applies to your own situation.

Self-Employed People

Self-employed people file either Schedule C or Schedule E (Supplemental Income and Loss) and, depending on which one you file (normally Schedule C), the deductions are indicated on different parts of the forms. As a self-employed person, you can take advantage of deductible mortgage interest, real estate taxes, casualty losses, and several other expenses.

Other home office deductions such as insurance, repairs, and utilities aren't allowed if you don't pass the initial general home office criteria test. If you do, though, go ahead and deduct away. If you rent your home, deduct a portion of that as well. Just make sure that these expenses don't exceed the deduction limit. If they do, they can be carried over to next year.

Employees

As a general rule, all employees must itemize their deductions on Schedule A (Form 1040) to claim expenses for use of a home office (and any other employee business expenses).

If you have employee expenses for which you were not reimbursed, report them on line 20 of Schedule A.

You generally must also complete Form 2106 if you claim any travel, transportation, meal, or entertainment expenses, or if your employer paid you for any of your job expenses that are reportable on line 20. (Amounts your employer included in box 1 of your Form W-2 are not considered paid by your employer.)

However, you can use a simpler form, Form 2106-EZ, instead of Form 2106, if you meet one of the following criteria:

- You were not reimbursed for your expenses by your employer.

- You were reimbursed for your expenses by your employer and the reimbursement was included in box 1 of your Form W-2.

- You use the standard mileage rate if you claim car expenses.

When your employer pays for your expenses, the payments will not appear on your form W-2 under these circumstances:

- You are required to account, and do account, to your employer for the expenses, and if you are required to return, and do return, any payments not spent for business expenses.

- You account to your employer and your business expenses equal your reimbursement.

- You account to your employer when you give your employer documentary evidence and an account book, diary, or similar statement to verify the amount, time, place, and business purpose of each expense.

- You account to your employer if your employer gives you a fixed allowance under an accountable plan that is similar in form to an allowance specified by the federal government and you verify the time, place, and business purpose of each expense.

For more information, get the instructions for Form 2106 and Publication 463 (Travel, Entertainment, Gift, and Car Expenses) from the IRS.

Although line 20 of Schedule A is used to deduct business expenses of a home office worker, employees with deductible mortgage interest should deduct both business and nonbusiness parts of the interest on line 10 or 11 of Schedule A. If the amount is higher than the allowed limit, you can't deduct the overflow on line 20.

Employees are also able to deduct real estate taxes and other expenses, including those not related to their homes, such as utilities, insurance, and advertising. These figures are indicated on Schedule A; casualty losses need to be indicated on Form 4684 (Casualties and Theft), section B.

Special Instructions for the Home Office Worker

Living and working in the same place can get very confusing come tax time. The lines for what areas of your home are used for business and what are used for personal purposes can get very blurry. Like it or not, it's time to divide and conquer. To be able to deduct expenses for the business part of your home, you have to separate the room or rooms that are strictly applicable to your life as a home office worker. The most crucial figure you need to calculate is the percentage of your home that is used for business. After that, figuring your taxes for a home office is relatively easy and similar to other small businesses.

Time to move on from definitions to deductions. We've already delved into the home-related deductions for home office workers, but the definition of a home office worker is so completely tied to deduction entitlements that it's impossible to separate the two.

What You're Entitled to Deduct

This section presents a complete list of deductions to which small business owners are entitled. Within this discussion, we touch on occasions when a general small business owner (the kind with a rented office and employees) is entitled to something that won't apply to a home office worker. Before we start, we need yet another definition—what is a deductible expense? To be deductible, a business expense must be both ordinary and necessary. An ordinary expense is one that is common and accepted in your field of business. A necessary expense is one that is appropriate and helpful for your business to keep running.

If you have an expense that is partly business and partly personal, you can deduct only the business part. Keep records of your business expenses separate from records of your personal expenses in Money, which was covered in Chapter 3.

Ready to use the minus sign on your calculator? Here are deduction opportunities for small businesses.

Bad Debts

Bad debts are just as terrible as their name. These occur when someone who owes you money can't pay you. A bad debt for business is one that was created or acquired in your business or that was closely related to your business when it became partly or totally worthless.

Your Car

You may use a car or truck for work purposes, such as delivering goods or meeting with clients. The expense of maintaining the vehicle can be deducted, as can any trips on local transportation made for business reasons. This does not include your commute to your office, if you have one. It refers to any trips you make from your office to an off-site meeting or appointment. When accounting for transportation expenses, you must choose to deduct either actual expenses such as gas, parking, and tolls (you'll need a receipt for each expense) or the standard mileage rate. For 1998, the standard mileage rate is 32.5 cents for every business mile. Tally up all the miles you've driven for business and multiply to get your final deduction.

Office Furniture, Including Computers

Let's say you just sprang for new office furniture for your whole company. The price tag was high, but look how great the place looks. Plus you can deduct the whole thing as a business expense. Right? Well, sort of. You can't deduct the total cost of the furniture in one tax year, because it will be with you for longer than that. What you can do is spread the cost over more than one year through depreciation. This rule covers computers, too.

The rule is: Any property used in business with a useable life longer than one year and that will eventually lose its value can be depreciated. This doesn't include land or inventory. Under the Section 179 deduction, you can choose to deduct up to $18,500 for depreciated property in 1998.

Insurance, Interest, and Professional Fees

Other areas with deduction possibilities include rent, insurance, interest on any loans taken for business purposes, legal and professional fees related to your business (such as accountant fees), and contributions to pension plans for retirement purposes. The latter includes simplified employee pension (SEP), savings incentive match plan for employees (SIMPLE), Keogh plan, IRA, and Roth IRA.

Insurance deductions have one qualification: Self-employed people can deduct only 45 percent of their health insurance costs. This number is due to increase for the 1999 tax year, so make sure to check with the IRS before you file for that year.

Business Taxes and Employee Salaries

You can also deduct taxes associated with your business, such as income, sales, personal property, fuel, and excise taxes. As an employer, you can deduct your employees' salaries as long as they follow the ordinary and necessary requirements defined at the beginning of this section.

Travel, Meals, and Entertainment

The area of travel, meals, and entertainment is the fuzziest deduction category. For instance, if you own a bookstore, can you deduct the cost of going to see movies that were made from the books you sell? Let's try to make some sense of this tricky area.

First, if you travel away from your regular place of business for business purposes, you can deduct the expense of that trip. This includes any transportation, lodging, meals, dry cleaning, telephone, tips, and other expenses you incur while on the road.

You can usually deduct 50 percent of the total cost of every entertainment expense, from a power lunch to an informal drink with clients at your local pub. As long as it's business related, you can deduct the cost of getting your customer a guest pass to your gym, floor seats to the Knicks game, or tickets to *Cats*. Anything associated with business-related entertainment is deductible. Even if you need to get some sleep and instead send an associate to catch the game with clients, you can deduct the amount you reimburse your employee for entertainment expenses.

You can see why there is a whole business culture built around playing golf. People like golf, so they turned it into a business deduction.

Home-Related Deductions

There are expenses that all small-business owners can deduct, and even though these are home-related expenses, they can apply to everyone. We touched on this in the home office worker section in an effort to come up with a definition, but this discussion presents a comprehensive list.

Remember that these deductions apply only if you can claim business use of certain home expenses. You must make sure to include only the business part of these expenses in figuring out the final amount to deduct. Keep in mind that you cannot deduct expenses that are related to tax-exempt amounts.

Home-related deductions include real estate taxes, deductible mortgage interest, and casualty losses.

Real Estate Taxes

To figure the business part of your real estate taxes, multiply the real estate taxes paid by the percentage of your home used for business.

Deductible Mortgage Interest

To figure the business part of your deductible mortgage interest, multiply this interest by the percentage of your home used for business. You can include interest on a second mortgage in this computation. If your total mortgage debt is more than $1,000,000 or your home equity debt is more than $100,000, your deduction may be limited.

Casualty Losses

If you have a casualty loss on the home you use in business, you can treat the casualty loss in different ways, depending on the property affected. The first is as a direct expense. You should use the entire loss as the business portion of the home office deduction if the loss is on the portion of the property you use only in your business. The second way is an indirect expense, where is the loss is on property you use for both business and personal purposes. In the latter case, use only the business portion to figure the deduction. The last way is as an unrelated expense when the loss is on property you don't use for business, so no loss should be figured into the deduction.

Be sure to check Publication 547 (Casualties, Disasters, and Thefts) to determine exactly which method describes your situation. If you are filing Schedule C for Form 1040, get Form 8829 (Expenses for Business Use of Your Home) and follow the instructions for casualty losses. If you are an employee or file Schedule F for Form 1040, you can use the worksheet near the end of Publication 547. You will also need to get Form 4684 (Casualties and Thefts).

Home-Related Deductions for Home Office Workers Only

There are other expenses that only home office workers can deduct. The business part of these expenses can figure into your deduction. These expenses include depreciation of your home, insurance, rent, repairs, security systems, utilities and services, day care, and business furniture.

Depreciation

If you own your home, you can deduct a portion of its value. In most cases, you can't deduct the whole thing in one year because you will own the house beyond that year.

Insurance

If you have insurance covering the part of your home you use for business, you can deduct that insurance. Make sure you check the duration of your policy. If it extends beyond the end of the tax year, you can deduct only part of the total amount paid for the coverage. If your policy extends into the next year, you can deduct that portion of the coverage in your return for that year.

Rent

Multiply your rent payments by the percentage of your home used for business to compute your deduction.

Repairs

If you fix or make improvements to your house, you can deduct the expense. But before you get excited, you can't go out and renovate your kitchen and expect to deduct the whole cost. First, you have to make sure the repair somehow relates directly to the well-being of the house or to your business. A new CD player for your son's bedroom on the second floor doesn't count. But putting a new sink in the bathroom closest to your office would apply.

To calculate the deduction, add up the labor and supplies used in the project and then take from that total the percentage of your home that you use for your business. Let's say you do put a new sink in the bathroom and it costs $500. But you use only 5 percent of your house for work purposes. You can only deduct 5 percent of the sink's cost—in other words, $25. Examples of common deductible repairs are patching walls and floors, painting, wallpapering, repairing roofs and gutters, and mending leaks.

However, repairs are sometimes treated as a permanent improvement, which is not deductible, because it increases the value of your property and extends its life. The IRS sees this as benefit enough. You need to be able to define the improvement as being essential for conducting business. See "Permanent Improvements" under "Depreciating Your Home" in Publication 587 (Business Use of Your Home) for more details.

Security Systems

You can deduct part of any security system you buy to protect your house. But again, you can deduct only the percentage of the total that accounts for the business part of your home. Security systems can also be used as a depreciation deduction.

Utilities and Services

Some home office workers spend all day under two or three glaring lights in a space furnished with a computer, a printer, a phone, and a fax machine. Talk about up-front expenses! Fortunately, that person can deduct a percentage of his or her total utility bills (including garbage removal and cleaning services), according to the percentage of the home used for business.

Along with all that hardware, you may also have two or three separate phone lines (not to mention the separate one you promised your kids). Your phone bill may be the scariest one in the pile. Aside from the basic local telephone service charge, including taxes, for the first telephone line into your home, you can deduct business calls made on that first phone line as well as the cost of a second line (or third or fourth or as many lines as you need) as long as those lines are used exclusively for business. You can also deduct any phone line you may have dedicated to a computer or fax machine you use for business purposes.

Day Care

I've been preaching that in order to deduct certain expenses, your house must be used exclusively for business purposes. Well, here's an exception: Part of your house can be used for business at one point during the day and at other times for nonbusiness-related activities. For example, you operate a small business that entails supervising three four-year-olds in your den at noon, then watch the evening news from the very same spot six hours later on your personal time and still take advantage of a deduction opportunity.

However, the day care services must be provided on a regular basis in that space and you, as a day care provider, must meet certain criteria: You must be in the business of providing day care for children, persons 65 or older, or persons who are physically or mentally unable to care for themselves, and you must have applied for, been granted, or be exempt from having a license, certification, registration, or approval as a day-care center or as a family or group day-care home under state law.

There are two different scenarios when figuring out your deduction in such a case. If part of your home is used exclusively to provide day care services, you can go ahead and deduct all the appropriate expenses that have been explained so far in this chapter. But if part of your home is used to provide day care but not exclusively for that purpose, you must figure out how much time you use that room or area for business purposes. If you use a room only occasionally for business, you can't deduct it. However, a room used consistently and for hours at a time for your day care business can be used as a deduction, even if you sometimes use the room for nonbusiness purposes. The good news is that you do not have to keep records to show the specific hours the area was used for business.

Business Furniture

Here's a deduction opportunity that probably far too few people know about: You can deduct the cost of business furniture or equipment even if you don't qualify to deduct other expenses for the business use of your house.

According to section 179 of the Internal Revenue Code (covered in Publication 946, How to Depreciate Property), you can deduct amounts associated with any of three situations. The first case, listed property, refers to any items used for entertainment, such as your new DVD player and 110-CD changer with souped-up hi-fi speakers. This category also includes computers that haven't already been accounted for in your total home office deduction (assuming you qualify).

Sounds great, right? Well, take the key out of the ignition. Before you run down to Circuit City to buy a TV the size of your wall, you have to put the equipment through the 50 percent test. If you can honestly say that spending more than half your day watching cartoons really does further your business goals (I know it does mine, though I'd swear I'm watching CNN), feel free to deduct the cost of the television.

But remember that any listed property bought in 1998 that is used less than 50 percent of the time for business cannot be deducted under section 179 of the Internal Revenue Code. You can, however, depreciate the property using the Alternate Depreciation System (ADS) covered in Chapter 3 of Publication 946 and, when doing so, also figure in the percentage of time you might use that piece of equipment to help manage your investments.

Let's say you have one of those bosses who screams to you just as you reach the elevator to head home for the evening, "Change in plans. I need that report first thing tomorrow." If you use any listed property at home, such as a computer, for your work as an employee, you have certain benefits as long as you use the equipment for the convenience of your employer and its use is required as a condition of your employment. This last requirement is a bit vague. It means that this piece of equipment is absolutely essential to doing your job.

If you don't continue to use a piece of listed property at the more than 50 percent rate, you can figure depreciation or figure excess depreciation. Look at "Years After the First Recovery Year" in Chapter 3 of Publication 946.

Property: The Section 179 vs. Depreciation Decision

If you bought property to use in your business, you have three deduction options: elect a section 179 deduction for the full cost; deduct part of the cost under section 179 and depreciate the rest; or depreciate the whole cost. Here's how each of the three options work.

Elect a Section 179 Deduction for the Full Cost   You can generally elect to claim the section 179 deduction on depreciable, tangible personal property bought for use in the active conduct of your business.

You can choose how much of the cost you want to deduct under section 179 and how much you want to depreciate. You can spread the section 179 deduction over several items of property in any way you choose as long as the total does not exceed the maximum allowable. You cannot take a section 179 deduction for the basis of the business part of your home. You elect to take the section 179 deduction by completing Part I of Form 4562 (Depreciation and Amortization).

There are deduction limits in this case, however. The section 179 deduction cannot be more than the business cost of the qualifying property. In addition, you must apply the following limits when figuring your section 179 deduction:

- **Maximum dollar limit.** The total cost of section 179 property you can elect to deduct for 1998 cannot be more than $18,500. This maximum dollar limit is reduced if you go over the investment limit in any tax year.

- **Investment limit.** If the cost of your qualifying section 179 property is over $200,000, you must reduce the maximum dollar limit ($18,500) for each dollar over $200,000.

- **Taxable income limit.** The total cost you can deduct each tax year is limited to your total taxable income from the active conduct of all your trade or business activities, including wages, during the tax year. Figure taxable income for this purpose in the usual way, but without regard to all of the following: the section 179 deduction, the self-employment tax deduction, or any net operating loss carry-back or carry-forward.

For more information on the section 179 deduction, see Chapter 2 in Publication 946.

Take Part of the Cost as a Section 179 Deduction and Depreciate the Balance This option becomes clear once you read the depreciation option.

Depreciate the Full Cost Use Part II of Form 4562 to claim your deduction for depreciation or property placed in service in 1998. This part does not include any costs deducted in Part I (section 179 deduction).

Most business property used in a home office is either five-year or seven-year property under the Modified Accelerated Cost Recovery System (MACRS), described in Publication 946. Five-year property includes computers and peripheral equipment, typewriters, calculators, adding machines, and copiers. Seven-year property includes office furniture and equipment such as desks, files, and safes.

Under MACRS, you generally use the half-year convention, which allows you to deduct a half-year of depreciation in the first year you use the property in your business. If you place more than 40 percent of your depreciable property in service during the last three months of your tax year, you must use the mid-quarter convention instead of the half-year convention.

After you have determined the cost of the depreciable property (minus any section 179 deduction taken on the property) and whether it is five-year or seven-year property, use Table 3-1 to help you calculate your depreciation.

Table 3-1 Half-Year Convention Recovery for Five-Year and Seven-Year Property

Year	Five-Year Property (%)	Seven-Year Property (%)
Year 1	20.00	14.29
Year 2	32.00	24.49
Year 3	19.20	17.49
Year 4	11.52	12.49
Year 5	11.52	8.93
Year 6	5.76	8.92
Year 7	8.93	8.93
Year 8	4.46	4.46

Here's an example of how to use the information in Table 3-1: During the year, Joe bought a desk and three chairs for use in his office. His total bill for the furniture was $1,975. His taxable business income for the year was $3,000, without any deduction for the office furniture. Joe can elect to do one of the following:

- Take a section 179 deduction for the full cost of the office furniture.

- Take part of the cost of the furniture as a section 179 deduction and depreciate the balance.

- Depreciate the full cost of the office furniture.

The furniture is seven-year property. If Joe doesn't take a section 179 deduction, he should multiply $1,975, the cost of the furniture, by 14.29 percent (.1429) to get his depreciation deduction of $282.23.

The Catch With Section 179 and Depreciation   One thing you should bear in mind about the section 179 vs. depreciation approaches is that the method of depreciation you use depends on when you first used the property for personal purposes. If you use property in your home office that was used previously for personal purposes, you cannot take a section 179 deduction for the property, but you can depreciate it.

Let's say you just traded in your three-piece suits and corner office for 10-year-old sweatpants and a finished-off section of your basement. You don't yet have the money to plunk down for a new computer system, so you're counting on your old PC to get you up and running. In this case, the year you began using the property (the PC) for personal purposes comes into play.

If you began using the property for personal purposes before 1981 and then start to use it for business in 1998, depreciate the property by the straight-line or declining-balance method based on salvage value and useful life.

If you began using the property for personal purposes after 1981 and before 1987 and start to use it for business in 1998, you generally depreciate the property under the Accelerated Cost Recovery System (ACRS). However, if the depreciation under ACRS is greater in the first year than the depreciation under MACRS, you must depreciate it under MACRS.

If you began using the property for personal purposes after 1986 and start to use it for business in 1998, depreciate the property under MACRS.

The basis for depreciation of property changed from personal to business use is the lesser of the following: the adjusted basis of the property on the date of change or the fair market value of the property on the date of change.

Here's another clarifying example: Jane bought a desk for $1,000 for her house on November 1, 1986. She began to use the desk in her home office on February 5, 1998, when it had a fair market value of $600. The depreciable basis of the desk is the fair market value of $600, which is less than its cost.

Under ACRS, a desk is five-year property. Under MACRS, it is seven-year property. Under ACRS, its depreciation is $90 (15 percent, the first-year ACRS percentage for five-year property, of $600). Under MACRS, its depreciation is $85.74 (14.29 percent, the first-year percentage for seven-year property, of $600). Because the depreciation is greater using ACRS, Jane must use MACRS to depreciate her desk.

Other Categories That May Not Apply to Everyone

Here are some less common but equally deductible categories of expenses:

Advertising

Charity trust fund contributions

Clean-fuel vehicles and refueling property

Donations to professional organizations

Educational expenses

Environmental cleanup costs

Interview expense allowances

Impairment-related expenses

Licenses and regulatory fees

Moving machinery

Outplacement services

Penalties and fines you pay for late performance or nonperformance of a contract

Repairs that keep your property in a normal efficient operating condition

Repayments of income (claim of right)

Subscriptions to trade or professional publications

Supplies and materials

Utilities

Don't Even Think About Deducting These

So you're brainstorming away, but before you include everything under the sun in your mental deduction checklist, examine this next list to make sure those items are viable deductions. The following are *not* deductible:

Bribes and kickbacks

Business start-up costs

Demolition expenses or losses

Dues to business, social, athletic, luncheon, sporting, airline, and hotel clubs

Lobbying expenses

Penalties and fines you pay to a governmental agency or instrumentality because you broke the law

Political contributions

Repairs that add to the value of your property or significantly increase its life

What's New for Small Businesses?

As in previous years, some of the new tax laws for 1998 affecting small businesses involve credits. The research credit, which was supposed to expire on June 30, 1998, has been extended to July 1, 1999. If you are thinking about trying to qualify for this credit, keep in mind that you will need to prove that you participate in an industry that depends on research and development activities.

The work opportunity credit was also recently extended to July 1, 1999. The welfare-to-work credit is new for employers who pay qualified recipients who begin work after December 31, 1997, and before July 1, 1999.

There have also been a number of deduction increases for 1998. These include upping the section 179 deduction to $18,500, the health insurance deduction for the self-employed to 45 percent of the total bill paid for family coverage, and the maximum net earnings of self-employed people subject to social security tax to $68,400.

Also introduced in 1998 were two new IRAs: the Roth IRA and the education IRA. You can make up to $2,000 in contributions to the Roth IRA, but these contributions are not deductible. This limit is also affected by contributions made to traditional IRAs and the income level of the person making the contributions. The education IRA allows up to $500 to be contributed per child until the age of 18 to go toward higher-education expenses. Again, these contributions are nondeductible and their amount hinges on the income level of the contributor.

For businesses that use transportation, the standard 32.5 cents mileage compensation rate can be applied to leased as well as owned vehicles beginning in 1998.

In addition to these tax law changes, new electronic filing methods have been introduced. Chapter 6 discusses how to use these options. Certain business-owning taxpayers can take advantage of an electronic payment system called EFTPS. Business owners can enroll in this program through a designated bank and make tax payments via telephone. The system is mandatory for businesses with more than $50,000 in payroll taxes, which accounts for 1.5 million businesses. Bear in mind no minimum tax level is required to participate in this program, so small business owners may want to consider this convenient means of payment.

For taxpayers filing their returns electronically, a test of paperless signatures is under way. In the past, e-file customers (as they're called) had to physically mail in an official signature document. This year, 8,000 practitioners are part of a program in which the taxpayer selects a personal identification number (PIN) that takes the place of an actual signature in terms of communication with the IRS. This test is part of the IRS's ongoing movement to accept digital signatures.

How to Track It All in Money

By the time you sit down to fill out all the right IRS forms—or have your accountant do it—it should be a matter of looking at the totals in your electronic files from your Money accounting and bill-paying software program, then importing those numbers into your electronic tax-filing forms with a simple click of a mouse. You should not be sifting through receipts and calculating at this point. Let Money do the ongoing calculations for you. What you need to remember in order to create the proper accounting system—"proper" meaning that it translates effortlessly to your tax forms—is to create expense categories for each and every deductible we've discussed.

It's relatively easy in Money, too, once you set up your Account Registers. Money divides your accounts into categories for a quick view. For tax purposes, you will also create a category for each deductible expense—meaning that you will keep a file for each deductible expense. Once a month, either you or your bookkeeper will input into Money how much was spent for each deductible category and create a worksheet file (a document saved in the category file) that shows the running total.

This is a cross-referencing method. You will, of course, have all these expense amounts embedded in your Money checking account register and your bill-paying registers. However, you want a quick view of each deductible expense's running total, and you want to be able to see only that expense, so you're going to create a file for each one. This means that once a month you or your bookkeeper is simply going to copy some of the line items in your checking account ledger to these deductible expense files. This setup will save you much time at tax time.

Some Perspective: What Accountants Advise

I believe in getting perspective from as many sources as possible. Aside from what the IRS dictates in its definitions and forms, the strategies best-of-breed accountants use specifically to help small businesses organize their taxes can be very helpful to understand.

This section is just a short summary of the many, many conversations I've had with accountants about the tax implications for small businesses. It offers a little insight into how to hone your financial management systems before we get to the nitty-gritty of setting up your accounts and ledgers electronically.

According to the typical small business accountant, there are several ways in which you can organize your taxes to better prepare you for April

15 every year. As a small business owner, you must remember to keep very detailed records of what you have (and don't have). Documentation will save you trouble and money when it comes to working with an accountant, as well as keep the IRS auditors at arm's length. This is where Money comes in. Accountants much prefer to see ledgers created on your PC than hand-written records. If for no other reason, PC records give you a greater chance that all the running totals are correct because the program does all calculations automatically.

Too Much Detail Ain't a Good Thing

For both small businesses and home offices, keeping an accurate finance log is key, but there's a fine line between records that are detailed and records that are *too* detailed. You should be sure to keep track of the major finance areas of your business, such as gross income, expenses, and payroll, but be careful not to go overboard. If you allocate expenses or add line items for every single tiny purchase, you can make your life and your accountant's life more difficult. Your primary function should still be to run your business, not be a bookkeeper. Be as accurate as you need to be so your accountant can tell what to derive on your behalf. Anything beyond that provides more info-glut through which you both must sift.

As a small business owner, you probably have an instinct to account for every little thing associated with your business—and until now, I've encouraged you to do just that, to think in terms of the IRS implications for expenses. That instinct, say accountants, needs some focus. First, you must account for cash through a bank account. If you are providing a service, you need to show that you earn fees. If your business is product-based, accounting for inventory is very important.

If you have employees, you must account for payroll taxes. But beware! This is a common area where small business owners have problems. Taxpayers negligent in this area often face the IRS in its strictest, most unforgiving mode. The IRS has been known to levy stiff penalties in ratio to the amount of tax owed.

Other areas for which you should account are customer or client lists and databases, bank loans or debts, and a record of the business's cash flow.

All of this activity is to streamline your tax-return preparation process and, of course, to avoid the dreaded audit. Although many taxpayers cling to the idea that the IRS chooses who to audit through a random, close-your-eyes-pull-out-a-folder method, there are ways you can reduce the odds of "winning" this painful lottery. Once your return is prepared, it's always good to take a step back and review it as though you were an IRS employee to see how reasonable the return. Does anything look strange, questionable, or in need of explanation? Many times large but legitimate deductions occur, and you need to be sure you can back them up with receipts and other documentation. If you think your return could look sketchy to the IRS, consult your accountant to see if you can do anything to rectify the situation before filing it.

Avoiding an Audit

You can do certain things on your own to avoid an audit. For one thing, make sure you pay your payroll taxes on time. If you recall, we mentioned that this is often a thorn in the IRS's side. Don't let the IRS catch you paying late or you'll have to suffer the consequences in terms of fines and the possibility of an audit.

You should also provide detailed reporting on your returns. This goes back to the issue of tracking your finances. It is a good policy to maintain solid records. That way, come tax season, you have the documentation to back up your deductions.

Many small businesses are in a position to take advantage of unique deduction opportunities. However, large deductions are bound to be noticed by the IRS. If you run your own catering business and recently purchased a van to travel to and from your various clients, make sure you can justify this as a business expense and that it is accounted for properly on your return.

Another area in which the IRS can be finicky is travel and entertainment. For small business owners, this category can create confusion about what you can deduct, because the line between friends, partners, and clients is often blurred. To make these deductions, be sure to back them up with receipts and a record of who was present and the business purpose of the occasion. A home office worker taking off to Las Vegas with three "clients" can look suspicious. Remember, the expense must be business-related in order to be a deduction. And while we're talking about deductions, remember that you can't deduct commuting expenses or daytime meals that can't be classified as entertainment expenses.

Tax Brackets

When you file your return, your tax bracket is based on the kind of business entity you run. As a sole practitioner, your tax bracket depends on how you file your personal return. Your filing status is determined by your marital status. This, in turn, determines your tax bracket.

With a C corporation (essentially a domestic corporation with an unlimited number of stockholders and that can issue more than one kind of stock, although there are other criteria), the brackets are better than for personal returns, with up to $50,000 of taxable income at the 15 percent tax bracket. The next bracket is $50,000–75,000 at 25 percent, then $75,000–100,000 at 34 percent, and on up. For an S corporation (a domestic corporation with fewer than 75 shareholders and issuing only one kind of stock, although there are other criteria), all income and loss are taxed at the owner's tax level, not the corporate level, so brackets are determined based on the owner's personal return.

By the way, if you're wondering whether to incorporate your business based on perceived tax advantages, you need to discuss it with an accountant. The process of incorporating is all about qualifying and filing forms, such as Form 8832 (Entity Classification Election). I don't advise making this decision without consulting a professional. For many small business owners, incorporating a business can be more trouble than it's worth.

Tax Changes for Corporations

If you already have corporation status, be aware of some tax changes: There is now no alternative minimum tax (AMT) for small corporations. For tax years beginning after 1997, the tentative minimum tax of a small corporation is zero. This means that a small corporation will not owe AMT.

For AMT purposes, a corporation is a small corporation if it meets any of the following tests:

- This is its first tax year.

- This is its second tax year and its annual gross receipts for its first tax year were not more than $5,000,000.

- This is its third tax year and its average annual gross receipts for its first two tax years were not more than $5,000,000.

- This is its fourth tax year and its average annual gross receipts for its first three tax years were not more than $5,000,000.

- This is its fifth or later tax year and it meets both of the following tests:

    Its average annual gross receipts for its first three-tax-year period beginning after 1993 were not more than $5,000,000.

Its average annual gross receipts for all later three-tax-year periods beginning after 1993 and ending before the current tax year were not more than $7,500,000.

For these tests, gross receipts for a short tax year are annualized.

Web Sites That Can Help

Unfortunately, this tedious process of being precise about taxes is simply one cost of doing business. Remember, like it or not, the IRS is your lifelong business partner; it's best if you know exactly how to communicate with it.

You may find you want to check out some of the information contained in this chapter, ask more questions, or keep updated about tax laws. Here are some of the best Web sites I've found to help you do just that:

Yahoo! Finance: *biz.yahoo.com/taxes*

Deloitte & Touche Tax Planning Guide: *www.dtonline.com/ taxguide98/*

H&R Block Tax Services: *www.hrblock.com/tax/*

Business Owner's Toolkit: *www.toolkit.cch.com*

Tax Prep 1: *www.taxprep1.com*

Tax Logic: *www.taxlogic.com*

Gilman + CioCia e1040.com: *www.e1040.com*

SecureTax.com: *www.securetax.com*

TaxCut.com: *www.taxcut.com*

FileSafe: *www.filesafe.com*

Electronic Filing Service Inc.: *www.efs.com*

OneTax.com: *www.onetax.com*

Tax Link Inc.: *www.autotax.com*

TurboTax.com: *www.turbotax.com*

In Chapter 6, we'll use some of these Web sites—particularly the IRS site for downloading forms—to get your electronic tax-filing system up and running.

Chapter 6

Setting Up Online Tax Filing

For the 1997 tax year, 24 million people filed their 1040 tax returns electronically (sometimes called *e-filing*). That number is expected to climb higher for the 1998 tax year. There's good reason that so many people are so hip to the e-filing idea: It's faster, more secure, and frankly, the IRS likes it because returns filed electronically tend to have fewer errors, because the calculations also tend to be done in tax software programs first and then sent to the IRS via modem, without the kind of human intervention that causes errors.

Yes, I did just say "more secure" and then skip right over it. I know the knee-jerk reaction to anything that's sent online is that it's a security risk, but in this case there's a reason it's more secure. First of all, the electronic transmission itself is secured by encryption, even if you send the return from a Web site service such as SecureTax (*www.securetax.com*). But, if transmitting your tax information over the Internet still bothers you, you can take it to an H&R Block office (or any of the other 1,500 electronic tax filers approved by the IRS) and have them send it via a private modem line that dials directly into the IRS's computer systems. Again, that transmission is secured by encryption technology.

Here's a reason electronic filing is actually safer for you: When you mail your income tax returns by, say, certified mail, the only guarantee the certified seal gives you is that the IRS received the envelope the return was in; there's no guarantee on the return itself. When the IRS receives an electronic return, it electronically sends a confirmation that the return itself was received. I know this sounds niggling, but perceptions of security are often little more than that. Besides, once you have your entire accounting, bookkeeping, and bill-paying systems in electronic format, you might as well go the distance and file taxes that way, too.

And don't forget perhaps the most compelling reason to file electronically: The IRS likes electronic returns. It makes their job easier, and if an IRS person is in a better mood, then so am I. There are even more reasons electronic filing is a good idea; this chapter examines those reasons and how you can go about e-filing your return.

Why You Should File Electronically

If you are entitled to a refund, you'll receive it much faster if you've filed your return electronically. Your refund for a traditional paper return that you mailed usually gets to you in four to six weeks (within 40 days). With electronic returns, 98 percent get a refund in 21 days or less; the average is 15 days or less.

There's a human contact point at the IRS when you e-file, so if there's a problem, you have the opportunity to resolve it up front. When you e-file, you get an acknowledgment, including a reference number, for your return. Say you forgot to do something simple, like sign your return. The IRS contact will catch that error right away and send you a quick note via e-mail. The bureaucratic process of correspondence is drastically reduced. Remember *The Odd Couple* episode in which Felix got a letter from the IRS saying he had to come to the IRS office to discuss his return? Felix panicked, thinking he was being audited. He went down to the IRS office a nervous wreck, and it turned out he had forgotten to sign his return. That won't happen with e-filing. You'll get an e-mail telling you of any such minor errors.

Speaking of errors, the published error rate is 20 percent for paper returns (communication exists for half those cases), while electronic returns have an error rate of 0.5 percent!

Furthermore, if you have a balance due (assuming you're paying estimated tax payments every quarter, which you need to as a business owner or home office worker), you could file electronically whenever you like before April 15 and then send the payment later, as long as the payment gets to the IRS by the 15th. With paper returns, you have to send your payment with the return.

Now you can pay your taxes electronically as well. This year the IRS is offering e-payment to everyone. E-payment is an Automatic Clearing House (ACH) authorized debit from your bank account. IRS and banking regulators worked out the system, and it's essentially a reverse direct deposit that can schedule estimated tax payments as well. You can actually set the e-payment system to pay the IRS as often as you like. You can set up this system at the IRS Web site.

By the way, e-payments are required if your business has more than $50,000 in payroll taxes. Another compelling reason to file electronically is new this year and is still in test mode but should be up and running soon. In past years, your signature had to be part of your return if you filed electronically. You had to first physically mail a signature document and then the IRS sent you back a card with a PIN number to use with your e-file. Now the IRS is doing a test of paperless signatures. Eight thousand tax practitioners are part of the test. As a taxpayer, you select a PIN number right off the bat—no requesting a signature document from the IRS and then waiting for the card—and that becomes your signature for your return. To find out information on these practitioners, go to the IRS Web site. This service may not be available in your area, in which case you need to still obtain that signature document by calling the IRS.

Over the long term, the IRS is examining the possibility of using digital signatures for e-filed returns so taxpayers won't have to mail in signature documents, but that may take a while.

Electronic Filing Options

As convenient as the process already is, filing taxes electronically could be easier. First of all, accounting software such as Money isn't yet integrated with the e-filing system. So, you're going to have to transfer your data into a tax software program and then send the electronic tax form in that software to the IRS. If you follow the guidelines in Chapters 4 and 5 to set up your tax totals in Money, they should be converted easily into any of the popular tax programs.

By the way, the IRS would like to see accounting software integrated with e-filing. To be fair, the IRS wants to be able to make tax return filing simpler for small businesses and take out as many steps as possible. But for now, you have two basic options for filing taxes electronically: go to a tax practitioner or buy tax software and file via the Internet.

Go to a Tax Practitioner

Your first choice is to pay a tax practitioner such as H&R Block (or any company that is e-file authorized will do) to file the return for you. You can also file with H&R Block electronically, and they in turn send your return to the IRS electronically, but not over the Internet.

Buy Tax Software and File via the Internet

You could buy tax software, such as Universal Tax Systems Inc.'s TaxWise, and use it to file your taxes yourself. Universal Tax Systems is also the developer of SecureTax.com, a Web site that allows you to file taxes electronically over the Internet. So, if you use TaxWise and then go to SecureTax.com (or MSN's MoneyCentral, *moneycentral.msn.com/tax/ home.asp*, which now lets you use the SecureTax.com service), you can file over the Internet. (Chapter 5 lists other Web sites that offer tax-filing services and tax software.)

Tip

If you want to use tax software but don't want to file over the Internet, you can do so. In fact, if you want to file your taxes electronically with a tax practitioner such as H&R Block, you'll need software and electronic IRS forms. But if you use a practitioner, call ahead to find out if there's a tax software program you need to use.

Don't Forget Your Estimated Payments

The easiest way to pay your quarterly estimated tax payments is by using an e-payment system, which allows you to simply schedule your bank account to be debited on June 15, September 15, and January 15 for whatever amount you or your accountant calculates you will owe in taxes. Tax practitioners such as H&R Block can set up this system for you.

A Note about Security

You should know that the IRS does a security check and screening process on practitioners before they become authorized to be e-file vendors. Because these vendors do not file your taxes over the public Internet, it is arguably safer for you to use a tax practitioner such as H&R Block instead of filing at a Web site on your own.

These authorized practitioners have tested the process of e-filing 1040s since 1985. The IRS claims there hasn't been a single breach of security. The IRS considers this method secure, and the IRS—not you—is at political risk if the system isn't secure.

In fact, the IRS argues that when a paper return comes into the IRS, the auditors have no way of knowing whether or not the signature on the return is really yours. Because of all the screening and checks the IRS does with e-filing, however, the IRS can make a strong case that the e-system is ultimately more secure than the traditional tax-filing route.

Here's the Catch with E-Filing

Businesses on the whole must file a variety of forms and, often, different returns. First, there is the basic business return consisting of Form 1040 plus Schedule C, CE-Z, and SE or whichever other form is accepted with the 1040.

Of the 180 standard forms a business may need to submit, roughly 50 of them are accepted electronically. That's not a great percentage, but of the 50 that are accepted, the majority of these forms are available for download from the IRS Web site. The catch is that all the forms that make up your return must be accepted electronically in order for you to take advantage of e-filing. You can't submit your return piecemeal, half electronically and half in hard copy.

The good news is that home office workers should have no problem; most other small businesses, depending on their size and complexity, should also be okay.

Remember that small businesses with employees must also file employment tax returns, including income tax, Social Security and Medicare taxes, and the Federal Unemployment Tax (FUTA). These returns can be filed electronically through a payroll agent such as ADP or another third party. Furthermore, the IRS has rolled out its Telefile program for Form 941 (Employer's Quarterly Federal Tax Return). In the Telefile program's first year, 582,000 businesses used the system and 1.1 million are projected to do so in the 1998 tax season. If your business is eligible, contact the IRS and it will send you the Telefile package.

For small businesses too small to qualify for Telefile or a payroll provider, a product is in development that will let those businesses buy software and transmit the return through a transmitter. Small businesses can look forward to this product being rolled out nationwide for next year's return season.

Chapter 7

Setting Up Analyses and Projections in Financial Manager

Let me start by saying that the material in this chapter won't be as daunting as it sounds. Or maybe crunching numbers in a spreadsheet analysis software program doesn't scare you, but it horrified me.

It simply sounded complicated to me—as though it would be more trouble than it was worth. But the opposite turned out to be true. It was simple to keep track of income statements, cash flow, and balance sheets. It approached magic when I could plug in numbers and get answers to my "what-if?" questions.

Before we start running through how to use Financial Manager, there's just one thing to remember, which may help you get your mind around the program: Essentially, it's a glorified Microsoft Excel program. In fact, Financial Manager is built for, and works in, Excel, and that means that you can export any spreadsheets you create onto anyone else's computer. as long as that computer has Excel.

Learn the Layout of Financial Manager

Once you've installed Office 2000 Small Business (or Office 2000 Professional or Office 2000 Premium) on your computer, you'll have everything you need to use Financial Manager. Simply click the Start button on the Windows taskbar, and select Programs from the Start menu. On the Programs menu, select Microsoft Office Small Business Tools and click Microsoft Small Business Financial Manager. That will start the program, which has a very clean, easy-to-understand Startup Screen with clear menu options, as shown in Figure 7-1.

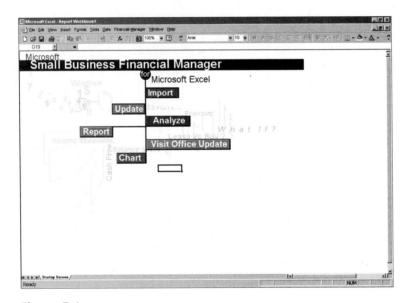

Figure 7-1
Financial Manager is easy to use.

You'll see several big button options: Import, Update, Analyze, Report, Chart, and Visit Office Update. Let's go through each button to see what it does. Remember, when you click most of these features, a wizard pops up that will walk you through the process of using that feature. The reason I like the program is that you are never "thrown to the software wolves"— the software always explains how to do what you need to accomplish.

Tip

When you start Financial Manager, a box pops up that asks if you want to disable macros or enable macros. The program gives you an ominous-sounding warning about computer viruses, making you think you should click on the Disable button. Don't. You need to enable macros in order to use the program. Most viruses are distributed through e-mail attachments or in programs or documents you might download from the Web. If you're careful about the files you open and have a good virus program on your PC that you keep updated, you should be fairly safe.

Import

Click Import and the Import Wizard appears. The first task it asks you to do is to create a password. I like this feature. Whenever we're talking about my money, I like to know that the information will be secure. It sounds obvious to say this, but don't forget your password.

You'll use the Import feature to bring your accounting files and data for charts, projections, and reports into Financial Manager. The wizard searches your hard drive to find files, including, of course, files in Money. This feature simply obtains the numbers you want to crunch.

Once you retrieve data, Financial Manager will ask what you want to do with it. You're going to want to use it for the Report, Chart, or Analyze features, which we'll get to in a second.

The only important thing to remember about Import is that it's how you bring into Financial Manager the files from your hard drive with which you want to work.

Update

Click Cancel on the Import Wizard and it sends you right back to the Startup Screen. Click Update.

Tip

Clicking Cancel in any of the wizards in Financial Manager takes you to the Startup Screen. If you're in a report or chart, you'll see a tab at the bottom of the window that says Startup Screen. You can click that tab at any time to go back, and it won't close the report on which you're working. The Startup Screen also has a tab at the bottom of the window that you can click to go back to the report.

A box appears, asking you to log in with your user name and password. Fill in the boxes with this information and click OK. Another box appears, asking if you wish to proceed with the Update. Because we're just running through this process and haven't done any actual analyses yet, you have nothing to update. Just click Cancel.

I point out the Update feature because it's crucial. Each time you work on a report or a chart, do an analysis, or simply import a file, you should click Update before you exit Financial Manager. Think of it as saving your work. If you're anything like me and make mistakes or have done work that you realize you don't want added to previous reports, don't click Update before you exit Financial Manager, and everything will remain as it was before you started that day's session.

Report

Here's where we get into the real work, or at least where the computer gets into the real work. You're going to be amazed at how little you actually have to do. When you click Report, the wizard pops up and allows you to create a Financial Report. The wizard gives you several options as to what kind of report you can create: Balance Sheet, Cash Flow, Change in Stockholder Equity, Income Statement, Ratios, Sales Analysis, and Trial Balance. For the purposes of this chapter, choose Balance Sheet. The wizard also asks you to select a company name. In most cases, you'll want to select the name of your business. For this chapter, however, select the sample business listed, Northwind Traders Sample Company, so we can do a run-through. Click the Next button.

The wizard asks you to select a particular type of report, such as a Balance Sheet with Scenarios. Just select Balance Sheet again and click the Next button. In the next step, you need to choose an end date for the report from the menu. Select March 2000 and click the Finish button.

Financial Manager displays a report showing the company's financial well-being. Look at Figure 7-2 to see what the sample balance sheet looks like. Notice it includes data on everything you'll want to track for your business—cash and assets, inventory, depreciation, accounts payable, accrued payroll, long-term notes, other liabilities, earnings—the works.

Depending on the size and scope of your business, you can use any number of these variables, but the important thing to remember is that even if your business is complicated, Financial Manager can handle it.

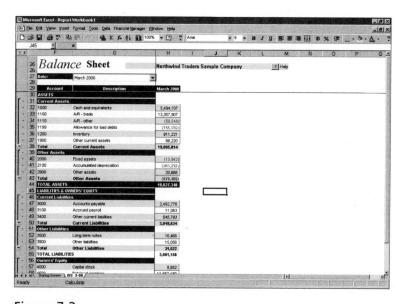

Figure 7-2

A Balance Sheet Report created in Financial Manager.

Keep in mind that you're essentially using Excel spreadsheets when you use Financial Manager. To make changes to a balance sheet—or whatever report you're working on—simply move the cursor to the line item and click it to highlight it. Then type your changes. Don't forget to click Update before you exit the program!

If you're done with the balance sheet and want to look at another automatically created report, go back to the Startup Screen, click on Report again, and select another kind of financial report—say, Cash Flow.

It is as simple as that. The beauty of the Reports feature is that it does the math.

Chart

The Chart feature makes pie charts from your reports, so we right-brained folks can get a visual of our financial reports. Print these charts for meetings for a snazzy visual aid.

When you click Chart, the wizard starts. It prompts you to select the type of financial chart you want to create and the company from which it should draw its data. To do a quick run-through, select Balance Sheet

Composition in the Financial Charts box and select Northwind Traders Sample Company. Click the Next button.

The wizard prompts you to select the values it should display on a chart: Assets, Liabilities, or Equity. Pick Assets and click the Next button.

The Chart Wizard then prompts you to select a date. Choose March 2000 and click the Finish button.

The wizard creates a cool pie chart from the data. In my case, the pie chart for my business assets is a little alarming. The pie has a tiny slice (a dieter's portion) for assets and a way too big chunk for accounts receivable. One look at my pie chart, and I pick up the phone to see when the publishers who owe me money will pay me.

I just hung up the phone. The checks "are in the mail."

You get the idea. Use the Chart feature to remind yourself to collect your accounts receivable, among other things.

Analyze

The Analyze feature is the coolest part of Financial Manager, if you ask me. When you click Analyze, the wizard pops up. You'll see several options for creating a Financial Manager Analysis Tool: Business Comparison, Buy Vs. Lease, Create Projection Wizard, Projection Reports, and What-If Analysis. Let's look at them one by one to see how these options work.

Create Projection Wizard

Start by selecting Create Projection Wizard. This is always the first place to start when you want to run an analysis of your finances, because it's where you plug in the data for whatever projections you're going to do. Click the Next button.

Select Northwind Traders Sample Company again in the Company drop-down box. Then click New and type Sample1 in the Projection Name box. Click the Next button.

The wizard prompts you to enter a period of time over which you want to project company finances. You can choose a period of time in the future ranging from one month to five years. For the purposes of this run-through, choose one month. You can create a projection using one of two options: Last Year's Activity or Last Month's Activity. Make sure that Last Year's Activity is selected. See Figure 7-3. Click the Next button.

The wizard gives you the option to see values or percentages for the company's growth rate in your projection. This is called *selecting parameters*. Make sure that By Percentage is selected. You'll also need to enter the

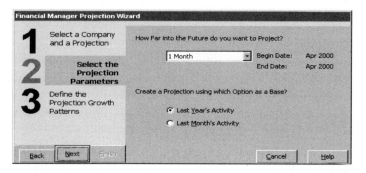

Figure 7-3

Select dates in the Create Projection Wizard to generate a projection of company finances over a certain period of time.

Estimated Annual Growth rates for Revenue, Cost of Sales, and Operating Expenses. Just for fun, click in the Revenue box, select the text, and type 15. In the Cost of Sales and Operating Expenses boxes, click, select the text, and type 5. Click the Finish button.

The Analysis Wizard then prompts you to go back and select the Projection Report Wizard in the Analysis section in order to see results. You do this by clicking OK and, on the Startup Screen, clicking Analyze and then selecting Projection Reports.

Projection Report Wizard

When you start the Project Report Wizard, a box appears, asking you to select a Projection Report (you can select from Projection Assumptions, Projected Balance Sheet, Projected Cash Flow, and Projected Income Statement) and the name of the company for which you want to create a report. In this case, select Project Assumption in the Projection Reports box and Northwind Traders Sample Company in the Company Name box. Click the Next button.

Next, you need to choose a type of report. Select Projection Assumptions in the Project Report Types box and click the Next button.

You'll see a box containing a list of Projection Reports you've created with the Analyze Wizard. Select Sample1, the projection report created earlier in this run-through. Click the Finish button. This will create the Projection Assumptions Report.

The Projection Report Wizard keeps track of the parameters you enter over time and calculates growth rates and dollar values based on these parameters. If you get in the habit of running Financial Manager once a month and entering the revenues, sales expenses, and operating expenses for your business, this analysis tool will track the growth of your business over time. See Chapter 20 for tips on how to develop good habits for tracking your revenues.

If you like, you can do analyses for Business Comparison or Buy Vs. Lease using the same process described above. Remember that you must enter data—as you did in the Create a Projection Wizard—for every analysis you want to do. Financial Manager can't analyze and make dollar comparisons without having the numbers to compare.

Business Comparison

A *business comparison* is a report that shows how your business is doing compared with others in your industry. In order to have the Projection Wizard do such a comparison, you will have to tell the wizard what kind of money the other businesses are making. This information may be difficult to obtain for many small businesses because they tend to be privately held. However, if you're in the Internet start-up businesses, where IPOs are the norm, you'll have an easier time finding this information.

Buy Vs. Lease

To create a Buy Vs. Lease analysis, you simply need to run this wizard and plug the costs of buying and leasing a piece of equipment or property, such as an office suite, into the parameters. The wizard gives you a report that will help you decide whether it's more cost-effective for your business to buy or lease.

What-If Analysis

When you select What-If Analysis as an Analysis Tool in the Analyze Wizard and click the Next button, you'll have the option of choosing Northwind Traders Sample Company. Select it and click the Next button.

In the Open A What-If Scenario box, click New and type Web store in the New box. The default value in the Begin Date box is the current month. For the purposes of this run-through, change the Begin Date to April 1999. The End Date box should show March 2000, which we entered earlier in this run-through. Click the Finish button.

The next screen asks you to save your What-If Scenario. You can select the folder in which you want to save it using the drop-down list in the Save In box, and you change its name in the Filename box. For this run-through, the default folder should be My Documents and the default filename should be Web store. Click the Save button.

The wizard generates the What-If Overview Report, as shown in Figure 7-4. Look at it and you'll see two columns of figures: Actuals and

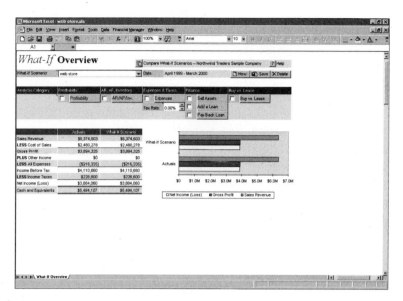

Figure 7-4

The What-If Overview Report can help you evaluate the potential impact of financial decisions on your business.

What-If Scenario. These figures are the same in both categories, because you haven't asked the wizard "what if?" yet.

Okay, here comes the cool part. Notice the options in the Analysis Categories: Profitability; AR, AP, Inventory; Expenses & Taxes; Finance; and Buy Vs. Lease. If you select one of these and fill in any information requested, the wizard then computes the financial situation of your business for that category. For instance, if you select Pay Back Loan in the Finance column, new figures in the What-If Scenario column appear, showing the effect upon your business if you paid back a business loan. I find the What-If Analysis Wizard an essential tool for business planning. I can see the financial picture if I buy a computer instead of leasing it or add to my expenses by going on a vacation or take out a loan to build my Web store.

A What-If Analysis helps me clarify my thinking and make sound financial decisions. The best part is that this Financial Manager feature is pretty easy to use. Yes, you do have to take the time to enter all kinds of numbers in the Create Projection Wizard for every aspect of your business you want to analyze, but you'd have to scribble down these numbers in one place anyway to track the finances for your business.

The benefit of all this data entry in Financial Manager is that once it's there, it's always there. You add to it, and over time your projections reflect the whole financial history of your business. It is a fantastic strategic system if you can get yourself into the habit of using it.

Visit Office Update

This isn't so much a feature of Office 2000 as it is a fabulous courtesy. To use it, you need an active Internet connection, however. When you click Visit Office Update from the Startup Screen, Financial Manager automatically takes you to the Office 2000 Web site to get information and updates.

Often, between releases of programs, Microsoft releases useful updates, such as new program features you can download from the Web site and integrate into Microsoft programs by clicking a button. In addition, this site offers information you may find helpful about using Office 2000.

The Keys to Planning Growth

I promise that after a few times of tedious data entry in Financial Manager, you will come to depend on the reporting, charting, projection, and analysis features to see how various aspects of your business are doing and to determine what you need to do to make them more profitable. You will also get a very detailed bird's-eye view of the overall health of your business.

These things are key to planning for the continued growth of your business, and the continued growth of your business means your continued freedom.

Chapter 8

Getting Started: A Real-Life Business Puts Its Accounts and Bills Online

So far we've gone through the steps of how to set up accounts, pay bills and taxes, and conduct strategic forecasts. But these lessons are still abstract as far as I'm concerned, for a couple of reasons: There's been no discussion of what to do when things go wrong or when you change your mind.

So now you're about to get the inside story of a day in the life of this author when I set up my office to run on all the systems we just explored. I'll understand if you skip this chapter altogether, thinking that this could get ugly. I include far more information about my messy office habits than you ever cared to know. But if you're brave enough to read on, I do promise to keep this chapter short, if not sweet, and I hope that my mistakes may be of some value to you. If you're anything like me, seeing the whole picture at once can be very illuminating; you may just be able to make your whole process shorter by looking at what I did wrong and avoiding making the same mistakes. Just to sweeten the pot, I'll share some tricks I use—especially to avoid being fined by the IRS—that I invented by creating a new kind of account in Microsoft Money. Okay, enough of my sales pitch. Read on.

Your Business Is an Extension of Your Life

In an attempt to take my own advice about thinking everything through— which, I have to admit, is a departure from my usual M.O.—I sat down one morning, coffee by my side, and stared at the mess on my desk.

In less than three months, I thought to myself, my patient and loyal accountant is once again going to sit across his desk shaking his head at me, staring at the big envelopes and shoe boxes overstuffed with receipts and watching me rifle through crumpled-up pieces of paper looking for the numbers he just asked for.

No way, I said. I can't possibly endure that humiliation again. Besides, a $2,000 discrepancy in my own business checking account is really making me take pause. I need to get this stuff in order; it's simply not enough to be earning money. At this point it's controlling me, not the other way around. Besides, how embarrassing is it that a journalist who constantly gives people advice about finances is such a mess herself? I understand these systems, so it's time to put my money where my mouth is.

Here's the log of that fateful day when I decided to move on from poseur to stand-up financial advisor:

8:30 A.M. Sitting and staring at my desk, I remember the central concept that I always give to entrepreneurs to use when they're creating money management systems: Business and personal life must be considered together first and then separated later.

Okay, I can do that. I write down everything that costs me money on a regular basis. I create that list in two sections, business and personal. But I put it all in the same list because some of the items will invariably end up being both business and personal—that is the essence of being an entrepreneur. My list looked like this:

- Computer and telecommunications systems, including computers, peripherals, phones, software, other electronics, tech support maintenance contracts

- Phone bills, including my high-speed ISDN digital line for Internet access
- Other utility bills
- My assistant
- My accountant
- My attorney
- Research, including books, newspapers, magazines, films, reference materials
- Office supplies
- Car expenses
- Travel expenses, both local and out of town
- Housekeeper/office-cleaning service
- My mortgage
- Food
- Clothing
- Entertainment
- My dog
- Taxes
- Homeowner's insurance
- Car insurance
- Health insurance
- Medical/prescription expenses

Then I made a list of how all these expenses appear in my life every month:

- Credit-card bills
- Utility bills
- Phone bills
- Cable TV bills
- Insurance bills
- Mortgage vouchers
- Monthly apartment cooperative fee
- Estimated taxes

- Housekeeper/office cleaner fees
- Invoices from my assistant
- Other random bills—accountant, attorney, magazine subscriptions, etc.

Then, after getting nice and depressed about how many people I pay on a regular basis, I thought about all the sources for my revenue:

- Publishers
- TV networks
- Filmmakers
- Corporations for which I consult
- Investments

Then, I thought about how that money comes in:

- Checks from all my business opportunities
- Statements from my investments

Then, in an attempt to bridge the two sides of the balance sheet, I thought about what bank accounts I have to process all this money:

- Checking account
- Savings account
- IRA account
- Investment account
- Bonds

9:30 A.M. I'm exhausted. But I do not give up. I get more coffee. I decide I should make a list of my life goals over the next year, including personal and financial goals:

Finish this book for Microsoft Press

Hire my assistant full-time instead of part-time

Finish the novel I'm working on

Write another film script that I did the research for last year

Travel to Greece, Italy, and Alaska

Accelerate my mortgage payments

Upgrade my computer systems

Put some money away

9:45 A.M. I'm overwhelmed. I don't even know how many of these goals are realistic, because I don't have a clue what my cash flow is. I spend an awful lot of time each month paying bills, yet searching through my desk I can't even make sense of the folder of papers I have. And from that need my first two systems are born.

Put It All Online, Ask Questions Later

I decide I need to set up all my bank and other financial institution accounts online so I can look at them. Then I need to set up my online bill-paying system. That way I will track my incoming revenue and my outgoing expenses. Then I will create a separate folder (a real-world, physical paper folder for my desk) for each account and each creditor. I will keep the paper records that I print from my computer as back-up, along with the bills I get in the mail.

I get out all my bank statements, credit-card statements, and bills from other creditors so I have account information for everything I'm about to set up (as we did in Chapters 3 and 4).

10:00 A.M. I start Money, and I go through the steps in Chapters 3 and 4 to set up all my accounts and bill-paying systems. While I'm at Chase, my primary bank, I also change my accounts around a little. I open a new checking account for business use only. One more thing I do: I add an account called "My Income" in Money so I can track my earnings. I put this account as a subset account under my checking account, since this is where all my checks from my work are deposited.

I divide my accounts into two major categories in Money: Business and Personal. This is really a matter of putting my Business Checking Account (including the subset of My Income) and Business Credit Card Accounts into one category and everything else under Personal. I'll certainly call on my Personal Accounts for business purposes because there are tax deductions to be had—for mortgage and insurance for instance—but because I work at home, their primary category is still Personal. If you have a small business in which these expenses are completely separate (such as a car used only for business purposes),then put them in a Business category.

But for many entrepreneurs, there is overlap. Health insurance is deductible, and so is a portion of your mortgage if you take a home office deduction (which you may do even if you have another office outside your home). That's the whole reason you have to think of your business and personal life together. Make loose categorical differences anyway—especially for the obvious ones like Business Checking and Business Credit Card—because it will make your expenses clearer to you.

Bring In the Bookkeeper

Noon. I'm kicking myself. Because I knew at the outset that I was going to hire a bookkeeper, I should have done that first and then sat down to do all this with the bookkeeper. Now, I'm going to have to explain this whole thing to that person.

Save yourself some trouble. If you have a bookkeeper, assistant, or spouse who will be a part of this process, sit down with that person while you go through these steps. There is no better way for that person to learn what is going on. Plus there's another benefit: Any quirky thing you do while you're setting up accounts will be in that person's head as well, so if something goes wrong later, then your helper will know why.

For example, my Chase business checking account is brand new. When I transferred funds from my existing personal checking account to get it started, I also set up my bill-paying system at the same time. I know all too well how the computers at financial institutions work—or don't work—so I thought it likely there would be a glitch. For instance, the Chase system may try to pay my bills from my old account and run into problems.

If my bookkeeper had been sitting with me when I opened the account, he would know later that if bills didn't get paid, he should call Chase and tell them about the new account number and what he suspects went wrong. He could do this without checking to see whether something was wrong with the computer (everyone's first guess), trying to figure it out himself because he didn't want to bother me, and then finally consulting with me.

Oh well, lesson learned. As it turned out later, I spent quite a few hours going over my set-up with a bookkeeper. Don't make the same mistake. By the way, a bookkeeper is a great thing if it fits into your budget. Once a month I pay $100 for my bookkeeper to come in and take care of downloading monthly statements and scrutinizing them for mistakes, checking to make sure bills were paid and checks cleared, keying in my expenses and tax-deductible receipts, and filing all the appropriate paper copies. It makes me proud of my online money management system—it's a perfect framework in which the bookkeeper can work. Because I set up the system, I can feel confident if I want to check up on him. Furthermore, if there's a problem with an account, my bookkeeper, not I, calls the bank and sits there on hold listening to bad Muzak. Ask your accountant for a bookkeeper referral.

Next I looked at all my nice new Account Registers, all organized in Money, and my bills that were scheduled to be paid automatically for the next year. Then I looked at all my account balances minus my total monthly expenses. That last move was plenty of motivation to stop for lunch.

1:30 P.M. I drag myself back to my desk, after doing everything to avoid going back to creating these systems. I even put in a load of laundry and did the dishes. The reason for the procrastination? It was time to set up my online tax-paying system.

Paying Taxes: The Secret to Not Getting Fined

The reason I decided to set up my taxes as an electronic system (my third money management system) is simple: By the time I set up my bill-paying system, I started to think of my taxes as another bill. It's a quarterly bill instead of a monthly one, but that doesn't matter. I set up a system to track my federal taxes using Money. (See Chapter 5.)

Bear in mind that this process took me just a few minutes on that day, but that's because I had already gotten the forms I needed to sign and sent them back to the IRS. If you sit down to do all this on the first day you think about it, you'll have to send those forms in and then do the actual tax paying after the IRS sets up an account for you. Still, you can go through the steps of setting up the electronic forms. You just won't be able to pay estimated taxes on the same day.

Now, remember, you shouldn't simply set up this arrangement in your bill-paying system, though that would certainly be nice. The IRS has its own system, and Money's bill-paying systems don't include vouchers for quarterly payments. In theory, you could simply write that information in on your electronic check forms, but it is really better if the IRS receives the vouchers.

Let Money Track It

For the sake of simplicity and easy tracking, I actually set up the IRS as an account in Account Manager in Money. I did this so I could think of it in terms of a balance due, not unlike a revolving credit-card account. Because there is no Money option for IRS Accounts per se, I simply made it into its own category, using the Other option.

I calculated my total yearly obligation (by adding up the quarterly estimated payments my accountant calculated for me) and started with that as what I owe (like a credit-card balance). Then each payment I make I deduct from the total, until I hit zero in April. Of course, this estimated number is based on the assumption that I will earn this year what I earned last year.

The IRS expects payments to be made by projecting earnings based on past experience. Fair enough. But the problem with this logic is that if you're wrong and happen to earn more this year than last year—even if there is no way you could have foreseen it—the IRS may fine you for low-balling estimated payments.

The law says that your yearly taxes are due in full on April 15 for preceding calendar year. (On April 15, 2000, your tax liability for all of 1999 is due). Say I go to my accountant's office on March 1, 2000, to review my earnings for 1999, and it turns out that I made more than I did in 1999, so the three quarterly estimated payments I've made so far for 1999 (one each in June 1999, September 1999, and January 2000) were low. In my mind, that simply means that the April 2000 payment will be bigger. No problem, right? That's when the tax is due, after all.

Nope. The IRS has the right to fine me for this underestimate—on a $20,000 miscalculation, it's about $100. To add insult to injury, if I earn more than I thought I would, I have to pay a fine even though I am still paying the full tax on time. My poor accountant can only take so many of my diatribes, so he just tells me that's the way it is. He usually takes aspirin out of his desk drawer around that point.

Check It Twice

For the time being, I am taking the Machiavellian approach and dealing with things as they are, not as they should be. So, to make sure the IRS doesn't fine me, I check my math.

I look at the total tax obligation number every quarter and compare it to my revenue in my earnings and investment accounts for that same quarter. For each quarter, I look at a quick total of all the freelance checks I've deposited (I set up an Account Register in Money for my work income), the taxable interest I've earned for that quarter, and any other monies that have landed in my pocket. Remember, the IRS rule of thumb is that if it looks like income and smells like income, they're going tax it like income. Then I make sure that the estimated tax payment I'm about to make is the right percentage of that quarter's income. If it's low, I add money to the estimated payment. I've noticed, by the way, that the IRS doesn't complain if the electronic estimated payment you send is a larger number than the voucher says it should be.

Setting Up Your Tax Payments in Money

When setting up a system for paying taxes paying from scratch—if you're actually trying to calculate your estimated payment instead of using the ones an accountant gave you—you will first need to set up your investment accounts in the Investments place in Money. Chapter 10 gives step-by-step instructions on how to do this, but it is the same process as setting up bank accounts in Account Manager. The important thing to remember about investment accounts is that they look very similar to the Account Manager accounts.

Your investment accounts, however, are not in Account Manager because Money separates earnings from expenses. Accounts under Account Manager are all expense-oriented accounts; accounts in Investments are all earnings. To keep it straight in my mind, I also copy the My Income account, which I keep in Account Manager, to the Investment place so I can look at the revenue side of my personal balance sheet all at once.

2:30 P.M. I stop to pet the dog. No one should go straight from setting up tax payment software to another system without taking a break. The dog wags his tail and looks like he wonders why I spend so much time pressing keys and staring into a glowing box instead of petting him. I wonder the same thing.

Using Financial Manager to Plot Your Course

2:45 P.M. Time for my goals. I start by congratulating myself for actually setting up three systems already today: my accounts, bill-paying system, and taxes. I have to admit that I didn't clean out my desk and create all the paper folders I need. I'll let the bookkeeper do that. If I had done it, it would be midnight right now and not 2:45.

Because I am now all too aware of what my revenue minus expenses are, I know that my goals seem lofty. Yet I don't want to guess. I want to know for certain the answers to the following questions:

Based on the period of time that it takes me to earn a certain amount of money, how many projects will I have to take on to hire my assistant full-time and have it be a good business decision?

Will there be enough hours in the day to do that much work?

How much will my productivity be increased if my assistant is working full-time—and how does that change the calculation of how many hours in a day I need to work?

If I stop all other work to finish my novel before I get a publisher for it, how will that change my earnings (and therefore my cash flow) and over what period of time?

How much will the trips I want to take cost me?

If I accelerate my mortgage payments, how much more of a tax benefit will I get compared with the financial hit I'll take every month?

Is it better to lease or buy more computer equipment?

How much will I have to earn to fulfill every goal on my list and have 15 percent of my earnings go into savings?

As we just went over in Chapter 7, I turn to the Analyze Wizard in Financial Manager to set up an Actuals vs. What-If Scenario report. Bear in mind that some of my questions are easily answered using the What-If Analysis Wizard, such as adding the cost of a full-time assistant or adding the price of a vacation and seeing my new financial picture. You can change all kinds of variables in your business finances to see how your revenues would be affected.

More complex questions such as, "How much more productive will a full-time assistant make me?" are much more elusive. Can you really use the What-If Analysis Wizard to get such answers? Well, not exactly. But What-If Analysis can get you started, and that's the point. Once you start thinking about these questions in an organized manner, following through is a matter of time. The tough part is getting started. Although Financial Manager can't give you answers to abstract questions, it can give you a framework for thinking about your business issues. That kind of organized thinking is really what sophisticated financial management, and therefore financial growth, is all about.

Using the example of a full-time assistant, this is how Financial Manager helped me think: First, I calculated what I would have to pay my assistant to work full-time. Then I created a What-If Scenario to see how this would change my overall liabilities. Let's say she makes $35 per hour. If I use her for 50 percent of the time, she makes about $2,800 per month. To hire her on a full-time contractor basis would double that monthly cost to $5,600. This is strictly for the hourly wage, not taking into consideration benefits I may need to offer her as a full-time employee. Say, for the sake of this example, that she would remain an independent contractor but work full-time.

Then I looked at how much work I did before I hired her and how much I did once I had her part-time. I decided to quantify that analysis in Financial Manager by using dollar amounts. Any time you can quantify things in dollar amounts to conduct analyses, do so to make it easier. I figured that I made $9,000 in one month without her and $14,000 with her working part-time the next month—$5,000 more. In that month she worked 80 hours—which works out to exactly half-time (two full work weeks out of four). She made $2,800 and I made an additional $2,200.

So I created another little What-If Scenario factor: without an assistant vs. with an assistant. The What-If Analysis Wizard told me that I make $2,200 more in profit per month when my assistant is around. Now, here's the question: If she worked full-time, would that mean that I'd make $4,400 more in profit per month?

I had to look at how many hours I worked to make that $14,000 in a month, because there are only so many hours in a day and I can't calculate this scenario in a vacuum. I found that in order to make $9,000, I had to work about 90 hours a month, or about three days a week (this is the work I'm paid for, anyway; there is plenty of other work for which I'm not paid). I find out that with my assistant I don't have to work extra hours to make another $2,200. In addition, she remembers things that I don't. She saves me time in so many unquantifiable ways that I can't even calculate them. I give special thanks to her in the acknowledgment page in the front of this book, but as I made these calculations I was suddenly overwhelmed by how wonderful she is, so I want to just say that my assistant Amy Oringel, also based in New York, is a lifesaver. This book would not be written without her.

Okay, I digress. Excuse the moment of love. Back to what I was talking about.

In my What-If Scenario, "The Amy Factor" now includes several pieces of vital information: the cost of her working part-time and then full-time and how many hours I have to work in order to make x dollars. As time goes on and various scenarios arise, I can see how this calculation will change.

For instance, working on my novel takes more time than anything else, and I'm not being paid for it at this point. So if I crank up the hours I work on it, how many more hours can I have for it if Amy works full-time? If Amy actually saves me hours and I don't take on more work (which is what raised my earnings from $9,000 to $14,000), then I can spend more time on my novel by sacrificing some income.

Looking at these What-If Scenarios opened up my thinking by giving me the foundation to make a decision. The moral of this story is to put as many things as you can quantify into What-If Scenario reports and then play with them.

Allow for Flexibility

The most important thing to remember about setting up these systems is that you will change your mind, just as I changed my mind about how to automate my mortgage payments after entering the numbers into Financial Manager. Allow yourself flexibility—whether you run a small business with a number of employees or are sole proprietorship in a home office.

Once you have the basic infrastructure set up for one of these financial systems, it is easy to make changes. You'll probably find that you'll keep polishing the systems you set in place for a while, learning how you really think and therefore how you want information presented to you as time goes on.

Relax. You've done the most important infrastructure work and you've gotten your business records in some kind of order. Now we can move on to some of the more complex systems, starting with investing.

Part 3

Investing

Chapter 9

Managing Personal and Business Investments Online

I'm about to sound like a cheerleader, so I'd like to preface what I'm going to say with a short prologue: I'm about the most skeptical cynic around when it comes to people telling me they have a great new service of any kind. I tend to have an actual physical reaction, such as indigestion, to terms like "new and improved" or, worse, "updated." Anyway, before I digress too much about my gripes with marketing "hype," I'll get back to my point: I always approach new services on the Internet with a great deal of caution.

The Right Tool for the Job

There are some things the Internet is good for and some things it isn't. For instance, I hope participating in chat groups will never be a replacement for actually meeting new people in a physical-world setting. I think Internet chat is some sort of weird fad that ignores our most basic psychological makeup as human beings: We are social animals and need physical contact. Moreover, no telecommunications network is going to replace simple chemistry between people.

However, when it comes to managing investments, I am humbled by the Internet's prowess. Investment management is an example of something for which the Internet is good. Furthermore, because I try to be careful not to cross that fine line between healthy skeptic and brooding pessimist, I am the first to admit when something is wondrous.

The greatest thing to happen to an individual's ability to manage investments is indeed the Internet. It has created more discount brokerage houses and a freer flow of information that was previously the sole birthright of institutional investors, and it has allowed virtually anyone to become a fairly astute investor. This is not to say that there are no limitations, no shortcomings. Believe me, I'll get to those. But the bottom line is that if I sound like a cheerleader, it's because I'm sold; investing online, and then managing those investments electronically, works.

Why Invest Online? Save Money, Gain Control

Here's the short answer to the question of why you should change your investment strategy to include the Internet: You will save money, learn an awful lot—including how good the advice you've been getting over the years from professionals really is—and gain more control over your investments.

Discount online brokerages, and I mean the reputable ones, offer stock trading for less than $15 a trade. You will never get a deal like that from a traditional broker you speak with over the phone and who then proceeds to make the deal for you. Buying into mutual funds, bond funds, and such may cost a bit more online, but across the board, buying investments over the Internet is cheaper than doing it any other way.

What About Good Advice?

You need not give up the benefit of professional advice just because you use an online broker. People tend to think the minute they go to a discount brokerage house—on the Internet or off it—they're on their own. Frankly, that has been the case until the Internet.

What the discount brokerage Web sites offer besides making trade requests via e-mail is information and advice—and tons of it: real-time stock quotes that are as "live" as trades made on the stock exchange floor; analyses of stock performance, including five-year charts; advice columns; top stock picks; and news that affects stock prices—the list goes on. All you need to do is click buttons, type in requests, and more information than your broker has ever given you—and in a more succinct fashion—will appear in front of your eyes. In many cases, all this information is free. You'll hear about stock indices such as the Internet Index and the Socially Responsible Investing Index and how they stack up against the S&P 500.

None of this new market intelligence means that you can't still consult with a broker, either the one that you already have or one who impresses you online. Many brokers and fund managers have their own Web sites, with their own market analyses and performance charts. One of the great benefits of the Internet is that it has created ferocious competition for brokers and fund managers. They are going to great lengths to give out information and prove how good they are with cold, hard numbers.

Web Site Resources

Brokers and fund managers aside, there are so many Internet resources—investment Web sites, like Zack's, which is a favorite of finance journalists—that offer investment advice and market indicators; checking a few out might make you realize that you need a broker less and less.

In some cases, such as on the Wall Street Journal Interactive (*www.wsj.com*), Zack's Investment Research (*www.zacks.com*), and CNN Financial Network (*www.cnnfn.com*), all the market indicators are charted and updated constantly, and the analyses are taken from a number of brokers, so you can see what the majority of brokers are recommending and why. You actually get the benefit of many top brokers' thoughts, instead of relying on a sole person's opinion. Furthermore, you can take a quick glance at current and past performance of a particular stock or mutual fund you're thinking about buying. At these Web sites, you can use interactive charts to look at performance over the past five years as well as projections. In a demonstration of the real prowess of the Internet, you can ask to see only the news about a certain genre of stocks or about mutual funds in general (top performers, for instance), and the search engine will cut out all the superfluous information and deliver to you only the information you want to see. You can get stock quotes and company reports that are up to the minute.

It's truly a brave new world. Perhaps the most interesting aspect of Internet investment is that you can start researching without knowing specifically what you want and find out what stocks are a good buy.

The Future of Online Trading

In the course of my journalistic work, which often covers investing on the Internet, I have spoken to numerous executives at the various regulatory agencies that police Wall Street. One of the clearest indicators to me that investing over the Internet is a great boon to the individual investor is how skittish these executives get when you paint them the following picture:

> Right now, 20 percent of the stock exchanges' trading activity comes from individual investors. The lion's share is from huge corporate investors—institutional investors—who control the stock exchanges' floors. The individual investor, as a result, has little power.

> But what will the stock exchange floors look like, I always ask, when individual investors aren't just logging on to the Internet as it stands today to do their own trading? What about when video cameras attached to consumers' computers actually let them sit in on the stock exchange floor and participate like those madmen traders you always see in movies, flailing with incomprehensible hand signals that look like some sort of secret code a baseball catcher might use to tell the pitcher to throw a fastball? Once individual investors can participate on the floor, there is no controlling how much power they will have over their own investments.

> For instance, a group of small business owners could decide to pool funds, elect a trader among them, and play with bigger bucks. This is the exact strategy corporate investors use. Those brokers you see on the floor represent the investment dollars of major Fortune 1000 companies. What happens, I ask regulatory executives, when small investors can get dealt into this game?

(By the way, the Internet is a good place to network with other small businesses in general, and pooling funds for investing is no exception. Even though you can't yet sit on the stock exchange floor, you invest collectively through a broker.)

The response from regulatory executives is invariably some speech about how the technology is not there and how the laws of broker representation and floor-trading participants will have to change. But the truth is that they don't know what will happen; they see the whole idea of investing changing at lightning speed, and they are scrambling to make sure that the systems still work. Think about it: Can you remember any previous time when pretty much anyone you talk to had such knowledge of the stock market and its activities? The reason for this newfound knowledge is simple: The free flow of information on the Internet is transforming people into stock market experts. The motivation to learn is there—after all, we're talking about money here—and it doesn't cost much to try it out.

A Little Bit of Knowledge Can Be a Dangerous Thing

I will add a caveat here: A little bit of knowledge is a dangerous thing, and playing the market over the Internet could involve some danger. In dozens and dozens of financial chat groups, rumors and gossip lead to really bad investments. The professional advice of brokers and fund managers should not be tossed aside in favor of advice heard in a vacuum.

One of the things people forget about information—no matter how free flowing—is that it takes a long time and a steep learning curve to take in information and transform yourself into a legitimate expert. Professional brokers have spent a long time understanding the market. You have an entirely separate career with a different expertise, and unless you plan to bail on that career to become a serious trader—which people do today with some enormous success, by the way, thanks to online trading—you will not accumulate as much knowledge as these brokers.

Frankly, you may find yourself spending more time researching stocks than you care to. It may occur to you at 3 o'clock in the morning, while you're sitting there bleary-eyed, surfing the Internet, that if you had wanted to become a stockbroker, you would have. Is all this knowledge and control worth it, you may ask? Wouldn't my broker come to the same conclusion in mere minutes that I've spent an entire evening working toward? And doesn't that make the fee I pay him well worth it?

Middle-of-the-Road Advice

The answer to those late-night questions, as is true with most things in life, lies somewhere in the middle. Using your broker's advice as a starting point, then doing some research, then checking back with your broker is probably a good way to start investing using the Internet.

You might even inspire your broker to open his mind and think in broader terms about your portfolio if you ask about certain investments you researched on the Internet, bringing ideas to the table yourself. Your broker will be challenged to explain why you should or shouldn't go with an investment you suggest, as well as challenged to come up with the best return possible. The more your broker thinks you know, the more astute he will feel he needs to be. If he knows that you have accessed information that compares the returns on investment of various mutual funds, for instance, he also knows that he can't simply send you a quarterly newsletter explaining that the fund you're invested in has done okay over the last five years. He is on the spot to get you a better return.

This advice is a little contrary to the common wisdom about how to use the Internet to manage investments. Mostly, you will hear that the way to go is to use an online discount brokerage for less than $15 a trade, giving up altogether your traditional broker at Merrill Lynch or Fidelity. Or you might hear the advice on the other end of the spectrum: Never trade online, but do enough research to have better dialogue with your broker.

My advice lies in the middle. Keep your account open with your traditional broker in order to maintain access to his or her advice. But at the same time, start getting your feet wet investing online, and see how you do. You may have a knack. Some people consider this rather sneaky advice. I think my own broker would flinch at it a bit, thinking that I will eventually wean myself of him, and in the meantime I'm milking him for advice—advice I may take from him and then turn around and go cut the deal myself online, cutting him out of the fee. Is that fair? Is it fair to keep an account open, ask for advice, and then not pay the broker a fee for that advice? I don't know if it's truly fair in the long run, but I do think it's your prerogative to test out any new investment tools in the short term, even if doing so takes advantage of your broker. The free market is a Darwinist paradigm; if the broker truly adds value to your investment strategy, you will be compelled to continue to pay him or her over the long run, but if the broker eventually adds no value, you will cut him or her out. In the meantime, the learning process is justifiable.

Online Discount Brokers: How to Tell the Good from the Bad

Sometimes fear is the best protection, and so if what I say here scares you, that's good. The Internet is plagued by frauds, particularly when it comes to investing. Pyramid schemes; unlicensed poseurs pretending to be independent brokers; con artists who actually just out and out lie, saying they are fund managers or brokers for reputable brokerage houses—the list goes on. And perhaps the scariest part of Internet fraud is how slippery the thieves are. They can disappear in minutes by simply pulling the plug on their Web site.

The short advice here is to go with a brand name when it comes to investing on the Internet. When your money is at stake, you don't have time for games and you don't want to take unnecessary risks. You need to stick with reputable financial institutions. This is not to say that the Internet hasn't given birth to a new breed of stock brokerage: online-only brokerages that are completely reputable. E*TRADE, one of the most popular and one of the least expensive such houses, is a classic example. You can surf to *www.etrade.com* and for less than $15 per trade, you can set up an account and use this discount broker via the Web any time you want.

The trick in online trading and investing is knowing the landscape and the credible discount brokerages. Don't feel the need to be a pioneer; let someone else discover the next E*TRADE, and you can jump on the bandwagon only when there is solid confirmation that it is a safe ride.

Aside from following the list of reliable brokers and other Web sites that specialize in investment information at the end of this chapter, as well as a list in Money in the Investment section, there are patterns for detecting the bad brokers in the bunch, just as there are in the physical world. The same rules apply. If you are flipping through the Yellow Pages or driving down the street and see a sign for Joe's Brokerage and that's all you know about the company, you don't bother with it. The same deal holds true on the Web—with one twist. Any Joe can make a Web site look legitimate. Any Joe on a Web site can make it appear as though he is affiliated with someone reputable, such as Merrill Lynch or Fidelity, by placing graphics on his site. The National Association of Securities Dealers (NASD) and the Federal Trade Commission (FTC) do have rather sophisticated Internet fraud watchdog groups, so con artists will likely get caught—eventually. The problem is that they often take in quite a few suckers before they get caught, or they get away with it altogether, taking in a few people and then closing up shop and disappearing before the FTC or NASD gets hot on their trail.

Remember, a Web site can disappear overnight. You can keep from being one of those suckers, though. It's all a matter of being extremely skeptical and doing your own due diligence.

Steps You Must Take to Perform Due Diligence

Before you open an account anywhere on the Internet—before you give away a single piece of personal information on an online form—do the following:

- **Go with a trusted brand name listed at the end of this chapter.** Call the reputable brokerage house and make sure the Web site address you're accessing is the correct one. An example of how tricky Internet frauds can be: If you surf to *www.whitehouse.gov* you go the White House's Web site. If you go to *www.whitehouse.com,* you go to a pornography site. The same can hold true with investment sites. One letter's difference in an Internet URL means you are surfing to an entirely different place.

- **Go to both the FTC's Web site (*www.ftc.gov*) and the National Association of Securities Dealers Inc. (NASD) Web site** (*www.nasd.com*) and see if the brokerage or fund manager in question is on a fraud-alert list. In addition, go the Investor Protection Trust's Web site (*www.investorprotection.org*). IPT is a non-profit investment watchdog organization that now specializes in Internet fraud.

- **Call the brokerage.** If there is no phone number for the brokerage on its Web site or no one answers the phone, don't use the brokerage. If you do reach the brokerage by phone, ask for license and insurance information. Call the FTC with that information to check the company's legitimacy. Ask to be referred to the regulatory body in your state so you can make sure the brokerage is licensed properly. Call the state regulator.

Finding the Right Type of Broker for You

Fraud worries aside, the good news is that whether you're a novice investor who needs a lot of guidance, a do-it-yourselfer, or a seasoned market player who wants a sharp broker to handle everything, there's a broker for everyone on the Web.

For do-it-yourselfers, the answer is easy: You find a discount broker-age you like, open an account, and start trading.

For novice investors, a good teacher is necessary; for the sophisticated investor spending a great deal of money, the broker must also be sophisticated, able to provide detailed analyses in a number of ways. These two types of investor will look to different places to find brokers and evaluate them by different standards.

Where to start? For whatever profile you fit, follow the guidelines outlined in the following sections.

The Do-It-Yourselfer

Given the self-service nature of the Web itself, it stands to reason that there are more resources for do-it-yourself investors than any other type of investor. Not only can individual investors easily find legitimate discount brokers—such as Schwab, E*TRADE, Ameritrade, and Datek—they can also get opinions about which broker is best suited for their needs.

The Gomez Advisors Web site, sponsored by the stock quote service Quote.com, rates the discount online brokers by their prowess. For instance, Gomez gives Schwab the highest rating for serious, high-investment traders and Datek Online the best rating for day traders. These ratings change as the online brokers add new features and services. Interestingly, for one-stop shopping, Gomez gives the top award to no one, even though most of the discount broker sites claim to be everything the individual investor needs.

The do-it-yourselfer will also want to look for tips, tricks, and market insight. Aside from Zack's, which is a must-bookmark site, Briefing.com is a market commentary service started by former senior managers at Standard & Poor's MMS International. The caliber of people running Briefing.com—such as Richard C. Green, president (and former MMS president in the early 1980s), and Greg Jones, chief economist (formerly the senior economist at MMS)—makes for a great broker-style virtual advisor service.

Or do-it-yourselfers can opt for the quintessential virtual broker at sites such as Investorama.com. This site, run by Doug Gerlach, author of *Investor's Web Guide: Tools and Strategies for Building Your Portfolio* and senior editor of the National Association of Investors Corp. (NAIC) Web site, is full of market talk, links to quote services, news, and new start-up company information. The most brokerlike element is the "Ask Doug" feature; investors can get advice from Mr. Gerlach by e-mail.

The Investors Protection Trust is also a good place for this type of investor to get in the habit of visiting. Because it is nonprofit, this organization's collection of financial news and information has no agenda, and its fraud-watch feature is worth checking periodically. Keeping an eye on what's new with broker scams can save investors a lot of headaches.

Novice Looking for Hand Holding

The do-it-yourselfer will find most resources he or she needs on the Web, but novices and sophisticates will also find some very important information—such as whether the broker they are considering has had any disciplinary action taken against him or her.

NASD has on the Web its Central Registration Depository (CRD) service, the Regulation Public Disclosure Program, which lets you find out whether any disciplinary action has been taken against a broker. Investors can fill out online forms and e-mail requests. This NASD service is the most important feature that helps investors find the right broker. Certainly, check with your home state's securities administrator via its Web site or phone, to make sure the broker in question is licensed, but after that go straight to NASD.

Before novice investors can check out the legitimacy of a broker, however, they need to find one. For starters, stick with referrals from big brand-name brokerage houses, such as Merrill Lynch or Fidelity Investments.

Seasoned Investor Looking for a New Broker

A seasoned investor may be a do-it-yourselfer as well, in which case the high-end options for the do-it-yourselfer would apply. The quintessential example is Schwab's Signature, Signature Gold, and Signature Platinum services, which are available for clients with $500,000 or more in qualified accounts. Prices vary, but the services give constant access to a broker by telephone and online trading through a dedicated modem line, instead of relying on the Web's accessibility.

Here's a good place to hear the limitations of Web trading, rather than dialing into an online brokerage by using your modem to dial a private phone line that gets you directly into their computers: When you trade at a Web site, you're essentially sending an e-mail request to the broker. Depending on how many people are sending requests simultaneously, a queue might form. Even though the online brokerages are proficient at putting through the orders quickly, the prices can change in just a few minutes. There is no guarantee that you'll get the price you thought you were getting when you sent the e-mail. You'll know what you paid when the brokerage sends you confirmation by e-mail. By contrast, when you trade electronically by dialing directly into the brokerage's computer, it is immediate, and you will get the price you asked for. The difference in the two levels of service, of course, is cost.

For the direct dial-in, you will pay a couple of hundred dollars for the package. (Prices vary, so do some research.)

The most helpful Web site for seasoned investors who want a new broker is NASD's. Most veteran investors do have a network of professionals to tap for a new broker, so the easy-access due diligence will make weeding out possibilities a faster process. However, a Web site with a comprehensive listing of licensed brokers in each state, categorized by specialty—international markets, for instance—would be helpful. The closest thing is the National Association of Personal Financial Advisors Web site. There investors can find a financial planner and in turn be referred to a broker. There is also the Securities Industry Association Web site, which is not broker specific but can guide investors to any one of its 700 securities firm members, who in turn can recommend brokers.

You won't be able to get a comprehensive listing of brokers on the Web until regulation concerning how a broker is permitted to advertise and market services and products are changed. Broad restrictions hold sway as to what brokers can say that would be construed as sales material. They can't create promotional materials not approved by their companies, and in a self-publishing environment like the Web, that rule hampers them. For now is that you'll have to do some legwork.

Keep a Paper Trail of Stock Trades

The next chapter provides a step-by-step procedure for setting up an account and actually investing online. The chapter will include everything you need to know. Here I'll mention one key thing you need to do, and this step is crucial. You must keep a paper trail of any investment deals you make online. Get used to hitting the Print button before you send any transaction request to a broker over the Internet. You simply print out the Web page. That printout is the best receipt you'll have. Also print out the online registration forms you fill out and save them to your Investment Account ledger, which you will set up in Money. There is no better protection than your own records.

Guide to Online Investment Resources

Here is a list of Web sites to help you get started with your Internet investment research. The list includes the reputable online brokerages as well as market information sites and regulators.

Online Brokerages

E-Line Financial: *www.e-linefin.com*

Gomez Advisors: *www.quote.com/specials/gomze/index.htm*

Schwab: *www.schwab.com*

E*TRADE: *www.etrade.com*

Ameritrade: *www.ameritrade.com*

Datek Online: *www.datek.com*

Market Information

Zack's Investment Research: *www.zacks.com*

CNN Financial Network: *www.cnnfn.com*

Briefing.com: *www.briefing.com*

Invest-o-rama: *www.investorama.com*

Merrill Lynch: *www.ml.com*

Fidelity Investments: *www.fidelity.com*

Wall Street Journal Interactive: *www.wsj.com*

DLJdirect: *www.dljdirect.com*

MSN Investor: *msnvestor.msn.com*

Fraud Watchdogs

National Association of Securities Dealers, Inc. (NASD) Regulation Public Disclosure Program: *www.nasdr.com/2000.htm*

North American Securities Administrators Association, Inc. (NASAA): *www.nasaa.org*

Investor Protection Trust: *www.investorprotection.org*

National Association of Personal Financial Advisors: *www.napfa.org*

Securities Industry Association: *www.sia.com*

Chapter 10

Getting Started with Your Investments

Even if you're not quite ready to take your investment dollars and completely transform yourself into an online investor, there's no harm in a little toe dipping.

This chapter begins by walking you through going to an investment Web site and setting up a portfolio of your existing investments (with no purchase of anything required). You'll see how to customize the information you get so you receive the stock quotes of your existing investments. This exercise will give you a feel for how online investing works if you simply track the performance of the investments you already have. The chapter also sets up a sample electronic portfolio in Money, which you'll need for filling out your tax forms anyway.

The chapter also walks you through the process of setting up an online stock trading account. At $15 or less per trade, you can even go buy one share of a stock just to see how the whole system works.

After that, you'll start to see how Money ties the whole system together: You'll track trades and other investments, get the numbers ready for tax filing, and transfer funds into your investment accounts using your Bills & Deposits setup in Money.

Your Stock Portfolio on the Web and in Money

The first thing to do is set up a portfolio at a discount brokerage on the Web so you can track the performance of your present investments. By setting up your portfolio on the Web—and not just in Money—all your investments will be logged and tracked in one area when you open a Web trading account to do some stock and mutual fund purchasing over the Internet. It might sound like a pain to set up the same portfolio information on the Web and then again in Money, but the two information sources really do serve different purposes, and it won't take that long.

Think of it this way: The portfolio on the Web is for playing: looking up your stock quotes, checking performance, comparing the performance with other stocks and funds you're thinking about buying, checking out any news about your stocks. The portfolio in Money is your permanent record: the numbers for each investment, ledger-style, and the dates you bought and sold investments, information in which the IRS is very interested.

I chose E*TRADE as the Web brokerage we'll use for both setting up a sample portfolio and opening an online trading account. I chose E*TRADE because I think it best represents what Web trading is—and it's cheap and reliable. E*TRADE is not a company, like Charles Schwab, which started out in the physical world and then opened an Internet branch. E*TRADE was born on the Internet. Don't worry; it is insured and reliable. It's also very simple to use, as any service on the Web should be.

Creating a Portfolio at E*TRADE

So, here we go. First thing is to launch your Internet browser and surf to *www.etrade.com*. Have your investment information handy. You do not need the account numbers of your investments, just the stock or fund names and the quantities you hold. Remember, this will not be your official ledger. You don't want to put account numbers on the Web, nor will there be a place for you to do so. Never give out more personal information on the Web than you need to in order to get service.

One thing to note about E*TRADE: When you do open an account there—which will contain only the account information for your E*TRADE investments, not all of your investments—E*TRADE does have a policy not to share your personal information with other companies. Bear in mind that whether you end up opening an account with E*TRADE or any of the other numerous online brokerages, always take a look at their "Privacy Policy," which should be a clearly marked link on the brokerage's home page. If there is no privacy policy, do not open an account with that brokerage on that site. This should be your rule of thumb for doing business on the Web altogether, but it's especially important when investing online. In order to open an investment account, the online brokerage must get all sorts of personal information, including your Social Security number, just as any other brokerage does. You don't want to be handing this information over to any company that doesn't promise not to sell your private data to other marketers.

Once you're on E*TRADE's home page, click the Portfolio & Markets and tab. It's not obvious once you get to the Portfolio & Markets page how you set up a portfolio without opening an account. But you can. Click the Sign Up For A Free Membership option. You'll go to a form that you'll need to fill out. Create a user name and a password on the E*TRADE site.

When you're done, click Continue. You'll link to a page that asks you to enter a name for your mailbox on E*TRADE. Fill out this information and click Done. On the next page, click Log On. This takes you to the E*TRADE Customer & Member Log On page, where you'll need to fill in your user name and password. In the Start In box, select Portfolio Manager from the drop-down menu. Then click Log On.

On the next page, E*TRADE asks if you want it to save your user name and password information for six months so E*TRADE will know you're a member when you surf to the Web site again. If you select this option, E*TRADE loads a cookie (a string of numbers—a code) onto your computer's hard drive. The cookie identifies you to the Web site on subsequent visits. That way, when you surf to the site, E*TRADE will recognize you and log you on automatically.

Some folks cringe at the idea of a Web site placing a code on their hard drive. But honestly, it doesn't mean that they can retrieve other information from your hard drive. That is not the way a cookie works. However, that's not to say that there aren't other ways the cookie technology can be used to invade your privacy, but that is not the way the technology is being used in this example. Still, if you feel uncomfortable—which, frankly, I do—you can opt not to have E*TRADE recognize you and instead simply go through the 20-second process of logging on every time you visit the site.

Chapter 16 goes into privacy issues on the Web in depth. The focus in that chapter is on what you need to do to make customers comfortable on your own Web storefront. I purposely wanted this chapter to precede the privacy chapter so you'll see the issue of privacy from the customer perspective before you make decisions as a Web storefront owner. Internet consumers are a very sensitive breed. When they don't like something, they spread the word. Just imagine the implications of word of mouth on the Internet. Any single person can broadcast a message to hundreds of thousands of people. The last thing you want is irate customers dedicated to giving you bad PR. It's best to get very familiar with the feelings you have as a consumer so you'll become a Web storefront owner who lures customers, not one who ostracizes them.

Anyway, back to creating your portfolio. Once you've chosen whether you want E*TRADE to recognize you or not, click Go To E*TRADE. This will take you to the Create/Edit Portfolio page, which will ask you to name your portfolio. Just pick any name you'll remember. You may want to create two portfolios if you have specific funds that are business-only investments. Eventually, you'll need to track business and personal investments—if your business actually purchases its own investments under an incorporated Federal ID number—in Money, so you may as well monitor the performance of these investments in separate portfolio folders. That way, the total value of each portfolio will appear separately as well, making it simpler to input the totals when it comes time to record them in Money.

Once you name the portfolio, click Create Portfolio. This takes you to the Portfolio Manager page. Click Add Entries. A chart will pop up; that will be your portfolio. Simply start keying in the information in the right boxes: stock ticker or fund symbol, number of shares, and so on. If you don't know a stock symbol, you can simply look it up by clicking the Find link and following the directions that appear. Do this for each of your investments.

That's it. Your portfolio is created. If you click the Submit button below the chart, you'll immediately get a chart of the stock price. (There is a 20-minute delay on E*TRADE, as there is if you look up stock quotes by dialing in from the Investment section in Money). You can create a customized chart as well, if, say, you just want to see the latest prices but not be bothered with news updates. To do this, just click Create Custom View and fill in what you want to see in the appropriate boxes.

To create another portfolio—for business investments—simply go back to the Portfolio Manager page and create a new one using a different portfolio name.

Now, every time you go to the E*TRADE site (and log on, if you don't opt to have E*TRADE put a cookie on your hard drive), you will simply go to Portfolio Manager and ask for your portfolio by name. You can add investments to your portfolio at any time.

You'll notice lots of options once you're in Portfolio Manager. You can look up market indexes, get news about certain companies, see the day's gainers and losers, and many other things. The whole point is to look at your portfolio in context of the entire market. Play around; get the feel of it. It's all free.

Opening an Online Trading Account

While you're at E*TRADE, you might as well open your stock and fund trading account. There's no obligation to do this, so if you're not ready and just want to see what it's like to play around on the site and track your present portfolio's performance, go straight to the section on tracking your investments in Money, later in the chapter.

But, if you're game, here's what you need to do: Click on My Accounts on the navigation bar. You'll see Open An Account. Click the Apply Online button. You'll notice that you must have a printer set up and ready to go to take advantage of this option. The reason is that you cannot do the whole process on the Web. Because the site will be handling investing your money at your request, it requires you to mail in an original signature on a form—not unlike the IRS's policy for setting up an online tax-paying account.

After that, you just follow the prompts, answering questions. One of the key questions will be how you'd like to deposit money to open this account; you can't buy and sell stocks or mutual funds with a credit card, you know (I think the government is scared the economy will collapse if people buy stocks on credit! That's a valid fear, if you ask me.) The cool thing here is that the bank you set up for online bill paying and deposits in Money likely deals with E*TRADE, too. That means you can simply deposit a minimum of $1,000 to open your account by transferring the funds online. Now, rest assured that if you transfer $1,000, that money does not go anywhere. You can have an open account without trading, so if you decide later that you want to close the account, you can simply do so, without losing your money.

Tip

E*TRADE will ask you at some point what other kinds of investment accounts you have. Leave this section blank. If you tell it—by, say, clicking Full Commission— later in the process E*TRADE will ask how you want your existing account transferred to E*TRADE. E*TRADE won't let you finish the process if you leave this set of questions blank and try to opt out of transferring your account. Tricky, yes, but not tricky enough. Just say you have no other investment accounts. However, if you want to open this account by transferring funds instead of sending a check with your printed application, you will need to fill out this transfer account option. Simply put the name of your bank and the type of account from which you're transferring the funds. My suggestion is that you still leave your other investment accounts blank. There's no need to give any more information than you absolutely have to.

When you get to the end, E*TRADE will prompt you to print out the form. Then mail it to E*TRADE and your account will be opened. You need to follow the steps on the E*TRADE Web site to actually make purchases. Bear in mind that each Web trading site has different steps for actually buying investments. Essentially, though, it is all a matter of filling out online forms and clicking the Send button.

Be sure to take the online tour of any Web trading site you are thinking of using. All of them have such a tour, which takes you through their particular processes for investing.

Tracking Investments in Money

Setting up ledgers and tracking both personal and business investments in Money is as simple as setting up the Account Registers in Chapter 4. Because E*TRADE is one of the institutions included in the Money list of financial firms that have online services, the whole process is really a snap. Once you set up your accounts, you can dial into E*TRADE from Money and download statements right into your Investment Account Register.

Start by opening Money and clicking Investments on the navigation bar, which takes you to the Portfolio place. In the left pane, click Holdings View, if it's not already selected. Then just click New at the bottom of the page, and the wizard will pop up and walk you through setting up your accounts, in the same question-and-answer form as the Money Account wizard.

Tip

Say you open two accounts at E*TRADE, one business and one personal, and you have two more accounts at Merrill Lynch, one personal and one business. Make sure when you name these accounts in Money that you add a prefix to each name, such as "A" for personal and "B" for business. Because the Portfolio Register in Money alphabetizes the list of your investments, if you use prefixes you can effectively divide your investments into two categories that you see at a glance . All your personal investments will appear first, and your business investments will appear after them.

To update prices in your Investment Register, simply move your cursor to the line where the investment account appears, click it, and then click the Update Price button at the bottom of the page.

When you create a portfolio file in Investments, Money automatically creates a Register in Accounts as well. (You can look at it quickly by clicking on Accounts on the navigation bar.) Anything you do in the Investment Register, such as update a price, is automatically reflected in the Accounts Register.

The key difference between the Investment Register and the Account Register is that the Investment Register gives you a quick view of the price and total value of your investments. The Account Register shows all the transactions in each account—information that you'll need later for filing taxes. Go ahead and create an investment account in Investment, and then click Accounts on the navigation bar. In the Accounts place, click an investment to look at it from that transaction-by-transaction view. You'll notice that there are spaces to fill in quantities, commissions associated, dates, and the like. All this is information you can easily transfer to tax forms.

Staying on Top of Taxes

To make it easy to transfer all the tax-related information from investments—and all other accounts we've created so far—into whatever tax preparation software you'll use (details in Chapter 6), you'll want to create reports as you go. Plan to fill out reports once a month (this is a good task for a bookkeeper). Go to the navigation bar and click Reports. In the left pane of the Reports place, you'll see a menu of choices. Click Taxes. Another list of choices will appear. Double-click Capital Gains. A chart will pop up that you can fill in with dates investments were bought and sold and other information for the IRS. The point of using this Reports section is that all the totals—the numbers you need to port into tax software—appear in one view. So, if you keep reports for each account you hold, when it comes time to do your taxes, you won't have to open each Account Register to get the totals.

On the Reports place, click Taxes again, and then double-click Tax Related Transactions. Another report will appear; in it you can enter every single tax-consequential transaction you make. This is most useful for home offices, where the scope of tax-deductible transactions will be more limited than small businesses with employees and office space. For the latter, creating this report may be more work than it's worth. It may be easier for these small businesses to simply take the information from the appropriate Account Register and plug it into the Tax Software Report option, which also appears on the Taxes page in the Reports place. The reason it may be easier is that so many tax-related transactions might be involved that weeding them out is not appropriate. The Tax Software Report is a simple report—it just asks for the tax line item and the amount. It's simply a way to get a comprehensive view of all the tax line items you'll put into a return. Think of the report as a scratchpad worksheet, except it's a useful scratchpad because you can simply port all the numbers into tax software.

There's More to Investments Than Stocks and Mutual Funds

This chapter has covered the basic elements of online investing and electronic tracking. Bear in mind that creating a portfolio and an accounting system for stocks and mutual funds you own and learning to buy investments over the Internet for a discount are just the first tasks with which you'll become proficient as you work through this book.

In the next chapter, we'll use the tools in Money to get a grip on insurance, employee benefits, and capital investments, which are all key components to any electronic investment-tracking system.

Chapter 11

Special Investment Tracking

This is going to be a catch-your-breath chapter. You should also consider it a nagging chapter. Those sound like opposing concepts, don't they? Well, not necessarily. The actual content of this chapter is a reminder to change the way you handle the management of all your investments—not just the stocks and funds you buy. Essentially, we will flesh out a system you can use to ensure that your investment management is comprehensive and organized.

The content of the chapter is little more than going through all the components step by step—the nagging part. The reason I find the nagging important is that good financial management comes down to remembering the details. A system is no good unless it's comprehensive. The reason I also call it a catch-your-breath chapter is that nagging shouldn't be all negative and tedious—it should be a jump-start when you need rejuvenation in order to remember those details. Call it a gentle nudge that prompts you to take action, remembering to include all the details. But also call it a gentle nudge to remind you to pause and catch your breath, think things through again while you're going through the fairly automatic process of including the details. Sometimes it's in the details that we see the biggest picture of all. Catching your breath while you're being nagged to do so is all about checking the work you've done so far to make sure it's comprehensive.

The most important part of this chapter is to dot all the *i's* and cross all the *t's* in your ledgers, and then step back and make sure that the accounting portion of your financial management systems look sound to you. Because after this chapter we're moving on to the living part of financial management, where we'll look at the financial management that actually can grow your bottom line—the revenue-building portion. I'm speaking specifically about how to open a Web storefront of your own and how to set up the systems that change your business from a cash-based system to one that accepts credit cards and other cash alternatives.

So, try and sit back and relax a bit as we go through the checklist of things to remember when it comes to tracking investments. Sit back and let yourself think—think whether you're forgetting anything that is vital to the day-to-day and year-to-year management of your business.

The Niggling Details: The Sustenance of Your Business

Many things you need to track as investments certainly don't feel like investments. An investment should be something you get a clear return on, right? Not necessarily. As a business owner—whether you're a lone home office dweller or the captain of a fully staffed ship—an investment is anything you put into the business in order to sustain it. The return on the investment is the existence of your functioning business and, you hope, its growth. That may sound like an abstract return, but it is one nonetheless—perhaps the most important one. The reason that these types of investment are hard to sink your teeth into and label is that we're accustomed to intellectualizing things in terms of direct cause and effect. For example, we understand a stock investment because we pay a certain dollar amount and then see the effect, which is either a profit or a loss, directly related to and quantifiable in terms of the dollars we put in.

The sustenance investments, as I like to call them, have no such clear logic. You invest in insurance, for example, and the return is that you're allowed to own your home, go to a hospital if you need to, or legally employ people. That's hard to quantify when you ask yourself how much insurance to buy, because you have to somehow get your mind around what portion of your revenues are directly attributed to this investment.

But there are ways to quantify such investments, even if they are more abstract. For instance, if you have a good health plan for employees, it may cost you more, but your employees may stay longer and enjoy better health while they're with you. (They could enjoy better health, for instance, if your health plan covers mental health therapy and eye care.) But these investments are expensive, so you have to see what you can afford if you plan to sink more into these investments and not just track what you have. Tracking, remember, is also a way to take stock of what you have and see if you need to change things. That's why I went into the whole process of using the analysis tools in Office 2000's Financial Manager, instead of just explaining how to keep better records and become more efficient using Money.

Saving these sustenance investments for the last chapter before we move on to revenue building was totally intentional. Before we move on to how to grow your business, you need to make sure you are sustaining it in a healthy manner. It's a matter of priorities that's important to think about methodically: Before reaching outward and upward with your business, make sure its infrastructure is as efficient and healthy as possible. Therein lies perhaps the most important concept of financial management—and one that is often ignored. It's the nature of people—myself included—to want to run before we can walk.

Well, we're going to walk for a while first. We'll stroll through the sustenance investments and get you thinking about whether you need to make any changes and whether you've forgotten anything.

Business and Personal Insurance

If you're a home office dweller, get all your insurance information together—homeowner, health, car, and any other you have. In Money, create an Investment account for them all called Insurance (remember that creating an Investment account will automatically create an Account Register, too). By looking at and tracking the total amount these insurance policies cost you, you'll see what kind of monthly expenditure you have.

Then think if you need anything else. Do you have a lot of computer equipment not currently covered under your homeowner's insurance? Look at your policy carefully and see if you need to boost the amount of insurance you have. If you know the rates that, say, an extra $1,000 worth of insurance will cost you per year, use Financial Manager in Office 2000 and do a cost analysis of how much more you'd need to spend on insurance to protect your business assets.

If you're a small business owner with employees, you should also use Money to keep track of your insurance, but create two Insurance accounts—one for personal expenses and one for business. If you have a home office filled with computer equipment that you use for your business, check your policies. You may want to buy extra insurance for your home using an insurance policy for your business. It may give you a better tax break to do so. While you're at it, check the overall coverage of your business insurance and make sure it's up to date—your business could have changed an awful lot in the past year, while your insurance, which you bought the year before, hasn't. If you've hired more people, expanded office space, or purchased more computers, the effectiveness of your present insurance can be diminished.

Employee Benefits

Next on the list are your employee benefits, should you have any. In Money, create an account in the Investments place that lists all the benefits you offer employees—health insurance (which will be redundant in regard to your business insurance account, but bear with me), 401Ks (also redundant), education reimbursement, and so on. The reason it's important to create this Investment account as a single entity in Money, even though some of the line items are redundant, is to get a comprehensive look at what you're paying to sustain employees. In order to do any analyses in Financial Manager to see whether you can offer employees more—or whether you should cut back on some benefits—you need to look at all the numbers that feed into this account.

Employee benefits can also apply to home office dwellers if you're incorporated as a business. Under an S corporation, for example, you can set up employee benefits that serve you well. Say you're going back to school for some reason—taking classes that directly benefit your business. If you set up an employee benefits program, you can make this school cost a tax deduction. The trick with employee benefits under an S corporation is that you have to offer all employee benefits to all employees. Furthermore, an S corporation requires that you have a board of directors with at least three members. If you're in a family that participates in your business in any way, though, you can put them on the board. However, in order to get the employee benefits for yourself, remember you have to offer those benefits to everyone. Be aware that some of your family may take you up on this offer!

The point, of course, is not to incorporate your business; we're looking at employee benefits. You do want to see, however, if you're spending money on things such as education that could be better classified under your business expenses.

Capital Investments and Depreciations

The trick with to creating accounts that track capital investments and depreciations is to know what counts as a capital investment. Look carefully at Chapter 5 again for definitive details before creating these Investment accounts. Do yourself a favor, though: Create just one Investment account for all capital investments. This means you'll end up with a sort of summary account in your Accounts place, with all the components (such as car loan and computer equipment leases) spread out under other accounts as well. But it's worth having as many comprehensive views of whole categories as possible, as well as the detailed tracking in other accounts.

Remember, in order to perform useful analyses in Financial Manager, you need to think categorically so you can include all the pertinent factors in your decisions. Creating these summary accounts—insurance, employee benefits, capital investments—allows you to do that.

The clear lesson here is deciding when and how to depreciate capital investments such as computer equipment. There are different tax implications for depreciating a piece of equipment over two years as opposed to, say, five years. At first you may think to take a more ongoing tax benefit by depreciating more slowly—the five-year option. But what if you make this decision—or your accountant makes it—without analyzing whether you'll be upgrading all your computer equipment next year?

Lump these capital investments into one Investment Account Register and then go through, line by line, and do your analyses.

Analyses Are Key; So Are Filling in the Blanks

I sort of tricked you and I feel kind of bad. I started this chapter telling you to relax and take stock—that the only activity would be entering more numbers in your Account Registers. But I quickly turned face, encouraging you to launch Financial Manager in Office 2000 and do analyses. Well, sorry if you feel duped and exhausted just thinking about it, but I did say I'd be nagging, too.

The truth is that these analyses are key to checking your work and making sure everything is covered. This is the time to create the spreadsheets and projections that you will refer to in the next section, when you're trying to figure out if you can afford a Web storefront.

Miscellaneous Investments You Think of as Regular Expenses

Perhaps thinking about cost analyses has already prompted you to think about all the accounts and reports you could add under Investments—ones that you thought of as mere day-to-day expenses. But just in case it hasn't, there are a few that you may want to add.

Employee travel and conferences—including your own—are often categorized only under expenses. But they are also sustenance investments, if you think about it. The amount you decide to spend traveling in order to build your business is an investment in your business. I urge you to create an Investment account that looks at the totals you spend on travel in the name of building business.

Another investment area is research. Sometimes you can invest a lot in researching something without ever creating product from it. Research can be as simple as buying some books on a subject or as complicated as traveling, going to seminars, and spending many hours investigating a marketplace. Try to quantify research in terms of dollars spent and create an Investment account for it. It may help you set priorities in terms of what kind of research you can afford to do.

It may seem weird at first to create a Portfolio account for each of these things in Money, but the point of an investment portfolio is to track performance and see totals. In Money, this seems to be the easiest way to track such things, even if it isn't the ideal method (remember that no software program is perfect). In any case, it will keep you thinking about sustenance investments as investments. Try putting all these accounts under one category, such as Sustenance Investments. That way, when you click Categories on Money's navigation bar, the view will include the sustenance investments as a separate entity. That way, when you're in the mood to do some analyses of sustenance investments, you can look at them all at once.

That's it for bookkeeping and bill paying. Time to see what options are out there to grow your business.

Part 4

Web Storefronts

Chapter 12

Why Do You Need a Web Storefront?

Y ou're probably sick of people asking you if your business has a Web site. You are probably sicker of them asking if you sell stuff over the Web. I'm not sure when Web storefronts—Web sites that sell stuff—became such a vogue topic of conversation, but at any cocktail party these days, you'll probably be forced to chat about the Internet. Sick of the topic or not, as a small business owner you've got to think about it. It's one of the few competitive advantages small businesses can obtain affordably, and it's a great leveler in that on the Web, a small business can "look" a lot like a big business. One statistic—which should be taken with a big grain of salt, like all statistics—points out just how much this competitive advantage can yield in terms of profits. Of approximately 7.4 million small businesses in the United States, the ones with Web storefronts have higher revenues, averaging $3.79 million in revenues compared with $2.72 million for small businesses overall. That's over $1 million in additional revenue, which is nothing to sneeze at.

I grant you that this statistic doesn't necessarily mean that these businesses sell an additional $1 million in goods and services per year via sales made on that Web storefront. Any number of intangibles might contribute to the additional revenue, such as market exposure and enhanced brand name gained from the Web and turned into profits elsewhere. That's not exactly the same as direct sales. But the fact still remains that the small businesses that have Web stores are making more money than those that don't have a Web presence. In some cases, the small businesses to which this statistic refers are lone home office dwellers. However, for the most part, the statistic refers to businesses with 2 to 100 employees.

This revenue potential is the reason you need to analyze the situation and see if a Web storefront could benefit your business, as well as determine whether it's economically viable for you to have one. Not every business will profit from a Web presence, but it can work to the advantage of a great many businesses.

Who Needs a Web Storefront?

If you operate a retail business and sell hard goods—shoes, socks, books, lawn furniture, candles, wind chimes, stuffed animals, lingerie, power tools, gourmet foods, plants, wood-burning stoves, pets, surveillance equipment, or antiques, to name just a few—chances are you need a Web storefront to go with your "physical-world" storefront. The reason? People buy hard goods over the Web. Hard goods are definable, and people are already accustomed to buying these same things from catalogs. The switch from buying a catalog item by phone to buying a catalog item by dialing into the Internet is not a hard adjustment. These consumers have already decided that they don't need a showroom or retail store to convince them to buy. They want convenience. They want speed. They don't want to park their cars or wait in line at the cash register.

Five-year projections—even the conservative ones—put the total Web retail market in excess of $1 billion. There's even a new trendy term for it: e-tail, if you can believe it. I'll stick with Web storefront for now.

Retailers are the most common candidates for Web storefronts. They make more money, on average, from the Web than do any service-oriented businesses. However, retailers aren't the only businesses that fit the profitable Web store profile.

Some Service Businesses Qualify

If you own a service business for which that service has a clearly purchasable commodity attached to it—travel agencies, database marketers who sell reports, secretarial services agencies—chances are you need a Web storefront.

The key deciding factor for service-oriented businesses is whether a Web storefront will make the customer payment process easier. Ask yourself: Can customers do everything they need on the Web in order to finalize a transaction? If your customers buy airline tickets or book hotel rooms and car rentals, the answer is yes. They pay at your Web site and the service is activated. If they're buying airline tickets, they pick them up at the airport; for hotel reservations, they show up at the hotel on the appointed day and give the confirmation number.

In the case of a database marketer or pretty much anyone who sells the written word, audio, video, or published data, the key is that not only do customers pay over the Web, they can get the good or service delivered over the Web, too. For example, reports are delivered to them in electronic document form via e-mail.

In the case of a Web-based secretarial service, the customer can send the company an audio tape to be transcribed, pay over the Web, and get the transcript delivered via e-mail. Photography development studios are other good candidates—customers send in exposed film, pay over the Web, and get pictures developed and returned to them. That particular service isn't delivered over the Web, but the Web makes the process quicker.

House- or office-cleaning services are other good candidates. The customer can pay for the service over the Web and the cleaning person will show up at the door on the appointed day. Alternatively, a customer can pay in advance for a series of weekly cleanings. Restaurants accepting to-go or delivery orders are also Web storefront candidates. Restaurants could arguably be put into the hard goods category instead of services, but restaurants aren't considered retail operations.

Does your business fit into this profile because you have a service business that people traditionally have had to comb through the Yellow Pages to find? If so, customers are just as happy to surf to one of the many Web site search engines, type in what they're looking for, and get a much bigger list of companies that can provide the good or service. You could get exposure and direct sales you never even considered possible.

Some Businesses Don't Need a Web Store

The small businesses that do not need a Web store are the service-oriented businesses in which the transaction will inevitably require your customers to come face to face with you anyway, and therefore paying over the Web doesn't add any convenience. Examples are dog walkers, real estate rentals, computer repair services, plumbing or air conditioning services, locksmiths, accountants, and lawyers.

This is not to say that these service businesses don't need a Web site at all. It's still great marketing to be visible on the Web, and you can provide customer service and other valuable services over the Web. But there's no point in adding that electronic commerce component—the ability to accept credit-card payments—to your Web site if it won't do you any good. That e-commerce component is what differentiates Web sites from Web stores.

When to Make the Move

Okay, so you have an idea as to whether or not you fit the Web storefront profile. Let's say that you do and that you believe it could be profitable for you to open a Web store. Everyone tells you that it's dirt cheap to create a Web store and every day you wait is another day you lose potential revenue and brand name to your competitors that are already on the Web.

Relax. The biggest problem with the Internet is that everyone acts as though your very ability to breathe depends on how speedily you are getting on the Internet. I'm sure you've heard the breathless, hyperventilating marketers who say that the first business that gets to the Web in any market niche builds the brand name people remember and therefore steals the lion's share of that market. That's not true. The Web is just beginning to explode. The media giants and mega-retailers are coming on strong now, and every so-called "winning" brand on the Web will undergo a new challenge as the populations of both businesses and consumers grow. What you need to do is make a *really good* Web storefront, sell quality goods and services, and build your brand on that foundation.

An old adage comes to mind that has perhaps never held as true as it does when it comes to Web storefronts: There's never time to do it right the first time, but there's always time to do it over. I'm here to tell you that there is indeed time to do it right the first time. So, take time to breathe!

Like a Good Joke, Web Timing Is Everything

The first thing you need to decide is, when will you launch this Web storefront? It's going to cost about $300 per month to get started. There may be an additional $1,000 or so in out-of-pocket expenses , depending on your graphic design needs. It's going to take you at least two months to work everything out, and then you're going to need someone in your office—namely, you—to be willing to baby-sit the whole thing during that month and to track its progress after launch. This is the key piece of information that may help you decide whether to launch a storefront now: Can you afford $300 per month? (Incidentally, that $300 per month figure can increase quickly, but by the time it does, the store should pay for itself. More details on that later.)

If you can afford the money but it would definitely mean sacrificing something else, here's a question that might help you decide: Can you project any revenue earnings right off the bat? Figure out the answer to that question by finding out how much your competitors are making on the Web. Call the trade association you belong to, or phone the National Retail Association in Washington, D.C., and see if they have any figures that pertain to your business. Jupiter Communications, a New York–based market research firm that specializes in Internet commerce, may also have some useful data specific to your business.

If you do have the money now, here's something else to consider: You can try out a Web storefront, one you wouldn't put a lot of effort into designing, for as little as $100 per month. Bear in mind that this would be a generic-looking store, with no special designs that characterize it as unique, but it would be functional. You can rent this storefront space for a month and see if you generate any income at all. It's a "put out the bait and see if anyone bites" approach. If people bite, build something more elaborate.

Yahoo!, the Web search site (*www.yahoo.com*), offers such a service. Essentially, you use Yahoo! software to build a fairly generic site and, using Yahoo! hosting services, you put your site out on the Web. You send product pictures and the text you want to Yahoo!, which posts it on your Web storefront. All the transactions come to your computer, though. Since Yahoo! hosts the site, your business name will also pop up on Yahoo!'s search site if a Web surfer types the kind of product you sell into a search query. For example, say you sell candles via Yahoo!'s Web storefront service. If a consumer is looking to buy candles on the Web and types "candles" into the search box on Yahoo!, your company's Web storefront name and Internet address will pop up as a search result. That's immediate marketing.

We'll go much deeper into how such marketing works and where else to go to market yourself on the Web, but for now the point is that you can sign on with Yahoo! for a month or two just to test the waters. It's not a huge investment, but it could be the best empirical market test you can get for your money. I'll go into more details about Yahoo!'s service in Chapter 13.

So, without knowing the details yet, you have enough information now to decide whether to go ahead with your Web storefront or not. That's the key decision. Don't be daunted by the fact that you don't know the steps of actually getting this Web storefront up and running. By the time you've read through Chapter 14, you will know precisely what to do.

That said, before I move on to getting started with the actual process, you should keep two other tidbits in the back of your mind as you learn the whole process. The first one is this: Expect that everything will go wrong, will take twice as long as you thought, and will cost twice as much as you thought. For instance, in tallying the Web start-up cost estimate of $300 per-month cost, $1,000 out-of-pocket expenses, and two-month creation time, I took into consideration that things will be more expensive and obstacle-ridden than I assume. But bear in mind that's an average. You may decide to start with something more elaborate than you could get for that price, which is a basic cost to merely be dealt into the game.

The second piece of advice is a little more detailed and more serious. It has to do with going overboard and losing money.

What You Must Consider in Order to Make, Not Lose, Money

When you have finished reading these chapters and are on the phone getting started with your Web storefront, you are going to be bombarded with advice. That advice will tend toward trying to convince you that what you need is to buy more stuff—more stuff than I've told you to buy, more stuff than the people trying to sell you the stuff in question are even capable of explaining, much less describing. Try to remember this fact as the unsolicited and alarmingly expensive advice starts pouring in: Most of the advice is entirely unnecessary in order to get a Web storefront off the ground. So try to stick to the basics. You can always add things later. That's one of the beauties of the Web—your store is *virtual*, and adding features means plugging some information into a computer, nothing more than that. It's not like renovating a retail store and trying to decide if you need to spend another $5,000 for that additional glass case before you design the whole thing. People who have made money on the Web without spending a lot of money did so by starting slow and building later.

Enough lecturing for now. Let's get started.

Chapter 13

When to Do It Yourself, When to Hire an ISP

The first thing you absolutely must decide about your Web storefront is whether you are going to take on the project in-house or whether you will outsource it to what's called a Web-hosting service. Your Web-hosting service can be your local ISP; one of the long-distance phone companies, such as AT&T; or one of the Web businesses that offers this service as part of its arsenal, such as Yahoo! or iCat.

Most small businesses opt for outsourcing the project—it simply costs far, far less to do so—but there are some reasons that businesses may need to keep the project in-house. We'll get to all of that in a second.

Before we do, though, you should know that the process of deciding whether to keep your project in-house or outsource it is going to take some planning, so get ready. To help you out, I'll review factors that go into the in-house or outsource decision-making process, then I'll present a real-life case study of two small businesses that decided to keep the operation in-house. Since the in-house operation is far more expensive and high-maintenance, it's useful to see what compelled them to make the decision, as well as what regrets they had after all was said and done. You'll also get some tips by reading about what they learned the hard way.

Your Decision: In-House Operation or Outsource?

The simple answer for small businesses today is to outsource. Unless you have a compelling reason to run the operation in-house, it does not make sense in terms of budget. Web-hosting services are cost-effective and offer such comprehensive service options, it's barely worth debating—especially if you do not have a full-time IT person on your staff. No matter what anyone tells you, you must have a full-time IT person to run your own Web site. Some hardware vendors may tell you that it's simple enough to run the thing yourself without an IT person, but that's a faulty theory—one of those things that looks good on paper but never works in reality. Of the hundreds of business people I've spoken to about their Web storefronts, not one has said the business could have done it smoothly without some tech-savvy person in charge.

And don't just consider a local or national ISP, such as PSINet, UUNET, or NetCom, for your provider. The competition from long-distance carriers, regional phone companies, and upstart Web-hosting consultants is creating price wars and a buyer's market.

Some Web-hosting services, such as Yahoo!, cost as little as $100 per month, including storefront design and handling all the credit-card transaction processing. iCat (*www.icat.com*) has a similar deal. Long-distance carriers such as AT&T offer à la carte menu pricing: $200 or so for network integration, $50 per month for monitoring the site (and handling all problems if the server goes down), $50 per month for extra layers of security (such as encryption), and so on. In addition, AT&T will refer you to Web design specialists if you need them.

National ISPs such as Virginia-based PSINet and UUNET offer similar deals. In fact, small business software packages from Microsoft, Netscape, and even Claris come with lists of ISPs embedded in them; for instance, on Microsoft's BackOffice, you can search among 75,000 listings for an ISP that meets your needs. Mind you, there aren't 75,000 ISPs in the

United States; that listing also includes licensed Microsoft resellers, training centers, and consultants.

Even with a conservative estimate, you should be able to get up and running for under $1,000 if you offload the work. Furthermore, you should expect server hosting, financial transaction settlement, reports of your site traffic (how many people are coming to your site), 7 × 24 emergency server maintenance, top-level security, and consulting services.

If you take on the project in-house, you're going to spend $20,000 or more up front on creating a computer hardware infrastructure.

Compelling Reasons to Keep the Project In-House

By now, you must be asking yourself what the big decision is all about— I've just told you that you have a choice between spending $1,000 on outsourcing or spending $20,000 in up-front costs. Decision made, right? Not necessarily. Although it's a hefty infrastructural investment for do-it-yourselfers to create an in-house Web store, there are reasons you might need to run the operation in-house.

Say your company is a financial services consultancy, accounting firm, or law firm that plans to interact with its clients on the Web. Your clientele might not like it one bit if you host your Web site with an ISP, even though the level of security at an ISP is far more sophisticated than the security a small business would set up in-house. Nevertheless, people's perception is that if their personal and financial information is living on a server at some phone company, their privacy and security are compromised, or at least potentially compromised.

Where their information actually lives is the key difference between having an in-house Web storefront or an outsourced one. When you have an in-house Web store, all your databases are stored on a server in your office. The only thing you lease from the ISP is a high-speed telecommunications line to connect to the Internet.

But it's not always skittish clients that drive small businesses to keep their Web storefronts in-house. Some business owners—including many retailers— want control over their databases and feel they can glean better marketing intelligence from all the Web customer information that starts to accumulate if those databases are in-house. For the case study at the end of the chapter, I purposely picked retailers—not the less common financial services firms—to give you an idea of the most common issues besides security.

What Are the Realities of an In-House Web Storefront?

To get a Web site up and running first means buying a server with the right Microsoft or Netscape merchant software—a cost of $4,000 to $6,000. Then there's the security system—at least $1,000 for a firewall (a software system that prevents unauthorized people from getting into your network). Then there's the design work, software programming, network integration, and ongoing upgrade add maintenance of the site; for a salaried person or a consultant on retainer with these specialties, you're talking about at least $10,000 to $50,000 more.

Aside from the basic hardware, the essential chore for an in-house project is setting up the credit-card transaction capability. Chapter 14 presents a step-by-step checklist of what has to be done to set up your store. Consider the list carefully before making a final decision—it may be far simpler to convince a skeptical client to trust the integrity of a Web host's security system (if that's the issue) than to grapple with setting up and maintaining all the financial transactions yourself!

Also note that this set-up procedure covers just the basics. Installing your own Java applets (for animated tickers and such) and adding fancy design and advertising elements only make the project more complex.

Made a Decision Yet? Don't Before You Consider Financing

Don't make a decision yet. No need to rush—there's more to consider than cost. My guess is that the sticker shock may have made the decision for you. But you may change your mind, so just keep in the back of your mind the fact that you can finance the cost of the computer equipment you'll need. Most major computer hardware vendors have financing options, so you can pay off the computer equipment once your Web storefront starts to earn its keep.

If, after you see the checklist in the next chapter, you start to say to yourself, "I really should keep the project in-house—if only I could afford it," you may want to calculate the average cost of the necessary equipment, call a major hardware vendor such as Gateway or Dell, get the terms of their financing options, and then go crunch the numbers in Financial Manager to see if it's possible for you.

No Room for Rookie Mistakes: Set Your Goals

The preceding chapter discussed taking your time, planning, and making sure you do your Web storefront right the first time. Here are some more considerations, aside from price, that you need to mull over before deciding whether to outsource or not. Say you're leaning toward doing the project in-house despite the cost; you need to know that some Web site features can be complicated to design and operate, and if you decide you want them, you'd better make sure you have the expertise in-house or are willing to hire it. Otherwise, you may want to outsource, even if it means that you relinquish control.

All the things you have to think about do get confusing, but the best way to dispel some of the confusion is to organize your thinking. You need to set goals for your Web site and then weigh the options and the prices.

The next section describes some of the options. Once you've evaluated them, you can set your goals accordingly.

Think Self-Service for Your Web Customers

Some popular goals of Web sites, other than being simple points of sale, are marketing oriented (with marketing defined as the relationship of your company to the customer). Because the Web is interactive—unlike any other form of advertising and therefore of marketing—it provides you with a unique opportunity to build loyalty to and involvement with your company. One way of marketing is offering customer service on the Web. Good Web-based customer service can endear your company to consumers as well as being an effective method of tracking customer needs, because it gives you a digital paper trail of what customers want.

In terms of goals that help the Web operation pay for itself, think about customer service types of tasks that are particularly time consuming for employees, such as answering questions about the company and products. Save employees' and customers' time with question-and-answer pages on your site, product or service demonstrations (via graphics) if appropriate, customer order tracking, and e-mail access to experts in your company; these options can go a great way toward improving the reputation of your business.

Whatever your goals—selling, marketing, or streamlining access to information—keep this mantra in the back of your mind: self-service. Take advantage of the interactive medium, and think self-service in every design element, every function. Self-service requires that you have *interactive databases*. Here's an example of an interactive database: You want customers to be able to find out whether products they ordered from you are on their way. You don't want to have to field phone calls to answer questions. You can allow customers to access the orders database on your server (whether the server is located in your office or at an ISP). They ask the database the question; it spits out an answer automatically.

To create such self-service functions in-house means paying a software programmer at a cost of a few thousand dollars up to $20,000, depending on how sophisticated a program you need. Some ISPs offer such database services for a monthly fee, but you'll have to adjust your needs to their systems. Furthermore, if you ever do want to bring the Web storefront in-house, you'll have to build this database first; otherwise, you'll interrupt the customer service process your Web customers will have come to expect from you.

You don't have to put all sorts of functionality into your Web storefront right off the bat, but it's important to think about it, because there are some functions that may be worth your while to have right away.

Case Study: Why They Became Do-It-Yourselfers

Will Pastron doesn't trust anyone to run his retail candy store business for him. When it came time to build a Web store version of Sweety's Candies, Pastron took on the burden of building the whole store in-house, struggling with electronic commerce software packages, linking the back end to the bank so credit-card orders can be processed—the works.

"I built my own Web storefront so we would have total control," says Pastron, partner of the L.A.-based candy store who claims that since Sweety's hit the Web (*www.sweetys.com*) in early 1997, it has grown to represent 25 percent of his estimated $1 million in annual revenue. "We want to be able to keep control on that kind of business, and keeping it in house is the best way, and in the long run the most economical."

Pastron's views fly in the face of conventional wisdom about building Web storefronts. When it comes to getting a Web store up and running, two-thirds of small businesses today are opting for the outsourcing option.

"When it comes to new projects, the traditional M.O. for small businesses has been to do whatever they can in-house because it is less expensive; outside contractors has always meant money," says Ray Boggs, small business analyst for International Data Corp. of Framingham, Massachusetts. "But the Web is different. Unless you have an IT expert in-house and plan to make a lot of updates to your Web site more than once a week, it is actually cheaper to outsource this one."

Small business owners who have gone the do-it-yourself route are the first to agree with Boggs on all fronts, the first of which is having the technical expertise in-house.

"If I didn't have personal knowledge of computers, it would change my entire view of building a Web site myself," admits Pastron, who claims that of Sweety's 30 employees, three are skilled technical people, not the least of which is himself. "If I had to hire someone, that would be a whole different story. I would go out in two seconds and spend the $300 or so per month for one of those services like Yahoo! Store that does everything and lets you access your own Web store with a password and ID."

Constant updates on a busy site were reason enough for Marc Arendt, president of Gotta Have It (*www.gottahaveit.com*), a Falls Church, Virginia-based online computer peripherals store, which sells everything that goes with computers, from printers to video accessories. "I decided to build it in-house because I have 8,000 items for sale on the Web and I update prices and inventory constantly, every day," says Arendt. "Yahoo! Store isn't sophisticated enough—they host baby sites."

Arendt admits that he is also a computer person, and even though his company has only three employees, he had friends who are also tech-savvy who helped him build his site. "But even if you're not a computer person, the decision should depend on how sophisticated a store you need," he says. Since Arendt's Web store went live in April 1997, he's made $3 million.

Know What You're Getting Into

If your company fits the do-it-yourself profile—you have some technical expertise or can afford to hire it, you want control, and you plan to have a busy Web store in need of constant updating—you're going to need to find some software to get you there. The prices listed in this section were accurate at the time the book was written.

Some key electronic commerce software packages on the market are a decent start. Two prime examples of the types of products you can buy are ShopZone from Breakthrough Software (*www.breakthroughsoftware.com*), which sells for $995, and Internet Creator E-Commerce Edition from Forman Interactive (*www.internetcreator.com*), which sells for $99.

Why the $900 difference in price between these two products? For the answer to that question, let's return to the players in our case study: Arendt used ShopZone to build his whole Web storefront, whereas Pastron used Internet Creator to hook up only the electronic commerce components of his site, defined essentially as the credit-card transaction mechanism for accepting orders, sending them to the bank, and receiving authorization.

The catch with the $99 software package's functionality is that if you use it to set up your site, once you get authorization for an order, sending the actual orders for clearance and settlement through the bank and credit-card settlement network has to be done manually.

"Breakthrough's ShopZone includes the CyberCash back end that lets you automatically send and route the credit-card transaction through the bank and credit-card settlement system," says Arendt. Pastron opted for the simplistic Internet Creator because he built the first brochure version of his Web site in 1996. "There weren't the same kind of off-the-shelf packages there are now," he says. So he cobbled the site design together with different programs in 1996 and added the electronic commerce component as an afterthought.

The $100 software products in this category tend to be for businesses just like Pastron's—businesses that have made a substantial investment in their Web sites and now need a quick fix for the electronic components.

ReadyShop from Commerce Market Inc. (*www.commercemarket.com*) costs $749 and falls into the category of new-and-improved, we-do-it-all packages. ReadyShop is an online store-creation system that allows merchants to build and maintain catalogs of products. It includes tools for site creation and management, sales and traffic statistics, secure encrypted transactions, and online order fulfillment.

Where ShopZone outshines the other robust packages is in its computational prowess. ShopZone is a little easier to integrate into your databases, and it has forms that will pop up so your Web site visitors can calculate shipping costs and taxes. ReadyShop will do this, too, but it requires a little more programming skill on the business owner's part.

GizmoSoft's WebGizmo (*www.gizmosoft.com*) Merchant Edition represents the middle of the road in terms of functionality. For $239, it adds some shopping cart technology to the $100-level software package functionality. Shopping cart technology lets you create a Web store around which customers can surf, browse, and add items they're interested in to a virtual shopping cart. They can see the items and prices in the cart at any time, and they can click to purchase everything in the cart or click to throw some items out before they make their final purchases. Online bookstore Amazon.com (*www.amazon.com*) is a prime example of how shopping cart software works.

Here's the Catch

All of these software programs have their limits and require time, programming, and database integration—which means big money.

"In the end, it took four months of development," says Arendt. "I estimate, with my time included, that the project cost between $10,000 and $15,000."

Pastron says that he is at a point where he needs more automation and more integration. "We want all credit-card processing to be automatic, so we're talking to programmers," he says. "To have a real integrated back end that would automatically accept and process orders is going to cost somewhere between $10,000 and $30,000."

Bear in mind that Arendt and Pastron are making substantial revenue on the Web, so their $10,000-plus investments will pay for themselves quickly.

Although similar projects, in their entirety, seem extremely daunting for most small business budgets to tackle, when you look out over the long term, you can start slow, with a software investment of less than $1,000—assuming of course that you have in-house expertise.

The key for small business owners who are considering the do-it-yourself route is some reasonable ability to project substantial revenue from a Web store—at least 15 percent of your revenue. Ideal candidates for making such projections are retailers, businesses that sell hard goods. Service businesses are not ideal candidates.

Remember, You Can Bring It In-House Later

Perhaps the most valuable lesson to take from this case study is that you can always bring the Web store in-house at some point down the road if you can't make the substantial revenue projections Pastron and Arendt were able to at the outset. For them, those projections clinched the justification for starting out in-house.

Taking over the reins of a profitable venture is a long-standing business practice, and Web storefronts are no exception. Businesses that start outsourcing a Web site and then later find it is suddenly responsible for 10 percent or more of revenues often pull the site in house.

With all this in mind, it's time to learn the actual steps you need to take for either outsourcing or doing the project in-house.

Chapter 14

Setting Up Electronic Commerce

You can set the wheel of a Web storefront in motion in several ways. They concern getting your bank involved, buying hardware if you plan to create and run your Web store in-house, finding the right Internet service provider (ISP), choosing a Web-hosting provider if you plan to outsource your site, designing the site for function, and understanding what you must do to lure paying customers. You need to get a handle on all these details before learning how the Web store fits into your electronic books. (Chapter 15 covers the details of setting up Web accounts and routing reports into Money.)

This chapter provides a checklist of things you need to do up front to set up electronic commerce in the form of a Web storefront. At the end of the chapter, a case study outlines ways you can lure customers to your Web site. This is important information that could influence you as you go about setting up your Web site—particularly in terms of design and level of interactivity (how many things people can do at your Web store).

This chapter lightly touches on two critical things that require a much deeper explanation: security systems for your Web store and how to respect customers' privacy at your Web store so you don't make them angry and alienate them. I skim over these issues here, but I think they're so important that I've devoted an entire chapter, Chapter 16, to discussing them in detail. That chapter covers everything you need to know about security and privacy as they relate to your Web store, including advice from the FBI on what to do if problems arise. This chapter simply makes you aware of the basic issues.

The chapter focuses on a checklist to give you the big picture of the process of setting up a Web storefront. That way, by the time we get to the in-depth issues, you can use the checklist to help you flesh out your plan.

So, get your pen and notepad ready, because here's the straight dope on what you need to do to create and run your own Web storefront.

Getting Started: Call Your Bank

Before you do anything else, you must establish a new Internet credit line; without one, the whole Web store project is moot. It's time to call your bank.

The bank your company currently uses may or may not be the one that ends up giving you the new credit line, Web merchant ID (similar to a federal ID number), and the back-end settlement link that you'll need. It depends on how your existing bank perceives the Internet's risk as a distribution channel. But call your own bank first. If you can get the credit line from an institution with which you already work, life will be simpler—simpler, but not simple.

Even if your existing bank extends the new credit line, you'll find that accepting credit cards over the Internet is a more expensive proposition than accepting them over the phone or at a retail outlet. First, your application fees will range from $50 to $1,000, depending on the bank. Then there are the transaction fees themselves. The per-transaction fee for a Visa purchase in the physical world costs the merchant about 1.5 percent, but the charge for the same purchase over the Internet can cost the merchant 2 percent or even 2.5 percent. Charges for American Express, which are higher than Visa's and MasterCard's to begin with, rise proportionately for Internet transactions; what's normally a 3.5 percent AmEx charge may be as high as 5.5 percent over the Web.

Credit-card charges on the Internet are higher than in the "real" world because of the banking industry's perception of unknown risk in a still-unproved marketplace, according to Visa, MasterCard, and American Express officials. If charge-off percentages (the number of credit-card purchases that are never paid) remain low for Internet purchases, per-transaction fees may drop. However, it may take years for card issuers to make such a decision, and officials are making no promises. These percentages don't take into consideration the costs of electronic fulfillment, either.

On the positive side, once you do get a bank to approve a new credit line, the bank usually does the rest of the work—establishing the settlement link, getting you a merchant ID number, and giving you a price for electronic fulfillment, along with anything else you'll need to get up and running.

Some Help Twisting the Bank's Arm

Getting started already sounds discouraging, doesn't it? It can be difficult to get up and running, but help is available if you're having trouble convincing your bank that your Web store idea is a good one. If you encounter difficulty convincing your bank to give your company an Internet credit line, call a company such as Redwood City, California-based POS Card Systems. For a $250 fee, POS will shop around for a bank for you. POS Card Systems has long been a merchant service provider in the physical world, setting up merchants with Visa and MasterCard links to Mellon Bank and First National Bank of Omaha.

Remember to plug the costs—application fee, fulfillment charges, additional percentage fees for individual transactions—into Financial Manager as you learn what they are. You want to track your expenses and calculate how much the entire Web storefront deal will cost, compared with your initial estimates. This is the only way to keep track of your budget, see how much of it you're using up and how fast, and avoid sticker shock later.

Also remember that the increased percentage fee for online credit-card transactions cuts into profits, so include that information in your revenue projections to ensure accurate forecasts.

For an In-House Operation, Follow These Steps

After calling the bank and getting an Internet credit line, your road divides into two paths—doing the project in-house or outsourcing it. If you decide to go the in-house route, here are the next 10 steps you must take. If you have decided to outsource, skip to the section called "For an Outsourced Web Site, Follow These Steps."

Ten Steps for an In-House Project

Follow these steps if you're doing your project in-house:

1. Buy a dedicated merchant server. It should be at least a Pentium II, with a minimum 96MB of RAM and 4GB to 8GB of hard drive storage space.

2. Buy a tape backup system, an uninterruptible power supply (UPS), and a level 5 RAID array. The tape backup should cost you about $500, the UPS about $200, and the RAID array about $2,000. A RAID array is a backup archive for all your data. RAID stands for redundant array of independent disks. A RAID array is essentially a collection of hard drives that stores a copy of all your data.

3. For a server operating system, many small to midsize merchants opt for Microsoft Windows NT Server, which offers Microsoft's Internet Information Server (IIS) Web server, FrontPage (An HyperText Markup Language editor and Web site creation tool), DNS server (the domain name is the name of your Web store; my domain name, for instance, is *ReportersInk.com* because my company name is Reporters, Ink.), and other Internet and network services all in one package.

4. Buy an e-mail server. Microsoft Exchange and Netscape Messaging Server are popular choices.

5. Contact your phone company or ISP and obtain a T1 line. A T1 line is a high-speed digital telecommunications line. It can cost up to $1,200 per month to lease.

6. To integrate this high-speed telecommunications line, you'll need a network router. Cisco's 4000 series or equivalent will do. The router will cost about $2,000.

7. Get a CyberCash merchant ID number from your bank. CyberCash is the back-end accounting software system that links your Web store to the bank. The bank obtains it as a matter of course when setting up your Internet credit line.

8. Go to *www.cybercash.com*, key in your CyberCash merchant ID, download the CyberCash cash-register software, and install it on your merchant server. This software enables credit-card transactions to leave your Web storefront, stop at your server (where purchases are recorded), and then link to the

bank-settlement system via a public/private key-encrypted message (a standard secret-code software program that scrambles the credit-card information for security as it travels over the network) that goes through your ISP.

9. If you're selling more than 10 products, consider adding shopping cart software for an easy consumer interface and good reporting controls over product information. Such software can cost between $1,200 and $3,500.

10. Make sure security systems are in place, including the Secure Socket Layer (SSL) or similar protocols on the merchant server. By the time you have linked with CyberCash, received your Internet access from the ISP, and set up NT Server, you should have security and public/private key encryption programs.

That's it. And yes, it is a lot to do.

For an Outsourced Web Site, Follow These Steps

To outsource your Web storefront project, you need to find an (ISP to host your Web store and provide the consulting services you'll need, such as Web site design.

The national ISPs and long-distance phone companies tend to be the best bets for business Internet access, e-mail, Web site design, and Web hosting. Local ISPs are fine for personal e-mail addresses and Internet access, and in some cases they try very hard to meet businesses' Web store needs. Generally speaking, though, they fall short. If your company is located in an area where a local ISP has a particularly good reputation among businesses, consider using that local provider if its prices beat those of the national ISPs.

Otherwise, start getting familiar with the national players: AT&T, Sprint, WorldCom/MCI/UUNET (now merged), PSINet, NetCom, and America Online (AOL). The catch is that national providers' services and prices vary, and providers are not all created equal. Even for packages of similar services, such as a trio of e-mail, Internet access, and Web site-hosting service, the prices and payment structures vary. Starter packages range from $400 to $800 for this trio's set-up, and they come with different ongoing monthly fees, which range from $100 per month to $600 per month. The one truism is that the more you pay up front, the less you'll pay per month, and vice versa.

Seven Must-Have Services for a Web Store

There are no panaceas in the ISP service game. So, where should you start? First, there are seven services you should expect from an ISP:

1. Guaranteed up-time for Internet access (in other words, you get money back if you can't access the Internet because the ISP's servers are down).

2. Web-hosting services, including site design, domain hosting, site visitor-tracking reports, credit-card transaction capability, and registering your Web site's URL with all the search engines for marketing purposes.

3. Phone tech support 24 hours a day, seven days a week.

4. On-site tech support within 48 hours.

5. Multiple e-mail accounts on one e-mailbox. This means that your whole office can be on a single e-mailbox, which makes it easier to add new e-mail addresses for new employees. It also ensures that all employees have the same domain name in their e-mail addresses. In other words, your employees will have consistent addresses such as *mary@companyX.com* and *jane@companyX.com*, instead of *mary@companyX.com* and *jane@aol.com*.

6. Guaranteed deadlines for delivering Web design and other value-added services.

7. The ISP must offer security measures in the form of SSL or a similar protocol for its commerce servers (what you run a Web site on), firewalls (protective software that blocks access to your server from the outside world) for all servers designated for your company, and encryption for all credit-card transactions that occur at your Web storefront.

Unfortunately, no provider offers all seven services in the base price for its business Internet service package. Some don't even offer emergency on-site tech support (a must if your business starts to depend on the Internet for sales!). At least, it seems at first glance that providers don't offer that option. It turns out that some providers, such as WorldCom/MCI/UUNET, can be coaxed into putting an on-site emergency service agreement in writing during negotiations. That kind of maneuvering—negotiating to have extras written into a service contract when you cut a deal with an ISP—is the key to obtaining good ISP services.

A Two-Step Strategy to Get the Best Deal

Here's a basic strategy to follow when looking for the right ISP: Start by assuming that you want all seven services we've discussed. Ask each ISP what it would take to get all the services in writing. Translation: You want to know how much extra, if anything, it is going to cost you to get the full monty.

Here's a tip: First approach the long-distance phone company that already handles your long-distance phone service. Try to leverage that account by saying, "Hey, we'd like to also give you our business for Internet services, but we want all these seven things." According to officials at these companies, if your company is of fair size and your phone business means serious money to the provider, the provider may just put all seven services in writing for no extra charge, so it pays to ask.

For small business owners, as always, it's a tough negotiation, even if you're a longtime customer. Still, it might yield you a better price for the extras if you mention that you want all seven services.

Which brings us to the second step: Let's say each of the ISPs wants extra money for the services it doesn't offer as standard fare, such as on-site tech support. But your budget doesn't allow for that extra cost, which for on-site tech support service alone can vary between $150 per month and thousands of dollars. Start picking and choosing among ISPs based on your immediate needs. Prioritizing isn't always an obvious process to Internet novices, however. Here are the key things to remember about each of our seven needs and how to decide which are most important to you. The two most elusive services are on-site tech support and deadlines for Web store design. Choose on-site tech support over reliable deadlines if you have to, even if you have a real sense of urgency about getting your Web store up and running. A lack of on-site tech support will give you more headaches in the long run, whereas if you have to wait a little longer to get the site up, you can live with that. If a provider won't offer on-site tech support, even for a fee, seriously consider going elsewhere.

Guaranteed up-time is a close second in terms of importance. If the ISP simply doesn't offer it, and you really like everything else about that ISP's service, ask the provider if you can sign a contract with a probation clause in it that states something like this: If you try the ISP's Internet access for a month and the service is down so often that you're unhappy, you can be released from the contract obligation. Because many ISP service contracts are for six months to a year, this agreement is worth trying to finagle. Nothing is worse than being stuck for a long time with a service you hate or that is causing you to lose business.

The good news—before you feel too daunted—is that it is easy to get certain services these days. All the national ISPs I mentioned offer Web design and hosting services and ample security systems for the services they provide. As for the remaining concerns: You can settle for phone support during office hours if you have on-site tech support, and all the national ISPs except AOL will give you multiple e-mailboxes.

Alternative Web Hosts

The preceding chapter mentioned that Internet companies such as Yahoo! and iCat also offer Web-hosting service packages for as little as $100 per month. (Prices depend on how many products will be featured on your Web storefront.) For many smaller businesses and home offices, this is the best choice when starting a Web initiative. You should be aware, however, that design and functionality will be limited, and you will still need to go to an ISP to get Internet access itself (the telecommunications link).

Review the case study at the end of Chapter 13 to get a feel for the limitations of such Web hosts. The common wisdom of folks who have launched Web stores is that these cheaper services are okay as long as you don't need to constantly update your Web store by sending information to the ISP via modem. Think of it this way: Using these alternative Web sites is like renting counter space for your products at another retailer as opposed to having your own store. You simply have less control. However, you've also made far less of an investment, and it's an easy way to test the waters for your goods and services.

Beware of one thing, though: Many Web hosts are popping up, some that look like Yahoo! and iCat. But many of these companies go out of business as fast as they come in. That's the main reason I hesitate to recommend non-ISP Web hosts. You don't want to go through the trouble of getting a Web store up and running only to have the host shut down. At least with the brand-name ISPs, you are guaranteed of their continued existence; they make their living primarily from selling high-speed Internet access, which means they have assets and an existing network infrastructure. They have a stake in the ground and are likely to be around for a while.

(continued)

Alternative Web Hosts *(continued)*

Many Web hosts, on the other hand, simply make their living hosting other people's Web storefronts and acting as a link to the banking system. It's a much more fly-by-night business model.

Both Yahoo! and iCat are safe bets, however, because their business model expands beyond this service. Try to choose a Web host by considering factors such as the stability of its business, which can be an elusive quality in the age of the Internet. If you do choose a Web host, try to limit the length of time for which you sign a contract; don't opt for a year-long deal. Remember, the point of using one of the hosts is to test the waters, so don't commit yourself for a long period.

Web Stores That Sell: Smart Design, Smarter Marketing

Now we get to the nitty-gritty. You need to decide how you want your Web store to look and what services you want to offer customers. Read this section before deciding what Web host or ISP to hire, because—depending on how elaborate you want to get with your storefront—you may need a sophisticated service provider.

The first thing to understand is that a Web store is not about frills and flashing lights. It's about smart, efficient, sensible design that holds function as the first priority and aesthetics a distant second. You need the basics for luring customers, then the tricks.

This is not to say that design isn't important. It is. But it's important because the Web store needs to be easy to navigate, easy to "shop." One of the biggest mistakes rookie Web store owners make is to overload a site with too much information and too many design elements. What you get then is a busy, confusing store that gives the customer a headache.

The goal of any Web storefront site is to make money, and as retail veterans will tell you, a customer has to be comfortable in your store and able to see the merchandise easily if you want to persuade him or her to hand over hard-earned cash. This means that despite site designers' use of the coolest Java applications, fancy graphics, or funky frames, if surfers can't find what they are looking for or can't figure out how to purchase it, they will go somewhere else.

Here, then, are some golden rules of Web store design, from those who have learned the hard way, so you can avoid all-too-common pitfalls:

- **Don't try too hard to impress.** The key to creating your Internet storefront is to design to serve—rather than impress—the customer. This means that easy navigation and fast page-download times are a must, so cut the extraneous images and clear a path to the cash registers.

- **Don't assume surfers understand page layout.** You should approach your page layout as though each visitor is new to the site and needs a simple guide. Links to a search mechanism (where users can type in the specific products they're looking for and find out if you have them) and a site map (a guide to everything in your Web store) are always good ideas for customers who know what they are looking for. For uncertain shoppers who want to browse, make sure there is a navigation bar highlighting product categories on each page so they can skip between sections. The most important buttons on any navigation bar should be those that allow customers to make purchases or add items to their shopping carts. A *shopping cart* is a software tool that allows a customer to click a product name or icon and add it to a virtual shopping cart. At any moment, the user can click a button to view the shopping carts and see how many items he or she has chosen. (To see an example, go to L.L. Bean's Web store, which is a great example of a classically designed, easy-to-use Web storefront.) How do you know when you need to spend the extra $1,000 or so on a shopping cart program? If you sell more than, say, 20 different products on your Web storefront, it's probably a good idea to use a shopping cart. Some Web hosts provide the shopping cart feature as part of their packages. Ask.

- **Don't teach people, sell them.** Some sites have adopted frames to ensure that site visitors have access to a menu bar at all times, but frames can cause problems in some cases. You may have to spend more time than it's worth explaining to customers how the frames work. The goal here is to make sales, not teach lessons.

  Frames pose another problem: Customers can't bookmark your Web store easily if you use frames. *Bookmarking* is the process of storing a Web site URL in your computer for future reference; you make a bookmark when you click a Web site page and the Web address of that page gets filed in the "Bookmarks" section in your Internet browser. Once you bookmark a site, you give the Web page a name—such as the name of the store—and then in the future you can just click it to go back to the store. Avid Internet shoppers use bookmarks to create a library of their favorite stores. This way they don't have to remember the Web store address; they just look up the name in their bookmark list and click it. If you use frames to design your storefront, however, some pages on your site won't bookmark, so you are making it more difficult for the customer to return to you.

- **Be sparing with precious screen real estate.** This is another warning about frames, among other things. Frames slice the screen into parts and restrict design significantly. Watch out for any programmer or Web host who wants you to use design elements that cut up the screen too much.

- **Ease up on the use of forms.** Whichever purchasing software you choose for your site, make sure that you never require a customer to fill out a form merely to put an item into a shopping cart. For example, the online incarnation of the WalMart mega-chain discount store (*www.wal-mart.com*) asks visitors to fill out an extensive form and create an account just for collecting items they may or may not buy.

  By interrupting shopping customers to ask for a commitment before they've made a decision, you run the risk of scaring them off completely. Customers will have to give you personal and financial information at the point of sale; don't make them do it twice.

  One side hint about the point of sale: Once an order has been processed, make sure that you generate a confirmation page for the customer. If a customer has to phone you to make sure you got the order, the customer might as well have used the phone to order in the first place.

- **Avoid long page downloads.** Product-oriented sites offer an obvious challenge: Designers try to keep page-download times low, while the marketing folks want to show off pictures of their gizmos and customers want to see what they are getting. But no customer wants to sit and wait at a Web storefront for a picture to appear.

The shopper will click away to another store if the wait becomes too frustrating. Where images are concerned, the smaller, the better; under 10K is preferable.

Should you need to use a larger photo, you can always provide the option for a bigger download without forcing it on the customer as the default. The *New York Times* (*www.nytimes.com*), for instance, has made very effective use of thumbnails, which give users the choice of whether they want to spend time waiting to see the whole picture. The common recommendation among top Web store designers is that a page should be a maximum size of 70K. Ask the programmers or Web hosts you end up working with if they're exceeding this limit, and make sure they don't.

It is dangerous to assume, however, that keeping the image sizes small will always solve the problem. Sometimes page construction, especially complicated use of tables, can slow a page download. Make sure that the largest graphics are not in the first table a browser reads; give users text to read while the images appear or they will get tired of waiting and leave.

- **Design for flexibility.** The site design should be flexible enough to allow fast changes. For instance, try using text titles or headlines instead of graphics; they allow the Webmaster to make urgent changes easily and without having to wait for the art department. Think about what might happen if product information can't be updated within minutes on your Web storefront: Customers will be annoyed if they try to make a purchase and at the last minute are told, "Oh, we ran out of that." Inaccurate price and inventory information makes customers feel misled.

- **Explain yourself.** A little reassurance never goes unappreciated. If you are using *cookies*—the string of numbers a site puts on a visitor's hard drive in order to identify the visitor to the site on future visits—explain what you will use the information for. If you do choose to use cookies, assure customers about the privacy of information they provide (see Chapter 16 for more detail). Such straightforwardness helps build trust with your customers. Publish all your Web storefront's business practices openly on your home page.

- **Don't skimp on security.** Remember that the words "secure server" can have a remarkably calming effect on surfers. An optional link to a "security practices" page is all that is necessary. You can also offer long legal notices for visitors to read, but don't make them a requirement before purchasing or they will slow down the process and discourage buyers. Internet shopping is an odd thing; it creates incredibly fickle consumers. They can be all set to buy something, but a little glitch on the site can make them click Cancel and move on.

- **Don't spam.** Finally and most important, never spam your own customers without their prior consent. *Spamming* entails sending unsolicited e-mail about promotions or other updates. Instead, offer visitors to your site the option of receiving notifications of sales or new products, but make sure you have permission before sending such e-mail. Unsolicited e-mail is more likely to generate annoyance than traffic and sales.

Web Store Checklist

The following is a useful checklist to follow in creating a Web store:

- **Internet access should be a T1 line.** Unless you have no intention of selling anything on your Web site (it's merely a marketing brochure), you'll need T1 access or at least a fractional T1 (which is one-half or some other significant fraction of a full T1). Any skimpier bandwidth and you'll run into traffic jams, forcing you to upgrade quickly.

- **Don't hire an outsourcing company that charges by the hour.** Whether you're outsourcing graphic design, programming, database development, network integration, or all of the above and more, make sure the integration company you hire is willing to charge on a project basis. That way, if you change Web site color, run into snags with the network, or any one of a million variables, you won't be "nickled and dimed to death" by incremental charges.

- **Make a two-year plan.** Web site maintenance and upgrading can easily cost double the original start-up costs. These costs often surprise people. Budget ahead of time with this caveat in mind.

- **Whatever you think the cost will be, double it.** This is the only way to avoid sticker shock.

(continued)

Web Store Checklist (continued)

- **Get function under control before you focus on form.** Design is a key element of a Web site—it's what lures random consumers to stay and shop around. But before spending a bundle on the latest 3-D characters, which can add a significant cost to your overall budget, get the basic functions down. Consumers will appreciate a site that functions properly and is easy to navigate more than they will one with bells and whistles but without the horsepower to keep it going.

- **Don't underestimate the horsepower it takes to run Web applications.** Don't skimp on servers or hard disk space if you run your Web store in-house. You need horsepower no matter what, and you may as well budget for it up front than make it the first item on your "what took us over budget" list.

Tricks of the Trade

Aside from simple design rules of thumb, some proven strategies will help you lure customers without annoying them. I suppose that's the essence of the art of marketing: to get customers involved with your Web store without making them feel duped or hassled.

In order to lure customers, you must first know who they are. In order to know them, you must gather information about them and what they want. To that end, here are five quick steps to creating a very useful information-gathering tool: a registration form. In the preceding section, I told you not to make customers register in order to choose an item for their shopping carts. But that doesn't mean they should never register. They should register when they actually make a purchase. Think about it: By coming to a Web site to shop, customers have accepted the fact that they will have to key in a credit-card number and address at some point. They've gotten their minds around filling out a form; they just don't want to do it 100 times, and they don't want to do it unless they get something in return. The registration form is the perfect opportunity to get more information about your customers. The trick is not to ask too much. You don't want to be intrusive; you want to get information quickly so you can better serve these customers in the future.

Remember, creating an effective registration form is just the beginning of the marketing process. So, this chapter ends with a case study on how to go about marketing your Web storefront. The case study includes advice from some veteran marketers. But first, let's examine the five easy steps:

The Perfect Information-Gathering Tools

The way you put together your Web store registration form is key to whether or not you gather good demographic and psychographic data about your customers. (*Psychographic* is the new hip term for people's buying habits and desires. See the "Glossary of Web Terms" sidebar for more information.) Remember, you can't analyze data that you don't have, and no privacy-respecting alternatives have been developed to gather data about people visiting your site—so you must use the current methods of gathering data until something better comes along. Taken from a consensus of Web merchants who have tested the waters, this list of guidelines and ideas will convince people to register at your site:

- **Have a contest.** If registered site visitors are eligible to win something, "surfers-by" are not only more likely to register, but they will answer demographic questions more often and more honestly. If people think they will jeopardize a prize by giving the wrong gender and address, for example, they will tell the truth. One other thing: You shouldn't require customers to purchase anything to enter a contest. Give them the option to fill out a registration form and enter a contest right off the bat—don't make it a requirement for browsing through your store. That makes for bad feelings.

- **Keep the form short.** If people see a long, bureaucratic, interactive process just to get to the heart of your site, they'll leave.

- **Psychographic data can be more important than demographic data**, so don't waste precious space asking for a lot of demographic information, such as income, that many surfers won't give you anyway. Furthermore, questions about behavior can be put innocently enough that you have the opportunity to actually engage the consumer. For example, you can ask, What is your favorite Web site, and why? What time of day do you Web surf most? Do you buy stuff on the Internet?

- **Remember that all interactive relationships in the commerce world are based on trust.** Ask one trust-inspiring question, such as, Would you prefer to use a password each time you log on, rather than have a cookie placed on your computer? Let the person specify an answer. Remember, though, not to be phony about your intentions. If you ask people what their preferences are, be prepared to offer them the things they prefer.

Glossary of Web Terms

In the course of talking to people about your Web store, you may hear any or all of the following common Web marketing terms:

- **Click-stream.** This is the series of links a surfer takes in a given browser session. It includes the links taken to get to a given site and the pages within a given site. Knowing your customers' click-stream will help you see what they're interested in on your site. Web-hosting services often offer click-stream reports.

- **The refer.** A part of the click-stream, the refer, or reference point, is the site from which a surfer linked to your Web store. It's important for Web store owners to know the refer because if there are a lot of refers from a single URL (another Web site), it might be wise to strike up a formal co-marketing deal or other business relationship with that site.

- **Read-through.** An advertising term; when an advertiser gets a read-through on your site, it means that the surfer not only clicked on the ad or banner but read it and demonstrated understanding (by answering a quiz, playing a game, filling out a form, or some other interactive activity).

- **Cookie.** A string of numbers that a Web site places on the surfer's hard drive via the browser, usually without the surfer's knowledge. This string of numbers identifies the surfer to the Web site on future visits. Cookies are also the subject of hot debate among privacy advocates. Most of today's software products designed for tracking activity on your Web site use cookies. Concerned visitors to your site will likely ask if you use cookies; answer them honestly.

- **Demographic data.** Age, gender, income, and address are the most typical pieces of demographic data. Any data that puts consumers in a defining socioeconomic context is demographic data.

- **Psychographic data.** Information on what sites consumers visit, what they buy, what they pass up, what search words they use, what chat rooms they hang out in, how often they surf,

(continued)

156

> **Glossary of Web Terms** *(continued)*
>
> what time of day they surf, their click-stream—anything that gives insight into surfers' Web behavior is psychographic data. Some Web merchants claim that psychographic data is more important than the traditionally coveted demographic data because it gives far more insight into what people will read, interact with, and buy.

Case Study: Marketing Your Web Site

Finally, you've got your Web store up and running. You think it looks good. You've heeded all the advice about a nice, clean design, and you're accepting credit-card transactions for the products and services you sell. You've built the electronic commerce Web storefront all the business consultants insisted you couldn't live without. Build it, they said, and the customers will come.

So, where are those customers? Where is all that delicious revenue those spreadsheet projections promised?

Perhaps the consultants, designers, ISPs, Web hosts, and random MBA-wielding advisors forgot to mention one key thing: marketing. Without marketing, your Web storefront is like an anonymous star on a clear night—one of millions, indistinguishable from any other, and impossible to find unless someone happens to look up and see it.

In order to actually see a return on your Web site investment and milk this new direct-sales distribution channel, you must become a marketer. The act of marketing, as defined by the Wharton School of Business of the University of Pennsylvania, is making contact with potential customers and creating a relationship with them. A TV commercial makes contact by coming into your living room and showing you products, reminding you of a particular brand name. The relationship is clinched when you later go to a store, recognize that product, and buy it. Marketing is accomplished. The same two-step approach applies to marketing through radio and print.

The Web, on the other hand, presents a different proposition for the first time in marketing history: This medium allows you to combine the initial contact with the clinched relationship, in one step. The Web is not just a display, it is a point of sale. Furthermore, in most cases, this double-play costs far less money than any TV commercial. The catch, however, is that a double-play requires a more complicated strategy to execute.

Even though the strategy is more complicated, it need not remain a total mystery. Already, clearly proven marketing strategies have been developed. So, here are the three steps to take in order to put your Web storefront on the Internet map, make contact with customers, and clinch those relationships that translate into revenue.

Step 1: Build Brand Name Through Co-Marketing Deals

What's in a brand name? Everything. Some people consider advertising—the key purpose of which is to make the brand a household word—a separate entity from marketing, but it's not. In fact, advertising is a subset of marketing because it is the step of the marketing process that makes contact with consumers.

Brand-building veterans say the company brand is even more important than the product. This is a lesson brand building in retail environments and on TV has taught the business world, and small businesses cooking up Web strategies may do well to take a page from this Madison Avenue school of thought: "Your brand name defines the relationship consumers have to your company, not just your product. If that brand name is good and the relationship a loyal one, you can build your business with a variety of successful products and services," says Thomas Quarton, former president and COO of Cirque Corp., the Salt Lake City–based start-up company that invented the technology for Apple Computer's Powerbook laptop touchpad pointing device (called the GlidePoint) that replaced the trackball. Within five years of its start-up date, Cirque commanded almost 50 percent of the touchpad marketplace.

Quarton, who has 17 years of consumer marketing experience under his belt, says the Web was a key marketing tool for Cirque. He has also built brand names for Clearasil, M&M Mars, Marriott Corp., and Vidal Sassoon. But getting the word out on Cirque was the first time Quarton has felt how much of a difference the Internet makes. "People buy based on the relevance your company has to their lives overall, not just because of one product or another. That's what brand name really is," he says.

So, how do you get your company brand name, and therefore your products' brand name, out there and visible in order to win the hearts of consumers? Co-marketing agreements with major community Web sites such as Yahoo! or co-marketing agreements with online services such as America Online provide some ways. People clamor to have their businesses appear on Yahoo! and AOL in particular because those sites get a lot of traffic—millions of potential consumers. However, they can also cost a lot. A banner advertisement on Yahoo! can cost $15,000 or more, and co-marketing deals with AOL can reach into the millions.

But don't be discouraged. The idea of leveraging a larger brand name—a community Web site—in order to boost your own brand can be bought for less, in many cases. Instead of shooting for general interest sites, you can forge a co-marketing agreement with community Web sites that represent a more specific, vertical industry community.

Say you're a travel agent seeking a Web presence. You can cut a deal with Travelocity (*www.travelocity.com*), which is a travel-specific Web site. Vertical-industry community sites tend to cost a little less, on average, and in some cases may yield a better return. After all, you start out dealing with prospects that have already demonstrated interest in your product category.

Quarton found that banner advertisements on computer community Web sites were central to Cirque's Web campaign because they targeted his audience in an efficient way. "Our $15,000 banner ad—which bought one fiscal quarter of banner ads—on a computer community site reaches techies," he says. Quarton also placed banner ads—at the same price—on the Yahoo! site (*www.yahoo.com*) to reach less technologically focused Netizens, but he had the budget to do both. If he didn't, he says, he would have gone with the computer-specific community site first.

Many small businesses don't have thousands of dollars to spend on banner ads on major community Web sites. The Wharton Small Business Development Center, which is a University of Pennsylvania–sponsored consultancy to 400 small businesses, says that small businesses in particular need to be careful about how much they spend on the Web. According to Wharton's estimates, you shouldn't spend more than 10 percent of your revenue marketing on the Web.

So, if banner ads on community Web sites are out of your reach right now, you can try the poor-man's version of co-marketing, offered by MSN Link Exchange (*www.linkexchange.com*). Link Exchange has a service called Banner Network, which it claims has 400,000 participating Web sites. The deal is that you display someone else's banner ads on your Web site, and they display yours in return. There are some catches, such as the sponsoring site gets to put its logo on your banner ad, but it can be a great way to start, especially because the service is free, so you have nothing to lose. The key is finding Web sites in that network with which it makes sense for you to cooperate.

Step 2: Become a Popular Link

Another service that Link Exchange offers is called Submit It, which for $59 lists your Web site address with all the major search sites, such as Yahoo!, AltaVista, Excite, HotBot, InfoSeek, MSN, and more. What this means is that when random consumers go to a search site and search for a product that you happen to sell, your company name will appear on the list of results. In a sense, this is a co-marketing deal. You pay to have the search engines list your company and the URL of your company Web site.

Here's a quick tip, too, to make your company name pop up more often during searches. Make sure that Submit It (and therefore a prospective customer) knows exactly what your Web site has to offer by adding as many keywords as possible to your Web site description. (Think of keywords as the words people will type into a search box when they're interested in your product.) The way you do this is to add *meta tags* to your Web pages' HTML code. Meta tags generally contain the name and description of a Web site, in addition to other information.

The following lines of HTMLcode, called the *header*, should appear at the top of your Web pages:

```
/*********************************************************************
<HEAD>
<TITLE>Name of Your Web Site</TITLE>
</HEAD>
*********************************************************************/
```

You add descriptions and keywords to the header by inserting these meta tags:

> *<META NAME="description" content= "xxxxx">*
> *<META NAME="keywords" content="yyy, zzz">*

Here's an example of a header that has meta tags:

```
/*********************************************************************
<HEAD>
<TITLE>Joe's Carpentry Books</TITLE>
<META NAME="description" content="The widest selection of books on
carpentry">
<META NAME="keywords"="books, carpentry, building, tools, woodwork,
furniture">
</HEAD>
*********************************************************************/
```

By adding as many keywords as you can think of, you have a better chance of being found by the search engines. The reason is that when seeking products, people think of them in different ways. Someone looking for carpentry information might ask the search engine to find "carpentry," or "carpentry book," or "woodworking," or any other number of related things. You want your carpentry bookstore to appear in every search, no matter what related keyword the searcher uses.

Ask Submit It how to optimize your search results. Also, be aware that not all search engines accept meta tags, but even if only some do, it's worth the effort to create them.

Step 3: Have Contests, Specials, and Other Interactive Features

The next step after making the contact through co-marketing deals and links is to engage the customer in a relationship. You can't just stop making an effort after initial contact on the Web. You need to incite consumers to engage with your company so that they will get used to interacting with you and hopefully end up interacting enough to think of your Web storefront as a point of sale and buy something—preferably more than once.

"The Internet lets us directly interact with consumers—showing demos of our product, amusing people with games on our Web site, having conversations over e-mail, being there live for them in as many ways as we can invent," says Cirque Corp.'s Quarton.

A couple of classic tricks of the trade are used to engage consumers: running contests and specials. Running a contest is an interesting concept because it can actually lure people to your Web site. Say you run a banner ad on a community Web site. Why not make the message of that banner ad say that people can win something by clicking it? By doing so, you get your brand name in front of consumers and you get people to your Web site, ready to interact. People expect that if they're going to win a prize, they are going to have to fill out a form of some kind. Give away airline tickets or something. Once people fill out forms, you also have another tool all of a sudden—a list of prospects in your database.

Recently, Volvo Cars of North America ran a contest on America Online (through a banner ad), offering a free car to the winner of a raffle. Volvo officials say they got 53 million hits on their Web site in something like three weeks, just because of that contest. They also got a list of prospects whom they could e-mail in the future about new products and services. Just make sure that on the contest form you explicitly ask consumers if it's okay to e-mail them later.

Along the same lines of running contests is running specials—offering some product at an irresistible price for surfers who click on a graphic and "buy now." This is exactly the same concept as the old Kmart "blue-light special" of the 1950s, when an announcement would come over the store loudspeaker that everything in the aisle with the blue light above it was discounted for a short period of time. When that light went out again, the deal was off.

One of the small business pioneers of Web marketing, 1-800-Flowers, uses this strategy all the time. Donna Iucolona, director of the interactive services division at 1-800-Flowers, says that running specials on flowers is key to business. "Holidays such as Valentine's Day or Secretary's Day are important, and we run specials" for them, she says. This florist is worth listening to when it comes to Web marketing. A couple of years ago, 1-800-Flowers paid AOL an estimated $25 million for a four-year exclusive contract to be the only florist available in the AOL Shopping Channel. The company made its investment back the next year.

The key marketing lesson here is that running contests and specials that require immediate action on the part of the consumer means you are engaging that consumer. Take this concept and think of other features that are engaging. One example is product demos. If you sell toys, you can have a picture of a jack-in-the-box on your site; when surfers click the image, the jack pops out the box. Another example is interacting by answering e-mails. Give Web surfers a place to e-mail questions to you, and make sure those questions are answered. Give surfers things to do, a way to connect with you and your company.

CD-Now (*www.cdnow.com*), the popular online music store started about two years ago by two twentysomethings, engaged the consumer by allowing people to listen to music on the site—very clever and very conducive to selling CDs.

Do All Three Steps, If You Can

Perhaps the most important thing to take away from all this marketing advice is that to do as much as you can is the best bet. If you can afford to take all three steps cited in this case study, your chances of attracting more paying customers will be the highest it can be.

If you can afford very little activity, your priority should be to make every contact with consumers include a chance for them to interact positively with your Web site and therefore your company.

Chapter 15

Tracking Web Storefront Transactions

Yes, you guessed it: This is going to be another nagging chapter. It's easy to get lost in the planning of a project, thinking about all the things you can do in your Web store, coming up with cool marketing and feature ideas. But inevitably you need to bring the project back down to earth and understand how this new store will fit into your financial management system. Don't worry, though, I'll keep the lecture short.

As a reward for walking through the accounting details of tracking your Web storefront, at the end of the chapter there is a section devoted to strategies for maximizing the profitability of your Web store by using it to streamline your internal business processes. Once the Web site is up and running, the technology itself offers businesses many advantages other than electronic commerce.

But first, on to the accounting chores.

Getting the Accounting Straight

You're going to need to get a little creative when it comes to tracking your Web storefront revenues. Money and Financial Manager certainly allow for revenue tracking, but you want to segregate the earnings from your Web store so you can see how much of your overall revenue is coming from that one source, and you then want to compare the revenue to your Web store expenses. You need to be able to determine whether the Web store is profitable and how long it takes to become profitable.

The first thing you want to do, then, is set up an Account in Money that's called Web Store. You'll go through the same process you did earlier, creating a new account. For the financial institution, use the bank that's giving you the credit line for your Web store. Make sure when you set up this credit line with the bank that you open a separate account for it. Make sure you open an account where you can write checks, pay bills, and get credit. The bank may get annoyed, but make the bankers do it as a separate account anyway. This way, the bank will send you separate statements that have to do with only your Web store.

This setup makes your life simpler in other ways, too. To understand how, you need to understand how the Web transactions are settled through your bank. Assuming you are outsourcing your Web store, know that the transactions go directly from the host's server to the bank for settlement. The bank then sends back a fulfillment report to the host (and in some cases, directly to you as well), and the host in turn sends you a statement about your revenue activity each month. If your Web revenue is isolated in a separate account, it will be easier to track. You will want to take the report from the Web host and do some projection analyses in Financial Manager, but we'll get to that in a second. Back to your separate bank account first.

Make sure that all the Web store–related expenses are paid out through this account. It will help you track revenue and compare that to expenses, but it will also help you keep all the Web store expenses together for tax purposes. Building a Web store is a capital expenditure (though it can be deducted in other ways; check with your accountant for the system that suits you best).

In this new account, you'll have a ledger that tells you your expenses and all the deposits; the deposits will be the revenue from the store.

Also set up an account for the Web store in the Bills & Deposits place of Money so you can automatically pay the ISP every month, as well as any other Web store–related expenses. This is also a quick way to view how often you're making deposits from your Web site—a glimpse at how the revenue is flowing in. You may even see patterns that help you with marketing: Are some months better than others? Are specific times of the month better than other times?

After you've set up both the Account and the Bills & Deposits functions, go to Reports on the navigation bar. When you click Monthly Reports, you will get charts that tell you your top expenses for the month. By looking at this presentation every month, you can see how much the Web store is draining you, and whether or not it continues to be affordable.

Financial Manager Crunches Web Numbers

Remember in the last chapter I talked about making a two-year plan for your Web store? Well, in order to do this, you're going to need to do the analysis in Financial Manager. You're going to take your Web store expense projections for the next two years and then calculate how much revenue the store will need to generate each month to make a profit. You can plan your marketing efforts accordingly.

Financial Manager becomes even more useful once your Web store is up and running. You can take the reports from the Web host—or the ones you generate on your own server, if you run the Web store in-house—and see at what rate your revenues are growing, if you're at least breaking even, and how much you can expect to earn over time.

This information will also help with marketing. Say the reports show that in the Christmas shopping season you are earning three times as much as you do in the spring. In fact, in the spring, you are earning less than your expenses each month. You know what you need to make each month to make the store profitable, right? So, it may make sense to invest more in marketing and advertising during the Christmas season, to boost that revenue as much as possible so the slump season doesn't harm overall yearly profits. Using Financial Manager, you can see how much you should spend on marketing. You can even do an analysis on past marketing efforts and the revenue they tend to generate. This way, you can create a reasonable return projection on a marketing investment.

The Database Connection

Don't forget about creating a customer database. Office 2000, aside from the Financial Manager tools we're focusing on in this book, comes with a suite of tools for creating databases. Use them. You need to create a Web customer database that's a little different from the database for your other clientele. You can cross-reference Web customers with other ones, of course, but your Web customers will tend to be a slightly different, and you have a unique opportunity to create a database rich with marketing intelligence.

For example, if you do get Web customers to fill out a registration form with their demographic as well as buying habit and product preference information, you'll want to organize that information and use it. Drilling into a customer database that contains buying preferences data will help you think up promotions, new products and services—the works.

If nothing else, you want a database of e-mail addresses so you can contact your customers—if, of course, they've given you permission to do so.

Maximize Web Store Profitability

I believe in the Japanese philosophy that most useful things have more than one use. This couldn't be truer when it comes to your Web storefront. Once you have the Web store up and running, you may as well get the most out of the technology. You may be very surprised what your Web store is capable of providing you, aside from strict revenue.

To get you thinking of other functionality you may want now or down the road, I end this chapter with six other uses for your Web store. Bear in mind that there are costs associated with some of these functions. But then again, some or all of the functions are ones you already have in place or need to have in place anyway. The point is that the Web store streamlines these processes. If it doesn't, it's not worth the cost and effort.

Take a look at some of these suggestions and think about whether any of them could actually save you money, depending on how you conduct business now, or whether they could make your business more efficient and more productive.

Six Uses for Your Web Store

Customer Service

Imagine if, when your customers had a problem or question, they could e-mail you instead of tying up your 800 number. I'm not suggesting that customers with complicated requests would give up phoning you directly any time soon—and tech heads who try and convince you of this likelihood are worth tuning out—but the Web is good for many customer service functions. The usefulness applies to the customer as well as you. For instance, for questions about inventory and what kinds of products you have, the Web is far easier to navigate than a catalog and far more effective than talking to someone. Some people even argue that the Web is one big searchable catalog.

Or think about order tracking. Federal Express pioneered this customer service application on the Web. With your tracking number, you can go to the FedEx Web site and see the status of your package instead of calling an 800 number.

You can set up return policies over the Web, too. Have customers send e-mail when they're returning something, and you can coordinate receiving the package with your mailroom by putting a PC there and having the mail staff check incoming packages against the e-mails.

Give customers a chance to tell you more about what kinds of products and services they want by offering a personal profile form they can fill out on your site . This idea is an extension of what we talked about in Chapter 14. Again, remember that this kind of information can be useful for marketing campaigns, too. But be careful with this one. People are touchy these days about their privacy being invaded by marketers on the Web, so state clearly your intentions regarding any personal information, and are sure to be respectful of consumers' privacy. One thing that is critical to remember about the Web: It is a close-knit but global community, where word of mouth is extraordinarily powerful. If you do things to anger consumers, they'll bad-mouth you by broadcasting to the whole Web community their intentions to boycott you.

The trick to setting up customer service applications is getting a software programmer to create interactive databases for you. This means that the consumer will actually ask questions and get answers automatically from the appropriate database. In the example of order tracking, this database would be the one that holds order information. In the case of checking inventory, it would be the inventory database, and so on. If you do this in-house, expect to pay $10,000–$20,000 for a decent programmer. However, don't be scared off by this amount of money. Many Web-hosting services offer such interactive features for a monthly fee, ranging between $50 and several hundred dollars, depending on the complexity.

Product Demos

Think of this application as making your catalog on the Web a dynamic tool. Say you sell telephone systems or electronic gadgets. You can show the features of your product through a step-by-step visual tutorial on your Web site. Consumers can click graphics on your site and see how products work. Or if you sell toys—jack-in-the-boxes, for instance. You can animate your Web graphics so that when someone clicks a picture of a jack-in-the-box, the toy pops open.

This application can also be used for internal purposes. If you design car parts, for example, you can put demos on your Web site for business partners or internal employees to see. You keep their access exclusive simply by password protecting this feature on your site. Think of your Web site as an office building with many different department offices, including of course your retail storefront. Each office, or store, has a virtual door that allows access. That "door" is a password. So, you can have graphic icons on your site that are only for internal employees and business partners. They'll access the site by entering a password and name ID.

To accomplish both consumer and external product demos, you again will need a software programmer's help or a Web-hosting service that offers such features.

Recruiting

Now that you're thinking in terms of internal business applications—for your employees and your business partners—the possibilities really open up. A very useful application is for employee recruitment. You can set up a place on your Web site devoted to telling people about job opportunities at your company. You can set up a form—again, by hiring a software programmer—that allows people to fill out a job application online. You can also ask for résumés to be faxed or e-mailed to you.

To make your human resources department's job easier, you can set this application up so that HR personnel have exclusive access to this information—again, using passwords. Or you can simply have all the résumés and other recruitment information that comes from your Web site go directly into their e-mailboxes.

To make online recruitment even more robust, you can sign up with Web services devoted to recruitment. One of the most popular is called the Monster Board (*www.monster.com*). You set up a link from Monster Board to your Web site; then the potential hires can proceed to fill out whatever applications you have.

This idea is a classic example of just what the Internet is good for: getting your ideas much more exposure. Registering on Monster Board, for instance, may help you find new employees far more quickly and efficiently than placing an ad in a local paper will, if only because you are exposed to far more people.

In-House Bulletin Board

Human resources departments can use the Web site for far more than just recruiting from outside your company. You can have a section on the site, accessible by passwords, for internal employees to see what job opportunities are coming up. You could take this employee service a step further: Let employees ask questions about their health care plan, for instance, on the Web. You can let HR set up a whole slew of information about employee benefits on the site, including interactive question-and-answer features so that HR staff doesn't have to field phone calls to explain 401K plans, health benefits, vacation and sick leave policies, and the like.

The in-house bulletin board isn't limited to HR functions. If you have company announcements or reports you want to share, you can post them on the Web site. You can even set up a shadow Web site—a site on which employees see a different picture of the Web site, with more options, than outside consumers see. You can do this by setting up password and ID access once the user get to the home page. If someone keys in the proper password once, he or she surfs to the site, then the Web site changes to show a whole different set of options. So, for instance, employees surf to the Web site, look for the little box that says "password and ID," enter them, and a whole new home page pops up, complete with all the internal company options.

You can even make the site employees see so different that passwords pop up different home pages. So, say you want business partners to see some of the internal options but not all of them. You can create categories of passwords that, once keyed in, yield different views. So if all business partners have a class of password that begin with a "B," for instance, the Web site view they'll get when they key in their passwords will be all the functions designed for their eyes. If all employees have a password that begins with "E," they'll get a view reserved for internal staff when they key in their passwords.

This is all a programming issue. On to the next item you can do yourself.

Salespeople on the Road

Here's one of the coolest internal applications that uses this idea of different classes of passwords yielding different views of the Web site: One of your salespeople is off-site visiting a client. If you have the proper databases set up, he can surf to the Web site, key in his password, see the client's account information, e-mail the accounting department his billable hours from the road, send in T&E reports, or any number of functions. By doing all these functions from the road, the client will get billed faster, the salesperson will be reimbursed faster, and the overall machine of your business will move faster.

This kind of application is simply a matter of tying in certain accounting department databases as well as the sales department's databases to the Web site. Say you're a publisher that sells advertising. If the salesperson on the road clinches a deal, he can surf to the Web site, go into the sales database, and mark the client as "sold." The other salespeople back at the office can know immediately whether that client has bought an ad. The production and art departments, in this example, could also use this information. If their job, for instance, is to contact the client once the deal is made—in order to schedule graphics for the ad, for instance—the client may well get a call while the salesperson is still on an airplane flying home. There's no doubt that your clients would be impressed with such efficiency.

The concept of this application is expansive. Here we've used the example of the salesperson on the road, but anyone can file T&E reports to their accounting staff through the Web. You can even set up a routing system so an employee's T&E report first gets e-mailed to the person who needs to sign off on it (it shows up in their e-mailbox). Then, after it's signed digitally, it can be routed to accounting.

The important concept here is internal communication. The Web is a perfect vehicle for interoffice communication.

Training

This last application is perhaps the most dynamic, one that will change the most over the next few years. Right now, the most realistic way to use the Web for training is to post reports, lectures (graphics and slides translate well to the Web and are easy to view with Web browsers), and even full-text books and instruction manuals. The beauty of training over the Web is that people can learn at their own pace. You don't have to schedule big meetings in conference rooms for things such as employee orientation. You just point your trainees to the appropriate function on your Web site.

This training idea will evolve over the next few years to include video and audio. For instance, say you need to train people on an assembly line. You can have a video available to show how the mechanism works. Right now video can be difficult to implement on your Web site, because you need serious high-speed digital telecommunications lines so that the video looks like video, not like some slow-motion mess. If you have the bandwidth, video is a real option—but not everyone has bandwidth.

Audio is more realistic right now. Except the expense of creating the recordings, it doesn't cost much and doesn't require an enormous amount of bandwidth. So, to add voice instructions to Web training is a matter of doing recordings that are similar to radio show recordings. You will need an audio expert to set them up. Expect to spend a few thousand dollars for such expertise.

Chapter 16

Plan Your Security or Lose Your Business

You probably need read no further than this chapter title to think that this is going to be one melodramatic section of the book. But that's simply not true. You need to be alarmed when it comes to the security of your Web storefront and your privacy policies for your Web customers. If you aren't alarmed, the simple truth is that you could lose your business—literally—to hackers who could steal it and in terms of potential customers who shun you.

The real benefit of this chapter is that the advice—which, by the way, is taken from a compilation of conversations I've had with the FBI—has a much further reach than your Web storefront. It is information to incorporate into your whole business. Bear in mind, too, that FBI experts say small businesses are at particular risk when it comes to security problems.

This chapter starts with a case study that characterizes the security risks your Web storefront poses. We start with a case study because I think it best paints a real-life picture. Then we'll move on to the preventive measures you can take to prevent security breaches—on your Web storefront and in your office. More than 80 percent of all security breaches are inside jobs. You need to protect your whole office.

After the discussion about security measures, we'll delve into one of the hottest subjects of debate on the Internet: customer privacy. You need to wrestle with some very touchy issues in this area if you want to have a Web store with loyal, happy customers, instead of an Internet population that hates you. Again, we'll talk about specific measures you can take to appease a scrutinizing public without sacrificing the marketing strategies you'll need to make your Web store profitable. In the privacy section, you'll also read a special article about what the legal community, and particularly what the Federal Trade Commission, is up to, so you can be aware of how your Web store might be scrutinized by the law as well as by the public. Finally, the chapter includes a Q&A with a privacy expert who talks about the most common complaints heard from Web shoppers—the inside story about what drives paying customers away vs. what endears them to you.

Case Study: Be Paranoid, Says FBI, About Web Commerce Security

Bill Myers wants to make his credit union's Web site a full-service virtual bank for its members, but after the incident with the e-mail virus that attacked his whole network, he's not going for a full commerce Web site until he's sure the security issues are covered. And that's going to take time and money.

"Someone sent an e-mail into our company e-mail system with one nasty computer virus as an attachment," says Myers, manager of the 27-employee, Ithaca, NY–based Alternatives Federal Credit Union. "The virus got through and onto our network. We had to turn off all the computers, and then turn on the one that the virus came in on and clean it. We tried to clean the computer with the network up—so we could continue to conduct business—but it was a robust virus and kept reinfecting the network."

Understandably, this incident helped make Myers security conscious, if not downright paranoid. He has gone so far as to hire a computer programmer on retainer to periodically try and hack into his network, Web site, and e-mail systems, just to make sure they're secure. (Web sites are as easy, if not easier, than e-mail to hack into, say FBI experts.) He's so hyper-aware, the credit union's Web site will allow members to place an order for checks, but nothing else.

"I want members to be able to do all their banking on the Web, but I have other priorities right now [budget-wise] and it can't just be done recklessly," says Myers.

Small Businesses Have Big Reason to Worry

Is Myers simply paranoid? Tens of thousands of businesses now conduct commerce over the Web; many of these businesses are much larger than Myers', with much more to steal.

"It is not paranoid at all to obsess about Web security breaches," says Dr. Bill Hancock, a forensic expert for the FBI and chief technology officer for Network-1 Security Solutions Inc., a firewall manufacturer and security consultancy in Texas. "It is rational, particularly for small business Web stores, which are targets because hackers use them to test things out to see what works and what does not before they go after the bigger fish."

It's like thieves who start out holding up 7-Eleven stores before they move up to robbing banks. Every profession has its apprenticeship, and for Web thieves and vandals, small business sites are it. There is a certain appeal to stealing from smaller businesses, explains Hancock. If the hacker is trying to steal money, The payoff may be less—fewer credit-card numbers to steal, for instance—but it's also an easier hack. Some thieves make a living knocking over 7-Elevens, without ever evolving to bank-robbing level.

For small business Web sites, the major problems are hackers stealing credit-card numbers and company information, as well as performing pure acts of vandalism in the name of sabotage.

The FBI also warns that random strangers aren't the only reason small businesses are particularly vulnerable. More than 80 percent of all network hacks are inside jobs, according to the FBI. Not only do disgruntled employees and ex-employees pose a problem, so do friends of perfectly satisfied employees who come in to the office to, say, meet for lunch. Anyone who wants it has easy access to a small business network and, therefore, its Web site.

"The biggest problem is incompetence—not doing the simple things like maintaining passwords, encrypting and password protecting the data that's critical to the business, monitoring everyone and everything that comes in and out of the office," says Charles Neal, supervisor of the FBI White Collar Crime Squad in Los Angeles.

"Vandals in particular are a problem," says Hancock. A small business site is an easy target for the Web version of spray paint because small businesses tend to be lax about security measures.

Small business Web stores are a growing target, too, according to International Data Corp.'s new study, *US Small Business on the Internet:* 36 percent of small businesses that plan to go online expect to use the Internet to sell products. And there's good reason for that trend. Small businesses that use the Internet have higher revenues, averaging $3.79 million compared with $2.72 million.

Eight Measures to Take to Protect Your Web Commerce Site

Before you give up on conducting Web commerce, here are eight measures Web security experts such as Hancock say you can implement to protect your site. "Remember," says Hancock, "there are no unrobbable banks and no unhackable Web sites, but you can make it tough enough so that they try someone else."

The good news is that the following measures will work for any functionality you'd like to have on your Web commerce site. So, if you want customers to be able to track orders and shipments (the way Federal Express allows), you need not be worried about letting the customers have access to that database. You can apply the same security measures for every server and every database.

The trick with allowing access to a variety of databases and servers, says Hancock, is to keep them on a local area network separate from the rest of your business. Allow purchasing, inventory checking, order tracking—anything you want—but keep the databases with your company's accounting, personnel, and strategic business files somewhere else entirely.

"It's not hard to create a separate network—you just isolate the Web server, with all the databases you want to allow access to, from the rest of your network," says Hancock. "Then you connect that Web server to the site and to the ISP."

Bear in mind that some of these measures are cheap, some are expensive. But you won't get the safe-site nod from FBI experts unless you do them all. You must consider taking these steps the cost of doing business on the Web:

1. Back up your Web site. If you own the Web hardware (have your own server), consider putting as much of the site on CD-ROM as possible and minimize magnetic media (such tape backup systems and hard drives on your network servers). It's really hard to hack a CD-ROM. Also, make the system disk a removable magnetic disk for temporary storage, operating system, and so

on so that it can be replaced quickly in an emergency (for example, if a vandal has posted nasty stuff on your home page) with a nice, clean operating system copy.

The good news here is that CD-ROM drives are fairly inexpensive ($40 and up at Fry's Electronics or CompUSA). And CD burners can be as cheap as $200. Blanks are about $2–$4 each, so it is very cheap insurance.

2. Protect ADMINISTRATOR (NT) and ROOT (UNIX) account usage. These are directories technical people use to administer your Web store. You should always create and post the Web goodies from a less privileged account and keep the system administrator accounts very carefully controlled. That way, if you are nailed by hackers, you'll get less grief. Make sure to ask the ISP or programmer you've hired what is being done to protect these directories.

3. Watch out for FTP "holes." These holes can occur if an FTP utility is used in conjunction with your Web stores and it does not stop someone from copying a file to an improper directory. Always check proper protection and access control lists (ACLs) for directories (or folders) and files. An ACL is the list of people in your company who are supposed to have authorization (password and ID access) to a given directory or database. If you don't password protect the ACL itself, someone could go in via FTP (an Internet protocol that allows access to Web sites) and simply add himself to the access list.

4. Be careful when your store uses CGI scripts (a type of program commonly used to create Web site features, such as shopping carts and forms). CGI scripts are notorious for allowing breaches. Consult with a security expert on how you set them up and what they can do.

5. Beware breaches and holes when using Java applets (small programs written in the Java programming language commonly used to create Web site features, such as animation). There are very few defenses for Java these days, and the number of breaches is growing. Java is also capable of writing to the client's hard drive as well as reading from it, so if a hacker gets into an applet on page on your Web site and a customer then surfs to that page, a variety of ugly things can be done to that customer's hard drive.

Control over applet facilities is critical to ensure someone does not put a hostile applet on your Web site.

Because Java applets are so popular these days, you need to be particularly careful here. Programmers like Java for designing credit-card transaction pop-up forms, animated graphics, and other commerce-oriented Web site features. Ask what security measures are being used to protect the Java applets used on the ISP's Web site.

6. Use Secure Socket Layer (SSL) or a similar protocol whenever possible. SSL is protocol that is built into many commerce software programs; it just needs to be activated. Although SSL increases stress on the server's performance (and may cause you to buy a higher-powered server), it also increases security and makes it very hard for hackers to detect credit-card transactions from your Web store.

7. Use a firewall and a router for security. Firewalls are software programs that prevent access to a server or particular database without a password and an ID. A router is essentially a network traffic cop—a box that receives all communication and decides how to route it on your network.

    This gets expensive, to be sure, especially for an in-house operation. Firewalls cost anywhere from $1,000 to over $10,000, depending on your network configuration, and so do routers. But together they provide a multitiered security method that keeps attackers at bay. If somehow the router is breached, the firewall still stops the attack and can also proactively notify you of a potentially serious security situation. You can set firewall software to sound alarms or use pop-up boxes on a computer screen if there's a security problem. You can even set them to automatically dial you on a pager if there's a security breach. If an ISP is hosting your Web site, they should have a firewall and a router in place.

8 If you are using an ISP for your Web site hosting and design or have outsourced these tasks to another company, make sure you understand the security methods, precautions, and technologies, used. You should have get a a list of people to contact at the ISP or at the other company in case you have questions or if there is a breach.

FBI Security Checklists: Some Preventive Medicine and What to Do in Case You're Hacked

The case study that appeared earlier in the chaper, along with the list of eight security measures you should take, can be rather frightening. It sounds like there is a lot to worry about. But if you're going to do business on the Internet, those are the realities. The Web store owners that run into trouble are invariably the ones who don't get a realistic grip on the costs of doing business on the Internet. Skimping on security is a very bad idea.

In the same vein, you should always be prepared to take the proper action in the event that you are hacked. Two checklists, compliments of the FBI, explain what you need to do to prevent security breaches, and what to do—instead of panic—in the event that your site is hacked. Perhaps the most important list is the preventive medicine checklist. It's always easier to prevent a problem than it is to cure it.

This can't be repeated enough: Although every company with a data network is vulnerable to hackers, small businesses are particularly vulnerable and worse off than most. First, intellectual property, not hard assets, defines a small business's jewels. Now that most strategic and mission-critical data is stored electronically, small businesses are more vulnerable than ever. How would you like your core business strategy traveling by e-mail to your competitors with just a couple of mouse clicks?

Second, people are far too relaxed in a small business environment— they don't use passwords, they leave important diskettes lying around, they don't worry about who sees what.

Okay, enough lecturing. Here's what you need to do to protect yourself and what the FBI recommends in the event that you are hacked.

Basic Network Security

1. Set up firewalls on servers.
2. Turn on the audit logs that come with every operating system. Audit logs track network traffic.
3. Maintain passwords (and have everyone in the office change their own often).
4. Encrypt and password protect the data that's critical to the business.

5. Keep off-site tape backup systems. Security also means no loss of data.

6. Get an uninterruptible power supply (UPS) and a RAID array backup hard drive system.

7. Monitor the people who come in and out of your office.

8. Set up antivirus software on all of your systems.

What to Do If You're Hacked

1. Secure and preserve all evidence.

2. Identify the origin and time of attack, if you can. A technical person can do this. If you don't have a systems administrator, an FBI agent can walk you through this process over the phone.

3. Keep detailed and dated notes of what occurred.

4. Prepare for repeat attacks.

5. Notify law enforcement. Many people worry about PR and spin control, but the FBI says it will keep the security hack confidential unless there's a trial.

6. Do a cost evaluation—property, time, and cost of buying new computer equipment and hiring a private security consultant.

7. Be prepared to assist law enforcement.

8. Do not correspond via e-mail with *anyone* about the hack. Don't keep any electronic information about it at all. Hackers systematically do surveillance to see if law enforcement has been tipped off about them.

Don't Forget Customer Privacy

Privacy on the Internet. No matter whom you ask about this topic, you'll get an opinion. And though the big technical and philosophical brains have been struggling with how to approach the issue since the invention of the Internet in the 1960s, you can trace the point at which privacy became a public scandal to one event: the arrival of the cookie.

Like many historical events that triggered widespread hype and even paranoia, the cookie's arrival a couple of years ago was blown far out of proportion. Although the Web cookie is certainly not as innocent as the

Keebler cookie variety, a cookie is also not the Orwellian invasion people make it out to be. A cookie is a string of numbers that is placed on your hard drive by a Web site and that identifies a vistor's browser. Imagine a browser flashing an ID pass when landing on a Web site that requires membership. So, say you own a site at which you ask visitors to register. Once they register, they can come back without signing on again. Like a human security guard, the Web server recognizes the cookie and waves the browser in.

Sounds innocent enough. It's not even easy for Web sites to swap cookies among themselves (though they can do that). So why all the public outcry? People are practically marching up the Capitol steps in Washington, D.C., in protest. A cookie arms race has started, too: You can now load a cookie "crumbler" on your PC to disintegrate any cookies placed there.

The reason for the outcry is simple: Cookies can be placed on consumers' hard drives without consumers' prior consent. The very notion of a Web site reaching into a person's hard drive is what causes alarm. The minute people feel that they can be sitting in their den at home, happily Web surfing, and some Web merchant can reach a virtual hand out of the Web and into their homes, placing some tracking or probing device on their PCs, they feel vulnerable. They feel watched.

But it doesn't have to be this way. The Web marketplace is perhaps the greatest opportunity for consumers to have access to worldwide products and services and for merchants to use consumer preferences to better serve customers. If we can establish solid, respectful interactivity guidelines between Web merchant and Internet consumer, the sky could be the limit for profitability and consumer satisfaction.

Two Critical Core Issues

Now that the cookie has opened the Pandora's box of privacy, two privacy questions now take center stage with consumers: If I give away personal data to a Web merchant, will that merchant turn around and sell my e-mail address, demographic data, and psychographic data to other merchants as it pleases? Will I even know when that merchant is taking my personal data?

The event that brought these issues to the forefront was America Online's public announcement several years ago that it would sell the clickstream data (the logs of the online places each account holder had visited) it had collected on its 7 million-plus account holders. As if struck in the face, people became outraged. AOL stock plummeted.

AOL responded to the fuss by backing off—the company said it wouldn't sell the data after all—and boom, the stock shot right back up. The company got another million users.

Make the Information-for-Goods Trade Wholesome

Between a merchant and a customer—whether in the physical world or on the Web—there is always a trade of personal information for goods and services. And that's okay. What is important from here on is to establish contractual guidelines for good business practices in a new electronic age in order to limit the possibility for corruption in commerce.

The core consumer issue now—will a merchant sell my e-mail address and personal data?—should get Web merchants' attention. The fact is that electronic commerce has woken up consumers to a lot of business-practice issues that go on in the physical world, too, and that awareness creates scrutiny. If consumers truly don't feel comfortable with shopping electronically, that will stunt the growth of Web commerce, and Web merchants can kiss good-bye the revenue they see from this new marketing channel.

The reason the Web has awoken consumers to privacy-invading business practices that have been going on for a long time in the physical world— after all, selling lists of prospects defined the 1970s era, when direct marketing was born—is that the vulnerability is so escalated on the Web.

The ramification for consumers is that they are suddenly afraid of viewing Web information that they think will make them a target for certain things. Say there's a health magazine owned by an insurance company and company is tracking click-streams on its site. The trackers notice that a certain consumer is reading an awful lot about AIDS or Alzheimer's disease. The insurance company might make assumptions about the person reading up on these diseases. Do those assumptions have an effect if the same person goes to the insurance company to buy a health policy?

That may seem like far-fetched speculation, but part of the reason this is an issue for businesses is that the Federal Trade Commission (FTC) is looking at whether it is okay for merchants to virtually stand behind Internet consumers and read over their shoulders.

It's not that this kind of information wasn't available before the Web. Consumer personal data was always available in some way or another. In every town, in every state in America public records of citizens are maintained. Public records are legal to sell, and corporations with target marketing programs have been buying them for a long time.

What's different today is that those records are digital, so the overhead cost of using those records has gone down and the records' value has gone up. Furthermore, the speed with which databases that contain these digital records can be dispersed is amazing. You don't need keypunch operators or anything to disperse a database; you need only a file transfer.

The lesson here is to respect the data your customers—Web or otherwise—give you. If you intend to sell that data, tell customers up front. Make your business practices clear, and no one can argue with the way you do business.

Down to the Nitty-Gritty: Consumers Will Find You Out

You may decide that you'll take your chances, that you've never worried about revealing your business practices before and a Web store isn't going to change that. But before making that decision, understand that you will have to address this issue.

Both Microsoft and Netscape, the makers of the two most popular Web browsers in use today, have added security options to their browsers that tell consumers things like when a Web site tries to place a cookie on their hard drives. This is important because if consumers mistrust one thing about your Web store, they are less likely to trust you at all. So, say your only trespass is to load cookies without telling consumers, but you're really good about keeping their personal data private and secure. If they find out you're lying about cookies—lying by omission—they won't believe you when you say you'll protect their personal data.

Internet consumers have a loud, bellowing, collective voice. The fact that the FTC is now pushing for Web merchants to publish their business practices on their home pages shows that consumers are voicing their concerns in a big way. Be aware that the FTC could list your Web store as a privacy-unfriendly place—the kiss of death on the Internet—if it finds out you're hiding your business practices that deal with privacy issues.

Remember this as well: The Internet is now a worldwide marketplace, and international interests will influence business practices on the Web. Europeans, for instance, are much more hard-line than Americans about respecting privacy.

The moral of the story about heated privacy debate is simple: Publish a privacy policy statement on your home page. Tell consumers up front what your business practices are and how they affect their privacy. Always make it the consumer's option to give you information or consent to your business practices. Do not make it the default situation at your Web store that consumers must do things that could compromise their privacy. That's why it's important not to force them to fill out a registration form just to browse through your store. Make it an option. Respect consumers by making the choices theirs, and they'll buy stuff from you in return.

The FTC Is Watching Your Web Store

The sidebar below is the result of many discussions with key policymakers, attorneys, and privacy advocates who are focused on the issues of Internet commerce. I offer it here because what the legal community is thinking will have a direct impact upon the way you conduct business over the Internet in years to come.

Aside from this sidebar, you can easily check up on how the issue of Internet privacy is evolving by looking at the FTC's Web site (*www.ftc.gov*) for updates.

Free Web Market or Stalking Marketers?

We are now facing the serious possibility that individual privacy will be a casualty of the Digital Age, much like the earth's environment was the casualty of the Industrial Age.

Picture this, because this is where we're heading: What if you get fired, or your start-up business falls a little behind on the bills—and all of a sudden this information is broadcast over the Internet to all your business partners and customers? What if your boss could log on to a Web site that tells him what kind of psychiatric medication employees and potential hires are taking? And what if information about your children—information that, say, a child pornographer might find interesting—was free for all on the Web?

Okay, here's the only thing scarier than these scenarios: If this kind of private information, the stuff that really matters to all of us— personal finances, medical, and children's personal data—is forsaken, we will have only our own business practices on the Web to blame.

Sound alarmist? Not to the Federal Trade Commission, which has recently given its last ultimatum to the Internet industry: Either

(continued)

Free Web Market or Stalking Marketers? (continued)

we self-govern our privacy policies—in other words, Web merchants willingly disclose business practice information to consumers, such as planting cookies, selling personal data to other Web merchants and governments, and gathering data behind site visitors' backs— or the government will do it for us.

Informing consumers is crucial, according to the FTC attorneys, because consumers unwittingly give away information all the time. All those contest and registration forms people fill out online, for example, are used to build marketing databases. Chat rooms and discussion groups you and your children frequent are monitored by lots of businesses—including your own business, perhaps—that collect e-mail addresses and personal interest information from the discussions.

Perhaps consumers wouldn't give away information if they knew what the marketers do with it, reasons the FTC. They could instead do what the FTC calls "opting out" of the interaction.

This issue of disclosure is so important to civil rights, in fact, that in late April the FTC did a "privacy sweep" of the Web. The sweep was a random scan of all Web merchants to see who had decent disclosure practices. So, if your Web storefront collects cookies and you didn't post that fact on your home page, the FTC has likely got your number now.

The FTC is honing in on Web merchant practices because the Web will soon coordinate with TV and all telecommunications media, creating the key marketplace in which all databases with personal data are be bought and sold, the place where people can be virtually watched. "The FTC is particularly interested in protected medical data, such as what happened at your last doctor visit, personal financial data, and information about children," says Christine Varney, Internet privacy activist and head of the Internet Practice Group at the Washington, D.C.–based law firm Hogan & Hartson.

But sadly, even if the FTC does lay down the law, it won't be an adequate solution. "Lawmakers may not be able to enforce the law easily," admits Terry Maher, partner at Abrahams, Kaslow, and Cassman of Omaha, Nebraska, and former American Bar Association chairman for the business law subcommittee on cyberspace commerce.

To force the situation in the right direction, consumers are going to have to get smart and demanding, says David R. Johnson, an attorney and director of the Aspen Institute's Internet Policy Project,

(continued)

Free Web Market or Stalking Marketers? (*continued*)

a non-profit Washington, D.C., think tank of sorts that focuses on self-governance. "Hey, if consumers really don't do business with you if you make them mad, then the market will change."

Now that the disclosure issue is a top government priority, consumers will know about it. So even though the government may not be able to enforce these rules, says Johnson, consumers are fast becoming aware of them, so the pressure is on businesses to disclose business practices.

And it could be good for business, he predicts. What if a small CD Web store offers this contract: "We won't sell your personal data or plant cookies, and we'll let a privacy group like TRUSTe or Electronic Frontier Foundation randomly do surprise searches of our databases to keep us honest. Will you do business with us now?" Maybe the store could endear consumers so much that it becomes competition for Tower Records.

Tell you what: I'll sing the praises of businesses like that every chance I get. And I'll also write about the ones I think are doing wrong. You know what they say about word of mouth …

What Drives Customers Away in a Heartbeat

Over the last year or so, the Internet has exploded as marketplace. During this time, I have spoken to hundreds of Web shoppers and merchants about their likes and dislikes related to playing in this brave new world. From these conversation came distinct patterns—patterns of what Internet shoppers dislike enough to make them avoid certain Web stores.

Before I go into what they hate most, I'd like to say that when I asked Web merchants to answer my questions from the point of view of a consumer (many Web merchants also shop online for themselves), they answered in much the same way as consumers who didn't own Web stores.

What consumers (Web store owners and others) tend to hate about the Web is the threat to their privacy. And everyone's privacy is at stake—yours, your customers', and your children's. All you have to do is think a minute or two about how much time kids spend on the Internet and whether or not you really would like it if marketers sold your own kids' names and e-mail addresses to, say, pornographers.

Enough said.

Here are the privacy-invading merchant practices that make consumers angry:

Cookies

Cookies are the number-one irritants. People don't want you messing with their hard drives without asking first.

Click-Stream Tracking

Click-stream tracking is a privacy-invading practice that raises the public's ire. In its simplest form, click-stream tracking occurs when a Web merchant audits his Web server log-in files to see the path surfers take through the site. The reason a merchant wants this information is simple: to see which icons on the site lure people to click and which they bypass. Simple marketing needs make click-stream tracking appealing.

What really started to bug Internet shoppers is a certain part of click-stream tracking, what's called the *refers*. A refer is the site from which the consumer surfed. Again, any marketer would want this information. If a Web storefront is getting a lot of traffic from a particular site, wouldn't it make sense to throw a banner ad on that other site and draw even more people? The reason people gave for not liking click-stream tracking is simple: If you drive up to a mall and go into a store, would you want the store owner to know where you had just come from?

You may say you don't care if the store owner knows where you just shopped. But people simply don't like being watched. Again, think of children being harassed. Say someone is tracking the fact that your child hangs out at a Web site where there are chat rooms. That person could actually go to that site and engage in conversation with your child. There's simply something too akin to stalking in this kind of tracking. It makes people nervous, especially when you consider that many so-called Web stores out there have innocent enough names but are con-artist scams. So, even if you, as a consumer, would trust a legitimate Web merchant to use the click-stream tracking information responsibly—to see how to improve his or her own Web store, for instance, based on learning what features of the site customers are totally ignoring—there's no assurance that the Web store you land on from a search engine site query is legitimate. You may be on the site for a minute or two, clicking away, before you realize the site isn't on the up-and-up.

Overall, among Internet consumers the perception is that those who track click-streams are being sneaky. The thing is that it can truly be a useful information-gathering tool for Web merchants. My suggestion is this: Just tell people you are tracking them within your own Web store only—that you are not looking at the refers unless the consumer specifies that looking at them is okay (you can have a little box pop up asking them to check Yes or No). Although doing so could limit the usefulness of click-stream tracking, the downside of consumers finding out on their own that you're "following" them and getting angry about it isn't a worthwhile tradeoff.

Spam

From cookies and click-streams, the privacy terms and debates started escalating. *Spam*—e-mail messages or posts to newgroups that are sent out indiscriminately to numerous users—was next on the privacy hit list. Spam has quickly been labeled the junk mail of the 1990s. Some Web merchants have spammed e-mail accounts by sending unsolicted messages offering free stuff or anything to lure consumers to their sites. The more people's e-mail boxes started overflowing with junk mail, the more the practice of spamming has been criticized as sleazy and cheap. Avoid spamming your Web site visitors.

Top Five Questions Consumers Ask a Privacy Expert

For some added insight, here are the top five questions consumers ask privacy expert Tara Lemmey. Lemmey is the executive director of the Electronic Frontier Foundation (*www.eff.org*), a privacy advocacy group that is focused on setting up guidelines for Internet commerce. She is also a former board member of the TRUSTe Group (*www.truste.org*), a non-profit organization for which the mission is to establish a new business constitution for the new Web commerce era—one that sets up privacy-respecting contract law between Web merchant and consumer. Lemmey provided the answers following the questions.

Q: If I download software, can someone stalk me?

A: I tell them, yes it's possible. Of course they are thinking about this question in terms of cookies. The point of a cookie is that next time the same surfer lands on that Web site, the server will be able to identify the browser by that cookie. Cookies alone aren't necessarily a bad thing—it makes registration a one-time chore. But consumers should know when this is being done—they should always have [the ability to give] prior consent. Otherwise, if you think of these interactions—registering and placing cookies—as the new language of business, placing cookies is rather like saying, "Hey, when you come to my site I'm going to wait until you're not looking and place an identifying device in your back pocket. You won't know it's there, but I always will." It's just better practice to tell consumers what you are doing and give them the choice whether or not to participate. That's the difference between a free market and being stalked.

Q: Can I turn off a cookie?

A: The minute they understand what a cookie is, people want it gone. It's proof for skeptical business owners that perception is indeed reality and consumers don't like the idea of no prior consent. I of course tell them about "cookie crumblers," a software utility you can run on your PC to delete cookies.

Q: What major technology company has the best privacy policies?

A: Netscape. They plan all security mechanisms around consumer privacy.

Q: What happens to the data I put on registration forms I fill out on Web sites?

A: That's the part that is starting to get to consumers. Aside from the obvious target marketing of products to fit their profiles, consumers are worried that people are selling their personal data to direct marketers. This is a tough accusation to dispel.

Q: Is the idea of selling my name and personal data on the Web any different than in the real world?

A: Yes and no. The main difference on the Web is that data is accumulated faster.

Be Sure to Cover Your Security and Privacy Bases

You don't have time for games. You want your Web store to make money and offer you a great marketing opportunity at the same time. That means going through the often tedious process of making sure your security checklist is completed, as well as creating and sticking to a privacy policy.

These are not places for shortcuts, even though they both may seem like a big pain in the neck while you're worrying about the details of getting your Web store in order. All I can say is that I've heard nothing but regret from Web merchants who skimped in these areas and invariably had to go back later and do them anyway. The regret comes in two forms: One, they actually experienced a security breach that almost cost them their business. Two, it's difficult to repair a marred reputation for, say, sneakily acquiring personal information from customers.

All that said, these last few chapters on building a Web storefront have posed more questions than answers. You know you're going to need resources for all of this—and not just money. You'll need to hire the right people and know where to look for all your Web commerce needs. So, to get you started, the next chapter is devoted to lists of Web store resources. They're divided into categories for easy scanning. Good luck.

Chapter 17

E-Commerce Resource Lists

This book has laid out many tasks for you to do in order to get your Web store off the ground, but those marching orders aren't worth much without some kind of road map. You need to know where to find the people and services and software to get you from planning to launch. You need options so you don't feel like you have to put up with a vendor or consultant you don't like. Fortunately, the Internet marketplace is booming, and for every task you need to accomplish, many competing services would like your business.

So, in the spirit of giving you enough options to get you started but not so many that they're more confusing than helpful, this chapter is essentially one big resource list of Web commerce consultants, Web-hosting services, Web commerce technology—the works.

This list is by no means exhaustive, nor is it an attempt to exclude vendors that may be good. It's a sampling, and that's all. I believe that exhaustive lists don't really help people get started. Instead, they are overwhelming. Would you rather read a magazine article that lists 15 trustworthy laptops you can buy, or one that lists 100? If you're a novice, 100 laptops will all start to look alike, and choosing one will actually be harder.

This sounds like a long-winded disclaimer, inserted here so that vendors not included in my list won't call me up and ask why they're not included. I guess in part it is. But its main purpose is to give you a few places in each category—Web-hosting services, ISPs, and so on—to check out, places that will provide at least some of the services you need. Once you're in the throes of opening your Web store, you'll come across other sources, many of which are quite good, many of which are not. The purpose here is to show you the ropes, so even if you don't choose any of the vendors listed here, you'll know what to expect from the Web store marketplace.

For comparison's sake, the last list in this chapter is a sampling of Web stores that I think are exceptional. By that, I don't mean they are most glitzy; I mean they are easy to shop at, that aren't too busy or too complicated or too annoying. I like simplicity and options and good prices when I shop, and so this list of Web stores that I think are worth emulating reflects those qualities.

Just a few more things before you get to the lists. First, each listed resource has a phone number and a Web site. I strongly suggest checking out the Web sites if you can; they give a lot of information up front.

Second, you should check out with the Better Business Bureau any businesses you find on the Web that don't have renowned brand names before you consider hiring them. Either call (703) 276-0100 or go to the bureau's Web site (*www.bbb.org*).

Third, you'll notice that some of the lists contain resources that could be in another list as well. For example, the Yahoo! store is listed under "Shopping Cart Software," but it's also a Web-hosting service. There is a lot of crossover in the Internet marketplace. Because competition is fierce, many Internet companies have diversified services. So, check to see if a company you are interested in for one reason can actually end up meeting more of your needs than you thought.

Internet Access and Web-Hosting Services

Below are lists of vendors that provide Internet access and complete Web-hosting services, including Web storefront design. Note that this category includes only companies that can offer both services. Yahoo! Store offers good Web-hosting services for a storefront, but it cannot actually sell you the Internet access you need.

If you're interested in learning about other vendors that offer these services, check out CNet's Ultimate ISP Guide (*www.cnet.com/Content/Reports/Special/ISP/index.html*). CNet did a great job with this list, and it's exhaustive, including ratings for each ISP.

Tip

When contacting the companies in the "Internet Access and Web-Hosting Services" category remember to ask about the security systems they offer for your Web store.

National ISPs

PSINet: (800) 395-1056; *www.psi.net*

UUNet: (800) 488-6384; *www.uunet.com*

Netcom: (800) NETCOM1 (638-2661); *www.netcom.net*

Phone Companies

AT&T Small Business: (800) 756-6700; *www.att.com/small_business/internet.html*

Earthlink: (800) 327-8454; *www.earthlink.com/business*

Others

@Work: (888) 988-WORK; *work.home.net*

Concentric Network: (408) 817-2800; *www.concentric.net*

CyberZone: (800) 668-4NET; *www.cyberzone-inc.com/services*

E-Commerce Software Products for Do-It-Yourselfers

Soup-to-Nuts E-Commerce Packages

Breakthrough Software's ShopZone: (408) 321-9300; *www.breakthroughsoftware.com*

Forman Interactive's Internet Creator: (212) 627-4988; *www.internetcreator.com*

Commerce Market Inc.'s ReadyShop: (801) 812-2222; *www.commercemarket.com*

GizmoSoft's WebGizmo Merchant Edition: (888) 781-0254; *www.gizmosoft.com*

Shopping Cart Software

PDG Software Inc.: (770) 270-0062; *www.pdgsoft.com*

Yahoo! Store: (408) 731-3300; *store.yahoo.com* (also does Web hosting)

SalesCart: (800) 826-6248, Ext. 105; *www.salescart.com*

Back-End Accounting Systems

There is only one listing here because the majority of banks that participate in Web store transaction settlements use CyberCash. However, if you go with a long-distance carrier such as AT&T or any other robust national ISP and Web host, it is likely they also have a back-end accounting software link to banks. Be sure to ask.

CyberCash: (703) 620-4200; *www.cybercash.com*

What Successful Sites Look Like

Amazon.com, a bookstore that now sells videos and CDs and hosts Web auctions: *www.amazon.com*

Barnes & Noble, bookseller: *www.bn.com*

CDNow, music store: *www.cdnow.com*

L.L. Bean, clothing catalog store: *www.llbean.com*

1-800 Flowers, florist: *www.800flowers.com*

BuyVideos.com, video movie seller: *buyvideos.com*

Staples, office supplies: *www.staples.com*

Gateway Computers, computer store: *www.gateway.com*

Beanie Babies.com, seller of the stuffed animal phenomenon: *www.beaniebabies.com* (here's a store where animation works—the folks at Ty Inc. know their audience)

Travelocity, online travel agency: *www.travelocity.com*

E*Trade, online brokerage: *www.etrade.com*

Part 5

Tricks for Today, Plans for Tomorrow

Chapter 18

Why Take Plastic?

If you've just finished reading the Web storefront section of this book and have decided to launch a Web store of your own, the question "Why take plastic?" has already been answered: You want to take plastic because it is the only way to make your Web storefront a point of sale.

But when it comes to Web storefronts or any other point-of-sale system, the question of plastic is larger than just credit cards. Today consumers are increasingly interested in using debit cards, which are glorified ATM cards that banks issue in coordination with one of the major credit-card associations—Visa or MasterCard—and which can be used for purchasing goods and services over the Internet as well as in the physical world. Does your business need to accept debit cards as well as credit cards? If so, how difficult is it to put that mechanism in place?

What if you've opted out of creating a Web storefront? Are there compelling financial reasons for you to accept credit cards in your business transactions anyway? What about debit cards? Or what about smart cards—the debitlike cards that have a computer chip instead of a magnetic stripe? Smart cards are useful only when a merchant sets up a particular mechanism for them and then issues the cards to its customers. Chapter 19 addresses the issue of smart cards; I mention them here because they are a form of plastic payment, but smart cards differ so much from other payment methods that they require a separate discussion.

For right now, let's focus on credit cards and debit cards. Many factors come into play in making decisions regarding whether you want to accept these cards as a form of payment in your business transactions. Keep one thing in mind: In general, if you sell goods or services to the general public—instead of, say, to the publishers that are my customers—taking plastic as payment may help you increase sales. If you sell any good or service that could be considered an impulse purchase, the likelihood of increasing sales becomes even greater if you offer customers the option of paying with a card. In the United States, being able to afford something is less an issue than having the mechanism with which to pay. That sounds cynical, but it's true. Consumers will be less likely to suffer from sticker shock if the cost doesn't necessarily have to come out of their pockets all at once. Getting cash from an ATM or writing a check to pay for something is immediate—people are conditioned to think of that debit from an account as money already spent. But charging a purchase on a credit card—even for people who generally don't revolve credit and live within their means—tells those consumers they have a safety net; they don't have to "take the hit" on the purchase all at once if they are a little short at the end of the month when the bills arrive. That safety net influences their purchasing decisions and makes it more likely they'll make spontaneous ones.

Still, accepting plastic isn't the right choice for everyone. You need to know what each option entails and whether or not you fit the profile that generally profits from taking it.

Credit Cards

This option, as we've discussed, is a must if you own a Web storefront. Furthermore, offering credit-card payment options is advisable if you want to lure customers into additional impulse purchases.

But accepting credit cards is also a must if you sell big-ticket items. There's simply too much competition in today's business world; that market fact forces you to accept credit cards for expensive goods and services. Even mid- to high-end restaurants that don't accept credit cards can have problems. Customers can always find another restaurant, and who wants to have to remember to go to the ATM and take out an extra $100 or $200 before going out to eat? What if there isn't an ATM nearby? It becomes a hassle to get cash to dine. As a small business owner who accepts credit cards, you remove the hassle from the purchase. The less hassle people have to face, the more they will be inclined to buy.

Even for small-ticket items, people are getting used to using plastic. You can thank the Internet, in part, for this acceptance. After all, if you buy a music CD at a Web storefront, even if it costs only $8, you're going to pay by credit card (or debit card, which we'll get to in a second). People are getting used to using plastic for their purchases and consider it an inconvenience if they don't have that option. This is particularly true of retail situations. As a consumer, if I go into a gift shop with exactly enough cash to buy some candles, and I unexpectedly see other items that I want to buy, I'm going to be irritated if I get to the checkout counter and I can't pay with a credit card. Retail stores bend over backward to encourage impulse shopping. If people with whom you do business must remember to stay within the limits of the cash in their pockets, it will hurt your sales.

A less obvious reason to take credit cards, but one that is relevant to many small businesses beyond the retail area, is that accepting credit cards lends you credibility. By taking credit cards, you're telling customers that they have a built-in guarantee. For instance, some furniture movers in New York City, where I live, are notorious for being con artists. People are terrified that once all their personal belongings are loaded on a mover's truck, the mover will announce that the total cost of the move is $400 more than they estimated, and the mover won't unload the truck until the customers have paid the difference. The customers are helpless in this case. Personally, I will not do business with any mover that doesn't accept credit cards—still a rarity here in Manhattan—because it means that I have no recourse in the case of a disagreement. When I need to hire movers, this criterion means that I have automatically and significantly narrowed the list of businesses I can hire. The movers that offer credit cards have a competitive edge.

People want guarantees today, especially when it comes to dealing with small businesses, which have to fight bigger, better-known brand names for credibility. Whether you own an accounting firm, teach piano, or sell consulting services for a living, accepting credit cards goes a long way toward establishing credibility as a solid, reliable business.

A sound financial reason to accept credit cards is that credit-card transactions are easy to track as you manage your finances, because they offer a built-in tracking system—namely, the merchant bank statement—that you can import into Money.

Who Doesn't Need to Worry?

At this point, you might be asking, who *doesn't* need to accept credit cards? My short answer is, people like me. I swear I'm not saying that because I'm too lazy a home office dweller to set up the credit-card system or too cheap to pay the 1.5 percent or so per transaction. It's true that I'm lazy, but the real reason I don't need to accept credit cards is that my clients are not average consumers. They are publishers, so my financial credibility is of little concern to them. (I do, by the way, take pleasure in the irony of that statement, given that a chunk of my journalistic writing entails giving financial advice.) My customers don't care whether I'm solvent, and a money-back guarantee doesn't help them, because my clients generally don't pay until they accept my work for publication anyway. True, I get advances on royalties, but the contracts I sign are so involved that my customers have more buyer protection than any credit-card company could ensure.

Suffice it to say that if you're like me and your customers are a small, controlled group that don't qualify as the general public and your payment is contract-dependent, you probably don't need to worry about taking credit cards.

Getting Started

If you decide you do want to accept credit cards, the first thing you need to do is call a bank. Start with a bank you already do business with, only because it is often easier to get that bank to extend a line of credit—which is essentially what you're doing in the eyes of the bank—when you have already established a business relationship.

You're going to need to show the bank the balance sheet for your business, which you can prepare in Money. You're going to need good credit, of course, and you'll need to show in your balance sheet an established ability to generate profit. The reason for your need to be solvent and credible is that the merchant bank is liable for credit-card transactions that consumers refute. In other words, if you sell something to a consumer and he or she claims not to have ordered it or received it, ithe customer could call his or her bank to cancel the credit-card payment. Canceling a credit-card payment works like this: The consumer calls his or her card-issuing bank. That bank calls you, and the burden of proof that you kept your promise to deliver goods and services falls on you. You will have to supply evidence that the transaction took place. Assume that you can't supply evidence and the credit-card transaction must be voided. The consumer's card-issuing bank must contact your bank (the merchant bank), and your bank in turn must get the money back from you if it has already paid you for the credit-card transaction.

That means if the consumer presses the dispute, the merchant bank is ultimately responsible for the refund. If the merchant banks considers you too much of a risk—meaning that you haven't demonstrated the ability to deliver goods and services as promised—it won't want to take on the responsibility and hassle of getting money out of you for constant disputes. Of course, the merchant bank has legal recourse to go after you in case you don't refund the money, but it's still a pain in the neck and requires legal action and lots of paperwork. Essentially, banks reason that avoiding headaches and paperwork is worth more than earning a relatively small amount of revenue. Let's face it; a small business's credit-card transaction fees represent a small amount of revenue for a bank compared with the money a bank earns from its large, established corporate customers that accept credit cards using the bank's fulfillment system.

The moral of this story is that a small business must look pure as the driven snow to get a bank to handle its credit-card transactions. That said, don't be discouraged if your bank won't cut the deal with you. Just as in the case of setting up a Web storefront, you can shop around to find a bank willing to handle your credit-card transactions. Many banks are trying to cater more to small businesses because small businesses represent the fastest-growing business market segment in the United States. So, although banks may distrust small businesses on a case-by-case basis, in general they want a piece of your action.

Debit Cards

Debit cards look like credit cards, with the same logos and so on; they are issued by a bank, and one of the credit-card associations—Visa or MasterCard—does their transaction processing. The difference between the two types of cards is that debit cards work like ATM cards in that the cardholder has a certain amount of money in the debit-card account and cannot spend more than that amount. So, if you, the merchant, take a debit card and put it through the approval process to see if the card is good for the transaction, the bank will see if the cardholder has enough money in the account to pay you for your good or service. If the cardholder's account doesn't have enough money, the card will be rejected, because the bank is not extending credit to the cardholder, only offering convenience in the form of a debit card.

Now, there is some danger for certain kinds of merchants when it comes to accepting debit cards. Say you own a hotel. When you submit a guest's debit card for approval upon the guest's arrival, what the system is approving is the cost of the room for the number of days the guest intends to stay. If the guest using the debit card trashes the room, and the cost of repair is more than the guest has in his or her debit card account, it will be harder to get the money than if the guest had checked in with a credit card. That's why most hotels won't take cash payments to begin with—they have no recourse for getting additional money if they need to. The same risky scenario applies to rental car businesses, where the customer can wreck the car. If you're in a business in which the sale or lease of your goods and services doesn't represent the end of the transaction and more costs could be incurred because of damages the customer could impose on you, debit cards might not be a smart idea for your business.

The risks aside, there are compelling reasons to accept debit as well as credit cards: You can attract younger customers, such as high school or college kids who can't yet get credit cards, especially at your Web storefront, where they can't use cash. You can do business with people who don't like credit cards. You can do business at your Web storefront with customers who don't have a good credit rating but have money in the bank.

You notice that the Web storefront scenario plays a big part in debit card transactions. The reason is that many people without credit cards who don't shop online and don't travel—and so don't need means to book hotels or rent cars—generally get cash from an ATM and pay with cash, or use their debit cards to conduct transactions. On the other hand, people of all ages are using debit cards more and more in order to establish credit so they can get credit cards.

Unless you're in a high-risk category of business, taking debit cards is generally good for business. It attracts clientele that wouldn't otherwise be able to buy from you if you own a Web storefront or are trying to cater to younger customers. Plus, if you're not in the high-risk category, you have nothing to lose.

You set up the debit-card system with the bank the same way you would a credit-card system, except that debit-card transaction fulfillment is easier to convince a bank to do for you because it's less risky for the bank. You won't see a case where a small business accepts credit cards but can't get the bank to set up a debit-card system.

Remember, though, that like credit-card transactions, you pay a processing fee for each debit-card transaction. So you do make less money per "cash" sale. But you can test the system by offering debit-card payments for a trial period and see if you sell enough increased volume to make it worth it.

Case Study: Accepting Debit Cards and Credit Cards Online

"Debit cards are great because like credit cards, they're cash in the bank for us the minute the customer places the order, with none of that labor for a cash system, and it's completely transparent to us—looks like a credit-card transaction in terms of processing," says Ken West, founder of the Arlington, Texas–based PalmPilot Gear H.Q. (*www.pilotgear.com*) a Web storefront that sells accessories for the popular electronic pocket organizer, the PalmPilot.

West also thinks he is reaching a wider market with debit cards because some younger people, such as college kids, may not have credit cards yet but are the prime target audience for gadgets like the PalmPilot.

"Because there's no signature capture with debit cards, there isn't the same challenge as there is with credit cards when dealing with overseas credit-card accounts like the Eurocards," says West. "The only time we ever have problems with credit-card purchases is foreign credit cards getting rejected, even though they're perfectly valid." The reason some of the Eurocards get rejected is that is no signature is captured for out-of-country credit cards on the credit-card network system. Although the network is supposed to recognize them as foreign but still acceptable, a few slip by.

West says that 30 percent of his revenue comes from overseas purchases, and about 5 percent of those orders are rejected the first time around and must be put back through the system.

"Still, it is well worth it. One of the biggest surprises to me was how much overseas business we started doing," says West. "Now that I understand more about the marketing, though, I see why. In many countries, they just can't go into a retail store and find these kinds of gadgets."

West was an insurance salesman and fully intended to remain one when he started Pilot Gear in July 1997 as a side business from his office. "I started this business to have fun, with two friends of mine," says West. "But in the first six days we did $27,000 worth of business, and in the month of August we pulled in $102,000."

September 1997 revenues climbed to $140,000. Only $550 of that was received in cash transactions. Today, West's business continues to thrive in a way that it couldn't if he didn't accept credit and debit cards.

Chapter 19

Smart Cards Ain't So Smart

Whenever possible, I try to avoid making sweeping generalizations—first because they rarely tend to be true, and second because people stop listening to you after a while if a generalization is the best argument you can make.

So I fully understand the risks when I make the sweeping generalization that smart cards are pretty worthless. There are some rare exceptions to that statement, and by way of a caveat, I limit my judgment of their worthlessness to business dealings within the United States.

In this chapter, I back up my sweeping generalization with some context so you can see that I don't have some irrational prejudice against smart cards. To be fair, later in the chapter I talk about some cases in which smart cards can be somewhat useful.

What Is a Smart Card?

Before diving into my generalization, I need to define what a smart card is. Smart cards are about the size of credit cards, but they generally have computer memory chips instead of the magnetic stripes you see on credit cards and debit cards. The purpose of the chip is to store information, far more information than any magnetic stripe could hold. This stored information can be anything—personal information, account information, dollar amounts, whatever.

Smart cards are used for purchasing goods and services from a particular merchant. For example, if you own a café and want your customers to be able to purchase items without needing cash, or if you'd like them to get discounts—such as a free cup of coffee after they purchase 10—you could issue smart cards. At some point, though, you need to sell the customers the card and store a dollar amount (the cost of the card) on it. Let's say you decide to sell each smart card for $20. When the customer uses the card, you run it through a reader that looks like a typical credit-card reader. The reader automatically deducts the amount of the purchase from the $20 starting amount and stores the new total dollar amount on the card.

The concept of a smart card—without the computer chip, which simply makes it more capable and more advanced—can be found in a lot of places. For instance, subway system cards, such as New York's Metro card, are sold in advance for any dollar amount. Say you choose to buy a card for $20. When you enter the subway, you swipe the card at the turnstile and it deducts the amount of a single fare, keeping a running total of the amount you have left in your "account." In New York, you even get a deal for buying a $20 fare card. When you pay the $20, you actually get $21.50 on the card—which amounts to an extra ride. Plus, you don't have to keep carry tokens or wait in line to buy a token every time you need to ride the subway.

Essentially, the most basic concept of a smart card gives consumers convenience and a means to settle a transaction with a single merchant.

The concept of smart cards has evolved from its humble beginnings, at least in theory. A couple of years ago in San Francisco, a group of retailers and café owners in the downtown area all bought into a smart-card system that Wells Fargo bank was selling. (I use the term "bought into" lightly, because Wells Fargo piloted the system using these merchants, so the merchants didn't have pay for the readers used to accept the cards.) This is how the system worked: Some customers at Wells Fargo bank received smart cards, which they could load with dollar amounts of money they took from ATM machines. Instead of receiving cash, the smart card just got loaded with credit. These customers also received a little cradle for their smart cards, called a "wallet." The "wallet" allowed these customers to give money to one another. The theory was that if your friend bought you lunch at a cafés and you wanted to pay the friend back, you could put your smart card in the friend's "wallet," enter your ID number, and request that a certain dollar amount—say, $10—be transferred to the friend's "wallet," which also has a memory chip. Then the friend could insert her own card and download the $10 onto it The participating merchants accepted these cards instead of cash. The merchants were paid by Wells Fargo in a similar way that credit-card transactions are settled and fulfilled.

You might be asking, What is the point? I have to say I certainly asked that question and am in fact still asking it. The point is you don't have to carry cash, but if you lose the card, you lose the cash on it (which is a lot like carrying cash). You also can get the discounts and free offers the merchants choose to market, such as a free 10th cup of coffee. The smart card can store any information that the merchant chooses to program into it. The card's chip has enough memory to store all kinds of information from any number of merchants, and the software that runs the show allows the card to "know" which information is applicable to which merchant. This is not magic, but simply software programming that uses ID numbers and passwords.

Smart cards are supposed to be convenient and add value to the consumer experience. Incidentally, this pilot project had some reported success in San Francisco, meaning that some people actually used the cards. But it hasn't caught on there or elsewhere. In fact, Citibank attempted a similar pilot in the Upper West Side of Manhattan and no one bothered using the cards.

Why don't these "innovations" catch on?

Why Smart Cards Missed the Mark in the United States

If using smart cards sounds kind of silly, it's because there's an ATM on every other street corner in the United States. In addition, many merchants accept credit cards, even for small-ticket items. So, where's the need for a smart card?

Banks such as Wells Fargo and Citibank, which were trying to make smart-card use mainstream, needed to get as many merchants as possible on board in order for the idea to fly among consumers. In this effort, the banks failed. For people to get in the habit of loading money onto cards and then using them instead of cash would require that the cards be accepted pretty much everywhere people shop. If you can use the card at Starbucks to get a cup of joe, but the drugstore next door doesn't accept the card so you have to go to an ATM to get cash to buy shampoo, you're not going to bother with the smart card. Mainstream smart cards are useful only if you truly don't need to carry around cash in addition to the card.

Eventually, banks and other proponents of smart cards came to believe that cash, and perhaps even ATMs, would become obsolete, that people could go to a Web site and simply download money onto their smart cards instead of going to an ATM at all. People would buy PCs that have smart card readers on them or are offered as an accessory, like a Zip drive is today.

I have to admit in some ways the whole concept is kind of cool. Getting cash without leaving your house is a neat concept. But I also get Orwellian chills thinking that those memory chips would also start to store all kinds of personal information about me, tracking my every move. One of the great things about cash is its anonymity. I know people argue that only criminals care about anonymity, but I am too much of a history buff to buy that argument. In too many instances, in too many cultures, perfectly innocent people have fallen prey to the political beliefs of fanatics—fanatics who gain access to people by tracking them. The proponents of smart cards universally claim that if and when smart cards end up with a lot of personal information on them, that information would be accessible only to people and institutions with the proper ID and password access—namely, the cardholder and whomever the cardholder wants to share that information with. Call me paranoid, but I have my doubts.

It doesn't look like smart cards will replace cash anytime soon, and if and when they do, it will likely happen because your credit card and your ATM card become the same card. The smart card will in fact evolve because there won't be a need for separate credit and debit cards. After all, bank-issued debit cards already exist, and if they had a computer chip on them they could store enough information to act as your credit card as well (and vice versa). That's when the whole smart card idea—including downloading cash from your PC—will make sense. One of the key factors in making smart cards mainstream is merchant acceptance. Millions of merchants already accept credit cards. It's a natural transition, much more natural than trying to sell people on a whole new reader and a whole new system when what you really want is to store cash on a credit card.

Specialty Uses: The Only Real Option

Mainstream use of smart cards as cash aside—at least for now, when the possibility of such a thing does not exist—the idea of storing discount, account, and coupon information has its appeal, especially for specific-function cards. If airlines were willing to cooperate with, say, American Express, you could conceivably store all your frequent-flier mileage information on a single smart card. and then trade in the points for tickets. A smart card for that function would be cool. You can probably think of many similar ways to take advantage of the memory chip on a smart card.

If smart cards do gain any momentum before a combination credit/debit card hits the market and goes mainstream, it will be for specialty purposes like frequent-flier miles. That makes sense, because that's how smart cards originated.

The Back Story: Smart Cards Take Europe

U.S. bankers and technology companies became interested in smart cards is because Europeans have long used them. In England, for example, some parking garages take only smart cards, not cash or credit cards. Part of the reason is that unlike U.S. parking facilities, garages in the United Kingdom aren't necessarily manned by people. In that case, a card that people purchase, loaded with a certain dollar amount, is useful because there is a reader machine at the garage, and people drive in, park, and then drive out when they need to, paying as they go.

Many more facilities and mechanisms in Europe take smart cards instead of cash. Our own subway and bus systems mimic the systems in Europe. Public transportation in the United States represents one of the few systems in which cash has been replaced with tokens or cards. Perhaps this is because these are some of the oldest systems in the United States, ones that were patterned after European systems.

But until the last 10 years or so, credit cards weren't as prevalent in Europe as the premier form of payment as they were in the United States, a far more credit-based society. Europeans tend to live within their means and not borrow as much money; Americans do the opposite, and our shopping habits reflect that difference. For example, a European is far less likely than an American to charge a small-ticket item—a movie ticket, for instance—on a credit card. A European would use cash. Because credit-card use is less ferocious in Europe, their smart-card programs are, in turn, more prevalent and more useful. Everyone runs across instances in which cash is inappropriate, and in the absence of credit-card acceptance at places like parking garages, smart-card systems stepped in to fill the gap.

It could be argued that if Americans adopted more smart-card programs before we became totally and utterly a credit-card based society, the concept Wells Fargo and Citibank were after would pick up a little more steam. Perhaps if Americans hadn't gotten so addicted to credit cards, we'd see the logic of smart cards as they exist now. But we've evolved the way we have, with our lightning-fast pace of life lending itself naturally to the convenience of credit cards. So, for mainstream smart cards that work like cash, we'll have to wait until we've evolved just a little bit more.

The Other Lemon: Electronic Bills and Coins

While we're on the subject of electronic cash stored on cards, I will address one other similar concept: the literal electronic bill and coin idea that has surfaced over the last few years, thanks to—you guessed it—the Internet.

Several companies, the best known being CyberCash, decided what the world needed was to be able to surf the Internet, go to Web storefronts, and purchase items with "cash." So, they literally invented a bill-and-coin metaphor. The idea is that you would buy electronic bills and coins from your bank, which you'd download from a Web site onto your PC. The cost would be deducted from your checking or savings account. When you surfed to a Web store that, say, sells wine, you could buy a $6 bottle with this "cash" via a little application that would pop up in your Internet browser. You'd click on the "cash" payment option, type in some ID number and password and the dollar amount, and these bills and coins (which in some prototypes looked like little dollars and coins moving across your screen) would be sent to the merchant. The merchant would, in turn, redeem that dollar amount from the bank, much in the same way merchants are paid for credit-card transactions. This electronic bill-and-coin scenario is another case where merchant buy-in is vital.

No Consumer Appeal Whatsoever

Why did this idea never take off? Guess what—there's no consumer protection against fraudulent merchants when you use bills and coins in their electronic form. However, you have protection when you use a credit card on the Internet. If you get ripped off, you can call Visa and complain.

Proof that this idea is all but dead is CyberCash. As discussed in the Web storefront section of this book, the company earns its revenue with its back-end accounting system that links your Web storefront to the bank. The founders of CyberCash started the company with the electronic bill-and-coin system as its brain trust. However, they were smart enough to capitalize on the other bit of technology they had brewing, flexible enough to see the way the wind was blowing and go with that alternative.

Will electronic bills and coins ever have a purpose? Not that I can see. In fact, when smart cards truly get smart enough to be our combination credit/debit cards, they will nail shut the bill-and-coin metaphor's coffin.

Chapter 20

Make Life Easier

In the introduction to this book, I swore that by the time you finished reading this tome you would know what to do in order to set up the electronic financial management systems you need for a smooth-running operation. I swore you'd have all the step-by-step instructions to invest online and set up a Web storefront. I also swore that you'd get past the hump of the steep learning curve for all this stuff and be comfortably sliding downhill on the other side—the side where you know what you're doing. I made a lot of campaign promises.

My guess is that now, as you read this chapter, you feel overwhelmed. As you read each chapter and learn the ropes of individual systems—paying your bills online, setting up accounts, opening an online stock-trading account, outsourcing a Web store—you probably found that they make sense in their own specific context. But once you step back and look at the enormity of doing all of these things, you can easily feel overwhelmed.

When I set up my systems, I wasn't sure I could organize the timing to get them all off the ground and running. The problem came down to this: I wasn't in the habit of doing any of these things electronically. I did administrative, paper-based tasks to keep my business running, and those were old, ingrained habits. I may not have always functioned efficiently under that system, but I knew how to handle my finances.

But the truth is that my old habits hadn't always been habits. I learned them and set them into place. Then once I learned the new, electronic systems and allowed enough time for their peculiarities to sink in, using them also became habit. It reminds me of how I learned to drive as a teenager. I remember driving with the driver's ed teacher in a manual-shift, double-brake car in which the passenger side also had brakes, so the teacher could slam them if I did anything stupid—which was often. In particular, I remember struggling to learn the right timing for stepping on the clutch and then releasing it so I wouldn't stall. It took all my concentration, and I still stalled out a lot whenever I changed gears or tried to move after stopping at a stop sign. I never thought that the clutch motion would become so ingrained in me that it would simply become instinct, requiring no thought whatsoever. But it did, of course—regardless of what anyone who has driven with me may tell you about my driving skills—and it did so much more quickly than I expected.

The same is true for the habits and instincts surrounding electronic financial management systems. Once you go through the often tedious processes of setting these things up, using them will create the habits, and the habits will form faster than you think they will. There are reasons for this, too. The systems become habit quickly when they make your life easier, when they simply make sense, when they are set up properly, and when you use them exclusively.

It is trickier, however, to get in the habit of new financial management systems than it is to use a clutch on a car. Although you may be quickly tiring of this analogy, just bear with me, because the concept behind it is important. In the car, using the clutch is a habit that forms fast because it is your only option in order to get the car to move. In electronic management systems, this isn't the case; you can easily revert back to your old ways and still function. If you're anything like me, which is to say you like to take the path of least resistance when it comes to tasks you don't like, obviating new systems whenever you hit a glitch can become a problem.

The truth is that I had Microsoft Money loaded on my computer for six months before I really got in the habit of using it. Every time I had to make a deposit or enter an expense but I was too lazy to boot the computer, I just shoved whatever receipt I had in a drawer. The receipts piled up and it took me a good deal of time to enter the data when I finally got around to it. Sometimes I forgot little details I wanted to add to my Account Registers or tax information I wanted to cross-reference in other registers.

I was sabotaging my own system. The truth is that my old system was so dysfunctional that I sometimes fell behind and made mistakes.

Once I got in the habit of entering my financial information into Money regularly, I felt like an idiot for not making it a habit sooner. Not doing so had made my life more complicated than necessary for way too long.

For this reason, this short chapter is devoted to discussion of some psychological tricks and the lazy man's shortcuts. Tricks are for getting yourself in the habit of using your new systems. Some of the shortcuts are for the same purpose. Bear in mind that I use the word "lazy" not as an insult, but almost as a compliment. I am lazy about management tasks of any kind because I find them tedious and unpleasant. Not only do I think there's nothing wrong with that, but I believe it says good things about me. I have more interesting things to think about and do. I don't want to waste my time keeping my books straight or dealing with the niggling details of new ventures, such as online investing or a Web store. I want to reap the benefits and move on to the work I love and the things I enjoy doing. So, it helps me to know that I'm lazy about financial management. Once I acknowledge that my laziness isn't going to change, I can set the right systems in place to help me get things done in spite of my laziness.

A couple of shortcuts covered in this chapter have nothing to do with getting yourself into the right habits. There are other reasons to take shortcuts—namely, to save time and energy if you can't afford a bookkeeper or an accountant.

Getting in the Habit

Let's start with habits. Even if it sounds stupid, do anything you can to make getting in the habit of entering your bank transactions in Money. For me, this meant leaving my computer on all the time so I didn't think, "Well, I don't feel like booting up right now, so I'll just shove this paper into my desk."

Set Time Aside Each Week

Ideally, you want to enter in an expense or transaction each time you have the piece of paper in hand, but realistically this doesn't happen. Don't force yourself to become obsessive; you'll get annoyed and bored too fast and then bag the whole system.

Instead, set aside a time each week—perhaps a time when you're already answering a batch of e-mails you couldn't get to right away or cleaning the paper off your desk. I use Monday mornings for these housekeeping tasks. Schedule this time to get your Account Registers in Money straight, enter all the data you need, and check to see whether automated bills you sent for payment have cleared.

If you have a bookkeeper, let that person set the schedule for doing these tasks. But make sure you update the person on the electronic transactions you have done yourself. Sometimes electronic transactions can be more elusive than paper ones because you do them quickly and forget about them. If you don't communicate what you've done—by e-mail, a note, whatever—the system can break down.

Set Time Aside Each Month

The bookkeeping and bill-paying tasks require weekly updates to be kept current and efficient, but the financial analyses and projection systems you set up in Office 2000 can be done monthly, as can the ones you set up for your Web storefront.

Again, set aside a time that seems conducive—maybe near the end of the month when you can glance at your Account Registers and see what your revenue and expenses look like for the month. Pick a time when you're thinking about how your cash flow is doing. I choose the last Monday of the month, right after I do my Account Registers. I can see what the cash flow for the month looks like, and if I spend an hour or two playing with some numbers, I'm already in the right frame of mind for planning.

Don't overwhelm yourself with too many financial analyses at once. You don't have to revamp the whole business each month. Pick something—such as Web store revenues—to look at. Depending on the size of your business, you may need to look at a slew of financial projections each month. But if you don't, I suggest you go slow and pick one area of your business to examine each month. I'm a big believer that too much information isn't good.

The important thing is the habit. Get used to doing these things and you will start to feel the urge to do them. You will become dependent on the information you get. That's when you know you're in the right place. Although it sounds simplistic, setting time aside is key. It's when you try and squeeze in these tasks without their own time slot that they fall by the wayside.

Web Storefront

Because the Web storefront should ultimately represent some serious revenue flow, tracking your Web storefront has to become habit fast so that when the revenue starts flowing in, you're not left overwhelmed.

This particular habit is one of the easiest to acquire, because you'll be inclined to want to check your revenues. It's much more inviting than brooding over expenses. But it's also easy because the Web host service provider you hire will send you monthly reports. The only habit to get into is checking your earnings against your expenses for the Web storefront. You do this in the Reports place in Money. Keep close track, because you don't want to continue to run the Web storefront if it's not earning you enough money.

Set Time Aside Immediately

A couple of habits are extremely important for online investing. First, always print out the Web page when you make a trade. It's your only receipt. Second, do not wait until the weekly time you've set aside for other record keeping to record your trades in Money. Do it right away, because stocks can be hard to track. You want the buy and sell prices and quantity logged immediately.

If you trade often, this will be simple; you just make it part of being on the computer and making the trade. If you buy stocks and mutual funds only occasionally, this will be a harder habit to acquire. Before I started using Money, I was used to just getting off the phone with my broker and waiting for documentation in the mail. The minute I hung up, I was done. If you seldom trade, make checking in with your investments part of that weekly time you set aside to look at your books, but log everything when you do your transactions.

The Three Checkpoints

If you can manage the weekly check of your books, the monthly projection and Web storefront check, and the continuous stock trade check, you'll have some good habits in place. The incidentals of managing finances— the inevitable and equally elusive things you cannot predict—won't seem alarming or overwhelming.

Using Shortcuts

You can have all the good habits in the world, but managing finances can still be a major headache if you don't have the budget for an accountant or a bookkeeper. These tasks can be time-consuming and somewhat confusing.

My shortcut tips for people who cannot afford a bookkeeper are going to sound redundant: Make sure you do your weekly checking. If you let it go and try and catch up after a long period of time, it will just be more of a mess. Read through Chapters 3 and 4 as well and make sure to create the category folders of expenses in Money suggested there. The reason for these folders is to create an overarching view of your revenue and expenses. If you have that view, it will be easier to see the big picture of your finances.

In the same vein, if you cannot afford an accountant—and I strongly suggest you try to budget for it—make sure to get accounting software and follow the instructions in Chapter 6 for online tax filing. The software will make the process so much quicker, especially if you have kept good accounts throughout the year in Money. After that, at the very least, go to an H&R Block and have them file electronically for you.

The bottom line for acquiring good financial management habits is to find a rhythm that works for you and then keep at it until it feels automatic. This is especially important if you don't have a bookkeeper or accountant, because there will be no checks-and-balance system for your financial management. Yours will be the last pair of eyes to see your Account Registers and ultimately your tax returns. You'll need to make sure you are consistent and that you keep track of details.

One more thing: If you initially set up weekly and monthly times that aren't working—for example, if you're picking days that you consistently have to do other unavoidable things—switch your schedule until it does work. That sounds like overly simplistic advice, but not switching the days and falling behind on bookkeeping is the most common problem in financial management. In order to create a rhythm that ends up being habitual, you must find time that settles into your life comfortably.

Chapter 21

The Road to Successful, Socially Conscientious Entrepreneurial Ventures

With little left to say about managing the revenues and expenses you have today, I'd like to wrap up this book with some information about what you can expect looking ahead. For the sake of optimism—an essential ingredient in any entrepreneurial recipe—I want to focus here on a discussion of the kinds of exciting opportunities there are now in investing and in attracting investors to your own business.

Let's face it: Playing with the numbers you have right now is not nearly as satisfying as adding to those numbers. Thanks to the Internet and the opportunities it has created in business, there are some creative new ways to go about becoming more successful.

But before I get to the good stuff, just a word or two about what to expect from the IRS in the near future: Online tax filing should get easier and easier, thanks to some of the new online filing features being developed by the IRS (flip back to Chapter 6 for some details). But even more than that, I believe the IRS will start to feel less suspicious about home office workers and start-up businesses. In fairness to the IRS, it really would like things to be simpler, and the officials there are very aware that small businesses are the fastest-growing market segment of businesses in the United States. It may not seem like it at times, but the IRS would like to accommodate the needs of entrepreneurs. It's just that IRS staff deals with definitions, and sometimes organizations like ours are hard to define, especially because so many expenses overlap our personal and business lives.

As far as the tools you need to make things like tax filing more efficient, integrating tax software with bookkeeping programs such as Microsoft Money is the top priority for financial software manufacturers. It's also a top priority for folks at the IRS, who would really like to see integration between the tax software programs and their own online tax filing systems. So bear with it; online tax filing should get easier.

So should software program suites such as Microsoft Office 2000 and Money, by the way. Office 2000 in particular will have more and more features to fit the needs of small businesses. The Financial Manager tools are just the beginning.

Now, on to what's new in investing.

Socially Responsible Investing

I could blather on for a while about how the Internet is changing investing. I could talk about how access to immediate stock market information and the ability to trade from your PC represent a huge opportunity to make a living as a day trader. I could talk about how the technology sector itself has added virility to the market and cite huge opportunities to make money by investing in the sector.

But aside from these overall trends, the most interesting thing I see going on in investing right now is what's called socially responsible investing, or SRI. SRI is a stock index that's fairly similar to the S&P 500, minus some companies that are considered hazardous to the environment, human rights, and the overall well-being of our world.

The reason I find this such a fascinating trend is not just because I am a die-hard liberal and believe in the importance of the private sector behaving conscientiously. It's also because it's a trend that can directly be attributed to the raised consciousness of civic responsibility that the Internet community has created. Everyone talks about how the Internet has raised the collective public consciousness regarding the issue of privacy (as I've mentioned in detail in this book). But this same community has also turned a scrutinizing eye to the behavior of companies beyond how that behavior affects investors' personal financial profiles.

One of the greatest aspects of this technological era, in my opinion, is that the creators of it belong to a generation of people who believe in independence—financial and otherwise—but who also believe that a great standard of living does not have to mean destruction of the world we live in or abominable treatment of the people who make up our societies. I think this is a great era because it shows that we have the ability to mature as a country and as a global society. The United States is truly the Great Experiment—a hodgepodge culture still in its adolescence, struggling to find balance between wealth and civility. A gracious, evolving society must have that balance. A culture that is, in its essence, the most sophisticated mix of ethnicities and cultures has the greatest potential not just for invention and creativity—diverse points of view brought together are naturally conducive to a rich well of ideas—but for humanitarianism. The wealth of worldwide experience tucked into every nook and cranny of American culture creates very fertile soil, in which an evolved society can blossom.

It doesn't hurt that we're a wealthy society. Wealth is means, and means are critical. I believe strongly in money and what it affords me. But I also believe that the United States is a smart teenager—idealistic enough to believe in good and in truth, but also reckless and forgetful and self-centered. One thing that's important to remember about teenagers is that infusing them with principles is the key to growing adults who lead examined lives and who give a damn about the world. Another thing that's critical to do with teenagers is to fill them up with information and history and let them have the freedom to make decisions about that information—in effect, to create the social contracts that will lead their generation as it reaches adulthood, when it will wield the power to make collective decisions about how society will evolve. Knowledge of history is critical, of course, because these teenagers can learn what mistakes have been made by societies over time and assess the results of those mistakes. They can consider that actions have consequences, sometimes serious ones, and they can apply that knowledge to their own conduct.

The worst thing to do with teenagers, on the other hand, is to allow them to be apathetic. This is not only dangerous to society over the long term, but it's dangerous to each and every one of them individually. An apathetic teenager is unmotivated. Lack of motivation may seriously affect that teenager's ability to go after what he or she wants in life, whatever that may be.

If you think about the United States as a collective adolescent, paying attention to history is critical. Lucky for us, we have built knowledge of history in our ethnically diverse population. We can choose to learn from historical experience and use that knowledge to build a better society, or we can be apathetic and allow only greed to rule us.

I think I've mentioned before—hopefully not too much—that I am the consummate cynic, meaning of course that I am a true romantic in wolf's clothing. I loathe apathy. I loathe the love of money over all else. And I see that love everywhere. I see it in the way we, as a society, get all giddy over oddly mild winters because we think it's warm and sunny and easygoing. We forget that it could be global warming. We were all in a lather about this prospect in the 1970s, but like everything else, we got bored with the marketing of global warming and moved on to something fresher.

Before I get too carried away with diatribes about short attention spans for what's really important—and seemingly endless attention spans for the petty and unimportant scandals we create, which, by the way, is typical of the dramatic teenager mentality—I'd like to say that it warms me to see this trend toward socially responsible investing. It warms me and gives me hope about our maturity, because it shows balance in thinking. It shows that we can be a generation smart enough to know that we need means and want independence, but that we also give a damn about the effect we have on the way companies conduct themselves by endorsing them with our investments. It shows that we're paying attention to history and attempting to use that information to create a better society. It shows that we care about who wields power.

The most important thing, perhaps, is that SRI doesn't mean giving up profits, which is why it is even more compelling. The following section presents a case study of sorts about SRI. It is an article I wrote a while back for *CBS Market Watch*. If you are interested in how SRI works and what it is all about, and even what its critics object to, read on. I believe SRI is a trend that's more than a fad. It's worth paying attention to.

Case Study: Where Your Wallet Meets Good Citizenship

Dr. Patricia Kenschaft invests her money only in companies deemed socially responsible by the Domini 400 Social Index, which is the S&P 500 Index of the politically correct liberal agenda.

"I get an important sense of personal satisfaction and empowerment," says Dr. Kenschaft, a 58-year-old professor of mathematics at Montclair State University in Montclair, New Jersey. "I want to be a responsible American."

Socially responsible investing (SRI) is the "feel-good movie" of the investment world. Individual investors, like Dr. Kenschaft, put their money in socially responsible companies via direct stock sales and mutual funds. They don't regret the price of admission; they tend to feel emotional and civic inspiration and find affirmation of the potential for a capitalistic democracy that is livable for all citizens, as well as it is profitable.

According to the Social Investment Forum (SIF), the Washington, D.C.–based, not-for-profit association of this blossoming stock market niche, investors like Dr. Kenschaft today account for $1.2 trillion invested in mutual funds and direct stocks. That is almost 1 out of every 10 professionally managed investment dollars. The SIF (*socialinvest.org*) has 50,000 individual investor members and 2000 business members.

"The idea is to mix personal beliefs with investing," says Elisa Gravitz, vice president of SIF and executive director of Co-op America, another consumer and investor organization.

"Whether your interests are environmentally sound policies, human rights worldwide, or antiwar, the idea is to put financial and personal goals together—to make money while building a better world," Gravitz says.

Sounds fairly lofty. "Yes, and some people think they can't have an effect on building a better world," she says. "But remember, when you invest, you pick companies that are creating tomorrow's products, services, and ideas."

To investors with strong beliefs in human rights, the environment, employee diversity, and corporate citizenship, SRI sounds great right off the bat, especially since the Domini Index (*www.domini.com*) is fairly competitive with the S&P 500. A quick comparison shows that the Domini Index return was 36.02 percent in 1997, when the S&P's return was 33.36 percent. A three-year analysis shows Domini at 30.33 percent and the S&P at 29.82 percent. A five-year outlook, however, leaves Domini behind, with a score of 22.55 percent, compared with the S&P's 22.82 percent. When it comes to an overall performance comparison since Domini's inception in

1990, the incumbent S&P is faring a little better, with a 19.97 percent return versus Domini's 19.14 percent.

Defining what constitutes a socially responsible company is tricky business. The Domini Index excludes tobacco companies, nuclear weapon manufacturers, and companies that deal in environmentally hazardous material (see Domini's Web site for full criteria). But ultimately, SRI means different things to different people. Although the Domini 400, produced by Kinder, Lydenberg, and Domini fund managers in Boston, is the only published index for SRI available today, the liberal agenda is not the only definition of what is socially responsible.

The Timothy Plan (*www.timothyplan.com*) mutual fund, for instance, adheres to a Christian, right-wing agenda, excluding companies that have anything to do with abortion rights, birth control pills, or pornography.

"It's all subjective, gray matter," says Lisa Leff, director and portfolio manager of the social investment awareness program at Smith Barney. "But the most popular definition of socially responsible investing has to do with the liberal agenda. And within that category, there are philosophical consistencies."

Smith Barney manages 3000 individual investor accounts in its social investment awareness program. "What this means is different for every client," says Leff. "Essentially, we analyze companies, on the Domini Index and otherwise, and then customize portfolios for each client's social agenda."

Some top companies that Leff says are popular among her investors include Xerox, for its superb policies concerning remanufacturing, minority hiring, day care, flex-time, job sharing, and mentoring; Dollar General, for corporate citizenship; American Express, for minority advancement, charitable giving, women's issues, and day care; Merck Pharmaceuticals, for reducing toxic emissions and encouraging strong employee diversity programs; Home Depot, for employee profit sharing; Enron Corp., ENE, for the world's largest investment in solar and wind-generated energy.

Show Me the Money

The concept of socially responsible investing does beg some important questions. The first one relates to market performance: Can you make as much money being conscientious as you can otherwise?

"I insisted on socially responsible investing, and my husband wanted bigger bucks," says Dr. Kenschaft. "But now he has watched how well my investments have performed and has switched some of his own money over." Dr. Kenschaft isn't specific about her return on investment, but she does say that one of her investments is Pax World, which is a balance fund that includes bonds.

"We don't find the socially responsible screens to be restrictive to investors," says Smith Barney's Leff. "When you throw out companies involved in tobacco, alcohol, gambling, pollution, weapons of mass destruction, and racial discrimination, what you find is that you've knocked out 30 percent of the large-cap stocks." That number gets smaller with mid-cap stocks, with 10–15 percent of companies kicked out. When it comes to small-cap stocks, Leff claims that the number of companies excluded is less than 5 percent.

"The screens can actually be very useful to choose companies that are well managed," says Leff. "The criticism comes because most of Wall Street isn't looking at the links, for instance, between environmental conscientiousness and performance."

Xerox, for one, saves between $200 million and $300 million a year because of its environmental initiatives. Baxter saves $150 million because of its environmental initiatives. In Baxter's case, that figure accounted for 12.7 percent of its earnings in 1996.

Criteria for Judging Companies for SRI

The top no-nos for socially responsible investors include companies involved in the following:

Tobacco

Gambling

Weapons of mass destruction

Alcohol

Heavy pollution

Labor issues, including unsafe workplaces, lack of racial and ethnic diversity, and human rights infractions

Righteousness or McCarthyism? It's a Fine Line

Scrutiny does indeed abound in the investing world. Interestingly, what raises the ire of critics has less to do with performance issues and more to do with the deeper philosophical question of the fairness of the Domini Index.

Analysts and fund managers—including Peter Kinder, a principal of the KLD, the creators of the Domini Index—agree that the screening process used for the index is subjective. Can such an index then be truly representative, or even fair? What if a company has exemplary hiring practices but has an offshore manufacturing plant that's a sweatshop? Are any corporate conglomerates pure as the driven snow when it comes to all categories?

"Standards are applied to each criterion, and if a company falls below [that standard], we drop it off the index," says Kinder. KLD makes adjustments to the Domini Index once a month, and all addition and deletion information is available at its Web site.

"For example, we dropped Nike at the beginning of the year, because despite positives in workplace issues, its performance in the Third World was sub-par," says Kinder. "We dropped Gannett 18 months ago because of its labor strike. That was a tough call because, with the exception of maybe Nordstrom's, Gannett has the best policies for women's issues. You have to make a judgment call."

Making "judgment calls" is precisely what Donald Yacktman, president of Yacktman Asset Management, finds appalling.

"When you attempt to have mass agreement on what is responsible—which is what the Domini Index attempts—it's impossible," says Yacktman. "At some point the index screening becomes arbitrary and irresponsible."

But Kinder says that KLD's methodology is neither arbitrary nor McCarthyistic. "The Domini Index is a representation of a broad set of screens, but we never say that if you don't invest in Domini stocks you're not investing responsibly," he says. "We also have a research service for institutional investors and money managers, called Socrates, which gives full profiles of companies not included in our index. So, even though a company such as DuPont is not on our Index, we facilitate investing in DuPont."

DuPont is omitted from the Domini Index because it is a chemical company. But, as Leff points out, it is a classic example of the definitional "gray matter" because the company has also invested enormous resources to make its chemical process more environmentally sound. So, even if it is categorically omitted from the Domini Index, for the right client's personal agenda, DuPont could easily be considered a socially responsible investment.

Perhaps Dr. Kenschaft has the most sage approach. "As an investor, I read the screens, look at the Domini Index, and then I see if a company is suited to my personal beliefs," she says.

Online SRI Resources

Guides:

Good Money: *www.goodmoney.com*

Green Money Online Guide: *www.greenmoney.com* (published by RCC Group: *www.inusa.com/rccgroup/index.htm*)

S-R Invest: *tbzweb.com/srinvest/*

Groups:

Social Investment Forum: *socialinvest.org/*

First Affirmative Financial Network (FAFN), nationwide SRI in the Rockies: (888) SRI-CONF

Funds:

Kinder, Lydenberg, Domini & Co, Inc. (KLD): *www.kld.com/wdomi.html* or (617) 426-5270 (based in Boston, MA)

Parnassus Investments: (800) 999-3505 (based in SF, CA)

Calvert Group: (800) 368-2748 (based in Bethesda, MD)

Meyers Pride Value Fund: *www.pridefund.com/* or (800) 410-3337 (based in Boston, MA)

Vantage Investment Advisors: *www.vantage-invest.com* or (212) 247-5858 (based in New York, NY)

Angel Investors, Venture Capital, and Other Financial Hope for Entrepreneurs

Aside from the SRI investing trend, another investment trend is booming: venture capital investments in small businesses. Venture capital firms consist of groups of individual investors who pool funds to invest in entrepreneurial ventures. Consider this the flipside of your investments in other companies. This is all about getting those with the dough to invest in perhaps the most important investment you can think of: you. It's one thing to raise revenue by investing in the stock market. It's another thing to have the market invest in your business.

Venture capital has been the cornerstone of new Web-based businesses since their inception. Today, it seems that for the right small business profile—Web based or not—these helpful dollars might be easier than ever to get your hands on.

Investment banking analysts tend to agree that there is a lot of opportunity for companies with a viable business plan. It gets better: Because of the boom of Internet IPOs, which prove to the investment community that inventions that make money tend to come from entrepreneurs, it's the smaller, more creative organizations that are now being favored by investment bankers and venture capital funds.

If yours is a small multimedia company, for instance, you have one of the best corporate profiles attracting venture capitalists today. You can look to larger corporations for funding your Web storefront, for instance.

Other types of businesses are attractive to investors as well. They tend to be retail oriented instead of service oriented—selling hard, tangible goods. Technology companies of all kinds, not just multimedia, are on everyone's radar. As the Internet develops, video companies, telecommunications companies, and companies with electronic banking technologies are also attractive. Or if you have a successful Web storefront, you are a likely candidate for a round of funding to expand that Web store or diversify a product line.

Venture capitalists come in all shapes and sizes. Some are part of large corporations or banks. Chase Capitol Corp., parent company to Chase Bank, has a $4 billion-plus venture capital fund. Others are individual investors who have formed a corporation to fund companies, such as the popular Silicon Valley firm Kleiner Perkins Caufield Byers. Still others are merely wealthy individuals who are looking for start-ups for their investment dollars. People tend to call the latter *angel investors*. However, angel investors, by definition, cover a broader group; they are really a subset of venture capitalists. Two defining characteristics of angel investors: They tend to put up seed capital—the initial money to get your company off the ground—and they tend to ask for less of a chunk of your company in return for the favor than most venture capitalists do. Definitions get a little gray here, though, because many venture capitalists put up seed money. The real distinction is in how much of your company they want in return. Angel investors tend to want less than 25 percent, giving them the complimentary title of angel. Venture capitalists in general have been known to appropriate 50 percent or more of the companies in which they invest.

The Catch

You may be starting to see that there is a price to pay for any venture capital dollars. The main price you pay is relinquishing more ownership of your company than you'd like. Some people liken venture capitalists to loan sharks, but not all of them are like that. Even if you end up relinquishing a portion of your company, the positive side is that you'll have resources to grow revenues faster, ultimately still creating a bigger pie and therefore a bigger piece of it for yourself.

The important thing to understand is that if a bank doesn't want to give you a loan or a line of credit you need to get your business going, there are other options. In recent history, there has never been a time like now, when venture capitalists are ready and willing to invest in small businesses. To get a list of some venture capital firms out there, try *www.capitalventure.com/cvvclinks*. Most venture capital firms have Web sites now, so you can see what kinds of companies they're interested in.

One crucial thing to remember before entering into any deal with a venture capitalist: Get your own lawyer, specifically one that specializes in negotiating with venture capitalists. Make sure this lawyer does not work for the venture capital firm. Furthermore, make sure this lawyer is willing to give you some business advice, too, such as "Don't be tempted by venture capitalists who lure you by promising more money than you even asked for, but who want you to make unrealistic revenue projections." One of the common mistakes entrepreneurs make is to go wild with revenue projections, thinking they will attract more venture capital dollars, and then they get ousted from their own companies when they can't deliver. A common clause in a venture capital deal is that the investors can take over the company if the founder doesn't live up to revenue projections.

Bottom line: Get a good lawyer.

Don't Be Daunted

I suppose it's only fitting that the last comment I will make in this book is to be careful, but don't be daunted. This book has been all about setting up systems to manage what you have so you can reach out and grow your business as much as you'd like. That means being careful along the way but not being scared off. In the case of something like venture capital, understand the dangers, but also understand that the dangers are what lawyers are for.

There are plenty of tools today for the entrepreneur to get ahead and thrive. Everything from software to a Web retail outlet to online access to the stock market to venture capital is there for your taking. The mood of U.S. society today, not the least of which is a healthy economy and an understanding that an independent lifestyle is a real choice, means it's not just the technological age, but the age of the entrepreneur.

I encourage you to take advantage of it. And good luck.

Index

A

N

O

Sample Chapter from

Smart Business Solutions

Direct Marketing and Customer Management

DOUGLAS GANTENBEIN

Want to learn about direct marketing and customer management techniques? Read on to see a sample chapter from SMART BUSINESS SOLUTIONS FOR DIRECT MARKETING AND CUSTOMER MANAGEMENT, a companion title from Microsoft Press!

If you find SMART BUSINESS SOLUTIONS FOR FINANCIAL MANAGEMENT useful, we'd like to suggest another title that can help you harness the power of technology for your business. The next chapter, excerpted directly from SMART BUSINESS SOLUTIONS FOR DIRECT MARKETING AND CUSTOMER MANAGEMENT, gives you the practical knowledge and skills you need to plan and execute direct-marketing campaigns and manage customers to make your small business grow and prosper. Case studies of successful small businesses and advice from an array of small-business experts show you how to find and maintain your greatest asset: loyal customers. And you get complete details on how to use popular software applications to make your direct-marketing and customer-management activities a success.

SMART BUSINESS SOLUTIONS FOR DIRECT MARKETING AND CUSTOMER MANAGEMENT covers topics such as:

- Planning and producing your way to direct-mail success with Microsoft Office 2000

- Designing and writing direct-mail pieces that sell

- Using mailing lists successfully with Microsoft Small Business Direct Mail Manager, Microsoft Excel, and Microsoft Word

- Anticipating, identifying, attracting, and managing customers with Microsoft Small Business Customer Manager

- Using the Web to manage and grow your customer base

Douglas Gantenbein has been the Northwest correspondent for *The Economist* since 1988. He has written articles on small-business practices and technology for *Small Business Computing, Home Office Computing, Success,* and *The Wall Street Journal.*

Contents

Contents

Part 3

Appendixes

Direct Marketing That Gets Results

Chapter 1

Direct Mail and the Small Business

Sur la Table is a Seattle-based store that is a cook's paradise. Whether it's the perfect potato peeler, the ideal roasting pan, or the latest Italian coffee-making accessory, a customer can find it at Sur la Table. From its start 27 years ago in Seattle's famed Pike Place Market, the kitchen-supply store has grown into a seven-store chain, with outlets in the Seattle suburb of Kirkland, Newport Beach, San Francisco, Berkeley, and Santa Monica in California, and now Dallas, Texas. Sur la Table faces a tough marketing environment as it competes against nationally known names such as Williams-Sonoma as well as regional cooking stores. And getting the word out is difficult. "We're a small company," says Carol Couture, Sur la Table's director of marketing. "We're not big enough to afford broadcast every day or do run-of-press in a newspaper and hope that someone opens the food section."

The marketing solution for Sur la Table: direct mail. Each year the company sends out 7 million catalogs as well as local letters to customers about in-store cooking classes and newsletters to tell customers about upcoming special events and demonstrations. The catalogs generate nearly half the company's revenue, create a large portion of Sur la Table's in-store traffic, and help the company target the best retail locations by providing feedback on customer location and demographics.

"In my mind, direct mail is the most efficient way to grow a business," says Couture. "I love being able to send a piece to someone's house and to predict what the response might be."

Sur la Table is but one of thousands of small businesses in the United States that have found direct marketing to be the most efficient and effective way to spend their marketing dollars. Chances are, it's the right approach for your business too, whether you own a corner floral shop, a chain of drive-through espresso bars, or a local clothing store.

What Direct Mail Can Do for You

Advertising is expensive. Take, for example, the 1999 Super Bowl. Advertisers spent as much as $1.3 million for as little as 30 seconds of air time. For that astonishing sum, advertisers were rewarded with a huge audience—128 million people tuned in to see whether the Denver Broncos or Atlanta Falcons would prevail. The ads that ran during the Super Bowl, though, were the marketing equivalent of a shotgun—broadly aimed, perhaps even barely aimed. They were solely the province of advertising's 500-pound gorillas, companies such as Budweiser, Federal Express, and M&M/Mars. No Sur la Tables there, nor any other small businesses.

For the small business, direct mail is the best way, as Carol Couture says, to "swim with the big fish." And to do so without their advertising millions. Here's why.

Direct Mail Creates a Response

Although it can do several things, such as generate store traffic or create leads that might later become sales, direct mail primarily is aimed at getting a *response*. No other form of advertising works as well at coaxing the consumer to take action. If you want a customer to visit your restaurant, purchase a sweater, try a carpet-cleaning service, or subscribe to a magazine, direct marketing is the most effective way to achieve your goal. That's a particularly important point for a small business, which does not have the luxury of waiting for an advertising campaign—even if it could afford one—to work its way slowly into the customers' consciousness.

Direct Mail Grows a Customer Base

In 1967, L.L. Bean had annual sales of $3 million. Twenty-four years later, in 1991, it hit the $1 billion mark. How? Largely by taking advantage of

4

powerful new database tools that allowed Bean to more carefully target and accurately measure its catalog sales campaigns. L.L. Bean is just one of hundreds of companies that have used direct marketing to greatly expand a customer base. Others include Lillian Vernon, Banana Republic, and Sharper Image—not to mention Sears & Roebuck, one of the first companies to understand the power of direct marketing.

Direct Mail Can Be Tailored to Your Business

As a small business, you have a particular set of goals and ideals. That you're an entrepreneur also means you have a particular business personality. Direct marketing can easily be designed to fit your business just as stripes fit a tiger. You can be aggressive, or folksy, or professionally slick, or casual and informal.

Direct Mail Can Be Measured

With most advertising, it's difficult to know if the ads have any real benefit. Has the public's perception of a company changed? Are customers more aware of a brand? Direct mail, on the other hand, can be precisely measured. You can easily calculate the cost of a mailing and the cost per response, and you can weigh those costs against the sales generated by a direct-mail campaign.

Direct Mail Can Be Tested

What offer works best? What design works best? Are flyers better than catalogs? With direct mail you can find out. Big catalog retailers such as Lands' End and L.L. Bean, for instance, send catalogs to the East and West Coasts with different offers—a different price, or a product that is given special emphasis, or even one cover for the woman in the household (with more colors) and another for the man (more businesslike). The sales figures then tell the story of whether that special price or special catalog placement was effective. (As a consumer, you *always* want to ask if a catalog item is on sale; it very well might be in a different catalog from the same company.) A small business can test many variables, too. It can change the copy in an ad, experiment with different formats, or change the offer from a 10 percent discount on an oil change to a free oil change with a complete service checkup.

Direct Mail Can Fit Any Budget

Direct mail can be tailored to fit the size of your budget, whether you want to mail postcards to 500 customers, reminding them to rotate their tires or

5

change their antifreeze, or print and distribute a full-color catalog of your new clothing designs. It's easy to scale up a direct-mail campaign, so if results from the first 10,000 mailings are good, ordering another 50,000 copies, purchasing or renting some expanded mailing lists, and making the campaign even bigger are simple.

Direct Mail Is Personal

A properly executed direct-mail campaign reaches a carefully chosen set of customers. Because of that, you can be very specific when you discuss how the product or service will address the recipient's needs. Your mailing piece and its copy also can be very direct and personal in addressing the customer, unlike a mass television, radio, or print campaign. This personal approach leads to one of the real strengths of direct marketing: its ability to help you develop a strong, long-term relationship with a customer. By tracking your customers' purchase histories, you can offer special incentives to your best customers, remind lapsed customers that you'd still like their business, or tailor offers and products to suit particular customers.

Direct Mail Is Hot

In 1998, according to the Direct Marketing Association, direct-marketing sales (which include direct mail and telemarketing) to consumers totaled $759 billion, or 12.4 percent of total U.S consumer sales of a little more than $6 trillion. (No wonder they say ours is a consumer-driven economy.) Direct marketing also scores well in the business-to-business category, with $612 billion in 1998 sales, 5 percent of the national business-to-business total of $12 trillion.

Direct-marketing sales are growing, too, by an average of nearly 8 percent a year since 1993. Although that growth rate has been tracked fairly closely by cost increases, direct-marketing experts predict that cost growth will decrease in the next few years even as sales growth increases to about 8.6 percent annually, resulting in strong earnings for direct marketers. In all cases—advertising spending, revenue, and employment—growth of direct marketing is expected to outpace U.S. economic growth.

Direct marketing accounts for a huge percentage of revenue for those companies that engage in it. Another recent survey, conducted by *Direct* magazine, showed that companies using direct marketing earn nearly half their revenue from that approach. In the case of business-to-business marketing, the figure is more than half, closely followed by consumer marketing. Twenty-three percent of the survey's respondents reported that direct marketing was responsible for *90 percent* of their total sales.

Direct Marketing: Fact and Myth

Statistics such as those just discussed debunk one common perception of direct marketing: that it doesn't work. It's true that some consumer surveys may indicate annoyance with the sheer volume of direct-marketing pitches many people face. Other surveys show that in any given year more than half of all Americans purchase something by phone, by mail, or via the Internet. Those are all direct-marketing sales, folks. It does work—and it works well. Consumers who have clipped coupons, ordered from catalogs, kept and used discount cards mailed to them by a restaurant, or checked sales at local stores that sent them postcards have responded to direct marketing.

Lois K. Geller, a New York–based expert on direct mail and author of the book *Response: The Complete Guide to Profitable Direct Mail*, lists some other common misconceptions about direct marketing:

> **It's easier to sell retail.** Not true, says Geller. Even though the retail setting seems to give you better access to the customer, you may actually have little control over where the product is placed in a store or how a store's sales staff presents it to a potential buyer. Moreover, selling retail forces you to manufacture enough of an item to fill shelves at multiple outlets. In contrast, direct marketing gives the seller great control over how the product is presented. It can also be much more efficient, allowing the seller to manufacture or purchase more of an item only as needed. This "just-in-time" production approach is what helped Toyota to succeed and what led Ford and other car makers to follow suit. You can benefit from the same approach when selling to a few thousand people.

> **I already advertise, and I'm doing well. I don't need direct mail.** Well, maybe you don't, says Geller. But how do you know your advertising is what's drawing customers? Send out a coupon that offers a 25 percent discount, and you'll know exactly what sort of response your advertising dollar—when used in direct marketing—is earning for you. Otherwise, you could be wasting

advertising dollars if location and word-of-mouth alone could generate traffic.

I tried direct marketing, and it didn't work. Fair enough, says Geller. But are you sure you got your pitch into the right hands? That you had the right offer and the right product to sell via direct marketing? Sometimes a detail as minor as the wording of a headline can make a difference. Try several approaches; one of them is almost certain to bring results.

Great Moments in Direct Mail

1450: Gutenberg invents movable type.

1667: English gardener William Lucas publishes earliest gardening catalog.

1744: Benjamin Franklin publishes a catalog "near six hundred volumes in most faculties and sciences." Franklin further develops the concept of guaranteeing customer satisfaction.

1830s: Several New England companies begin to sell sporting equipment, fishing gear, and marine supplies.

1867: Invention of the typewriter makes it possible to print small quantities of material cheaply and relatively quickly. Alas, early models struck paper from the bottom, making it impossible to proofread.

1886: Richard Sears, a railroad station agent, enters the mail-order business to sell watches refused by an addressee. He joins with Alvah Roebuck in 1887 and six years later prints a 196-page catalog.

1912: L.L. Bean founds a successful mail-order company on the promise of a guaranteed waterproof boot.

1926: Neiman Marcus mails the first catalog with expensive, high-end clothing and gifts.

1950: Diners Club mails out the first credit card.

1982: Dr. Roger Breslow, a New York internist, keeps every piece of direct mail he receives in a year. His collection weighs 509 pounds.

1992: The number of Americans shopping from home exceeds 100 million.

OK, It Isn't All Great News

Direct marketing is a proven, effective, and growing method of spending your marketing dollars. But all is not instant profits and cheer. There's the "J" word, for instance. That's right, junk mail. Even people in the industry use it—at least, most of them do. Bob Hacker, a Seattle-area direct-mail consultant whose campaigns for clients such as IBM have resulted in tenfold response rate increases over previous efforts, notes one unavoidable fact: "Nobody," he says, "likes direct mail." In fact, in even the most successful campaigns 90 percent of the people you reach *will throw your message away.* That's right. Throw it away. As garbage. In a reasonably successful campaign that figure jumps to 98 percent.

One reason might be that people sometimes seem overwhelmed by direct mail. In 1998, for instance, catalog mailings jumped by 15 percent, according to the *Wall Street Journal*, with the typical "prime" catalog customer—a working couple with young children—receiving nine catalogs a week. Many stores that were strictly bricks-and-mortar retailers only a few years ago, such as Saks Fifth Avenue and Dillards Department Stores, now have entered the direct-mail fray with catalogs. Increased competition has made it more difficult for even well-established direct-mail marketers to maintain growth and profit rates. The brutal competition of recent years savaged highly respected Lands' End, the catalog clothier, resulting in shakeups at the top and layoffs among the employees. Then there is the proliferation of credit-card offers, magazine subscription offers, and record club enticements. The fact is that it's difficult to cut through the clutter.

You should consider other issues as well before launching a direct-mail campaign.

Higher Postage Rates

Through the early 1990s, rates for third-class mail (usually used for direct mail) increased by 16 percent. Rates stabilized during 1997 and 1998, but they increased again early in 1999. Higher mailing costs, of course, increase a direct marketer's cost-per-thousand, meaning that each mailing must show an improved return to make a profit. What's more, an increasing number of direct-mail consultants say that using bulk mail all but guarantees that your piece will be thrown out. Some even use high-end carriers such as Federal Express to ensure that a mailing gets to a selected group of readers.

Higher Production Costs

Along with higher postal rates, costs for paper, printing, and other production-related items have gone up as well. The good news, as the Direct Marketing Association's 1998 industry report notes, is that those costs are expected to grow at a slower rate than sales during the next several years. Still, postal costs and production costs can account for up to 90 percent of the total cost of some mailings. Any jump here can be substantial.

Privacy Concerns

Face it—some people simply don't want unsolicited advertisements. To date the direct marketing industry has done a poor job dealing with this issue. It's true; consumers can have their names taken off mailing lists.

The Industry Itself

Sometimes direct mail shows a remarkable ability to take direct aim only at its foot. How many pieces of mail do people get each week that are stamped "Important," have fake postal-handling instructions all over them, and contain assumptions about the recipient that reveal the hand of a giant mailing list that does little to differentiate among potential customers' actual needs or wants? As *Direct* magazine columnist Herschell Gordon Lewis recently noted, too many direct-mail offers start out with patently absurd lines such as "Make $1,000 weekly stuffing envelopes!" or "New money-making concept makes all others obsolete!" or "I made over $1 million cleaning dirty mini-blinds!"

Wrote Lewis: "We're regarded as sharpies, as fast-buck artists. The great unwashed public, with its great unwashed mini-blinds, lumps us all into one cauldron. Direct marketing, direct response, direct mail, mail order, telemarketing—it's like that line from the old comic strip 'Pogo,' 'We have met the enemy and it is us.'"

The message is not that direct mail doesn't work. The message is that direct mail must be done well. And when it is done well, direct mail becomes a genuine customer service, not an intrusion.

Is Direct Mail Right for Your Business?

Direct mail's adaptability makes it suitable for nearly any business. Here are some examples of direct-mail campaigns from companies big and small:

- To help introduce its new M-class sport utility vehicle in 1997, Mercedes-Benz developed an elaborate direct-mail campaign, beginning in October 1995 with a 400,000-piece mailing sent to prospective customers (mostly well-to-do suburbanites). Using surveys and including in its mailings some interest-piquing items such as bits of sheet metal said to be from an M-class prototype, Mercedes-Benz generated response rates as high as 50 percent and created considerable buzz for the new $45,000 vehicles, which proved to be a smash hit for Mercedes-Benz.

- In Seattle, the locally owned Schwartz Brothers Restaurants perked up sales during the slow January-February period with a colorful mailer with a handy business-card-sized tear-off stub good for up to $66 in discounts at the chain's eight restaurants and delicatessens. The result was a 6 percent response, adding tens of thousands of dollars in revenue to an otherwise dead time in the restaurant business.

- In Westport, Connecticut, upscale clothier Mitchell's assembled a mailing list of customers who had not been in the store for two years and who tended to spend less than $900 for a suit. The mailing offered special discounts. Mitchell's sent out 3,000 pieces, generating 438 trips into the store—an impressive response rate of nearly 15 percent. Those returning customers spent more than $300,000, income for Mitchell's that far exceeded the cost of the mailer.

In short, direct mail can work for virtually any business, with offers and products big and small. Here are just a few of the things you can do with direct mail:

- Sell a product or service
- Generate store traffic
- Thank customers for business
- Tell customers about new merchandise, a new location, or new employees
- Sell supplies and accessories to recent customers
- Offer special discounts
- Conduct customer surveys
- Retrieve customers who have not shopped with you for a while

- Persuade good customers to be better customers
- Introduce yourself to prospective customers
- Announce a store opening
- Build a mailing list of potential customers
- Excite customers about an upcoming product

How Microsoft Office 2000 Can Help

Microsoft Office 2000 can be a valuable tool in developing and executing a direct-mail strategy. It includes useful upgrades to many of the programs you already are familiar with and that can help you write and design direct-mail pieces, such as Microsoft Word and Microsoft Publisher. In addition, Office 2000 Small Business, Professional, and Premium versions include the Direct Mail Manager. This powerful Internet-based tool uses Microsoft wizard technology and the expertise of the U.S. Postal Service to make it easy for small businesses to develop precisely targeted and cost-effective mailings. The Direct Mail Manager includes the following:

- Access to targeted prospect lists from InfoUSA, a respected provider of mailing lists for direct-mail users. Office 2000 users can employ the Direct Mail Manager to access InfoUSA's Web site to scan available lists and costs, and then purchase and download names directly into a Microsoft Excel spreadsheet. Special discounts and offers apply to users of Office 2000.

- Tools that allow you to verify addresses against the U.S. Postal Service national database. The database will check addresses for completeness and fix incorrect addresses.

- Word or Publisher mail merge. This feature helps users send their documents or publications or hand off mailing tasks to an outside mailing service such as Pitney Bowes or Neopost.

Direct mail, Office 2000, and your small business—a profitable combination.

Get technical
help and support—
direct from Microsoft.

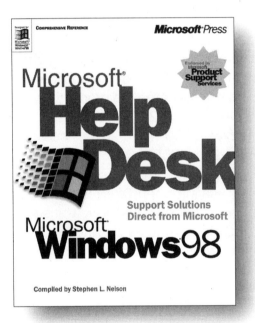

U.S.A. **$49.99**
U.K.   £45.99
Canada $74.99
ISBN 0-7356-0632-3

The Microsoft Windows 98 operating system is the upgrade to Windows that makes computers work better and play better. MICROSOFT® HELP DESK FOR MICROSOFT WINDOWS® 98 puts a portable, rich source of Microsoft product support solutions at your fingertips. Written in the clear, understandable language characteristic of the Microsoft Help Desk series, the book covers key Microsoft Windows 98 support issues and their solutions. It is the only Windows 98 Help Desk resource based directly on the archives of Microsoft Product Support's KnowledgeBase.

mspress.microsoft.com

See clearly—
now!

Here's the remarkable, *visual* way to quickly find answers about the power-
fully integrated features of the Microsoft® Office 2000 applications. Microsoft
Press AT A GLANCE books let you focus on particular tasks and show you, with
clear, numbered steps, the easiest way to get them done right now. Put Office
2000 to work today with AT A GLANCE learning solutions, made by Microsoft.

- MICROSOFT OFFICE 2000 PROFESSIONAL AT A GLANCE
- MICROSOFT WORD 2000 AT A GLANCE
- MICROSOFT EXCEL 2000 AT A GLANCE
- MICROSOFT POWERPOINT® 2000 AT A GLANCE
- MICROSOFT ACCESS 2000 AT A GLANCE
- MICROSOFT FRONTPAGE® 2000 AT A GLANCE
- MICROSOFT PUBLISHER 2000 AT A GLANCE
- MICROSOFT OFFICE 2000 SMALL BUSINESS AT A GLANCE
- MICROSOFT PHOTODRAW™ 2000 AT A GLANCE
- MICROSOFT INTERNET EXPLORER 5 AT A GLANCE
- MICROSOFT OUTLOOK® 2000 AT A GLANCE

Microsoft®

mspress.microsoft.com

Stay in the *running* for maximum productivity.

These are *the* answer books for business users of Microsoft® Office 2000. They are packed with everything from quick, clear instructions for new users to comprehensive answers for power users—the authoritative reference to keep by your computer and use every day. The Running series—learning solutions made by Microsoft.

- RUNNING MICROSOFT EXCEL 2000
- RUNNING MICROSOFT OFFICE 2000 PREMIUM
- RUNNING MICROSOFT OFFICE 2000 PROFESSIONAL
- RUNNING MICROSOFT OFFICE 2000 SMALL BUSINESS
- RUNNING MICROSOFT WORD 2000
- RUNNING MICROSOFT POWERPOINT® 2000
- RUNNING MICROSOFT ACCESS 2000
- RUNNING MICROSOFT INTERNET EXPLORER 5
- RUNNING MICROSOFT FRONTPAGE® 2000
- RUNNING MICROSOFT OUTLOOK® 2000

Microsoft

mspress.microsoft.com

Register Today!

Return this
*Smart Business Solutions for
Financial Management*
registration card today

Microsoft®*Press*
mspress.microsoft.com

OWNER REGISTRATION CARD

0-7356-0682-X

Smart Business Solutions for Financial Management

_____ _____ _____

FIRST NAME   MIDDLE INITIAL   LAST NAME

_____

INSTITUTION OR COMPANY NAME

_____

ADDRESS

_____

_____

_____ _____ _____

CITY   STATE   ZIP

_____ (_____) _____

E-MAIL ADDRESS   PHONE NUMBER

U.S. and Canada addresses only. Fill in information above and mail postage-free.
Please mail only the bottom half of this page.

For information about Microsoft Press®
products, visit our Web site at
mspress.microsoft.com

Microsoft·Press

NO POSTAGE
NECESSARY
IF MAILED
IN THE
UNITED STATES

BUSINESS REPLY MAIL
FIRST-CLASS MAIL   PERMIT NO. 108   REDMOND WA

POSTAGE WILL BE PAID BY ADDRESSEE

MICROSOFT PRESS
PO BOX 97017
REDMOND, WA 98073-9830